CORRUPTION AND RACKETEERING
IN THE
NEW YORK CITY CONSTRUCTION INDUSTRY

D1565917

ORGANIZED CRIME TASK FORCE

Ronald Goldstock, Director

CORRUPTION AND RACKETEERING IN THE NEW YORK CITY CONSTRUCTION INDUSTRY

Final Report to
Governor Mario M. Cuomo
from the
New York State
Organized Crime Task Force

RONALD GOLDSTOCK
Director

MARTIN MARCUS
First Assistant
Organized Crime
Task Force

THOMAS D. THACHER, II
Executive Director
Construction Industry
Project

JAMES B. JACOBS
Principal Draftsman
and
Consultant Coordinator

NEW YORK UNIVERSITY PRESS
New York and London

Library of Congress Cataloging-in-Publication Data

New York (State). Organized Crime Task Force.
    Corruption and racketeering in the New York City construction
industry : final report to Governor Mario M. Cuomo / from the New
York State Organized Crime Task Force.
        p.   cm.
    ISBN 0-8147-3033-7 (alk. paper) — ISBN 0-8147-3034-5
(pbk. : alk. paper)
    1. Construction industry—New York (N.Y.)—Corrupt practices.
2. Trade-unions—Construction workers—New York (N.Y.)—Corrupt
practices.   3. Organized crime—New York (N.Y.)   I. New York
(State).   Governor (1983- : Cuomo)   II. Title.
HD9715.U53N4556   1990   90-41594
364.1′6—dc20   CIP

New York University Press books are printed on acid-free paper,
and their binding materials are chosen for strength and durability.

TABLE OF CONTENTS

ACKNOWLEDGEMENTS

This Report reflects the combined efforts of many persons. Its observations, conclusions and recommendations are a product of intensive investigation, painstaking data collection and analysis, and thoughtful and extensive drafting and editing. So many people deserve credit that it is impossible to identify all of them individually. It is nonetheless appropriate to single out certain individuals and agencies for special recognition.

Construction Industry Project Staff

Thomas D. Thacher, II, Executive Director of the Project, not only led the investigative and prosecutorial efforts underlying this Report, but also provided extraordinary leadership to the shaping and writing of the Report itself. His inexhaustible capacity to motivate, coordinate and facilitate communication among members of the law enforcement community, academics, industry experts and public officials has been critical to the development of the broad perspective necessary for a comprehensive analysis of the industry's crime problems.

James B. Jacobs, Professor of Law and Director of the Center for Research in Crime and Justice at the New York University School of Law, was tenacious in the application of his incisive analytical mind and his deft writing skills to the seemingly endless drafting, redrafting and editing processes. Applying his high academic standards to our work, he sought preciseness and integrity in every assertion we made.

Joseph A. DeLuca's exhaustive efforts in coordinating the collection and analysis of data were indispensable. Wilda D. Hess, aided by Claire Collier, not only provided research support to the preparation of this Report, but—to the very end—questioned every word and comma for content, grammar and good sense.

I am indebted to these members of the Project Staff (along with their families), and to Helen D. Groh and Mary A. Mills, the Project's secretaries, for the countless evenings and weekends they dedicated to this Report.

OCTF Executive Staff

Martin Marcus, my First Assistant, has been tireless in providing outstanding direction, support and guidance to the Construction Industry Project, and to this Report. His exceptional ability to bring intelligence and imagination to both the largest issues and the smallest details has been essential to the success of the Project, the thoughtfulness and clarity of the Report, and to OCTF in general.

Indeed, the practical knowledge and intellectual stimulation provided by the entire executive staff, which reviewed and made contributions to the Report throughout its preparation, has added immensely to its quality.

District Attorney of New York County

Robert M. Morgenthau, District Attorney of New York County, and Michael Cherkasky, the Chief of his Investigation Division, have played a substantial role in this effort. Initially, District Attorney Morgenthau provided staff who were cross-designated by OCTF and joined in its construction industry investigations. Thereafter, he formed a Labor Racketeering Unit, directed by Robert Mass, one of those cross-designated assistants. Members of that unit then became an integral part of the Construction Industry Strike Force. Their work has provided valuable insights into corruption and racketeering throughout the industry. The success of the Strike Force demonstrates the potential for such long-term joint undertakings, and is in no small part a tribute to the spirit of good will and cooperation that Mr. Cherkasky fostered.

State and City Police

Superintendent Thomas Constantine of the New York State Police assigned a contingent of his Special Investigations Unit to

participate in many of the investigations undertaken in further-
ance of the Construction Industry Project. They and detectives
assigned from the New York City Police Department by former
Commissioner Benjamin Ward contributed skill and dedication
to those investigations.

Federal Law Enforcement

The Organized Crime Unit in the Southern District of New York,
and particularly its former Chief, Barbara S. Jones, and the Organized Crime Strike Force for the Eastern District of New York and
its former Chief, Edward A. McDonald, provided information
and insights to the preparation of the Report. So too did the Federal Bureau of Investigation and the Office of Labor Racketeering (OLR) of the U.S. Department of Labor, which shared with us
some of the vast knowledge each has gained from its substantial
investigative experience in this field. In addition, OLR has
assigned investigators and an auditor with substantial expertise
in labor racketeering to work with us in a number of cases.

State and Local Governmental Agencies

A project of this magnitude necessarily required the assistance
of many agencies—many of them outside of law enforcement—
which had few or no previous dealings with OCTF, and which
may have had understandable reservations about contributing
their time, effort and candor to this venture. John Poklemba, the
Director of Criminal Justice for the State of New York, like his
predecessor, Lawrence Kurlander, used his considerable talents
to smooth the way and make cooperation of such state agencies
the rule rather than the exception. His City counterpart, former
Criminal Justice Coordinator Kevin Frawley, did the same for us
with agencies of the City of New York. The support of Mayor
Koch for this project was, of course, essential.

Among the agencies that have been the most helpful are the
Office of the Mayor of the City of New York, the City's Department of Investigation and the Inspector General of the Department of Environmental Protection, the New York State
Department of Transportation and the Metropolitan Transportation Authority. The Revenue Crimes Bureau of the New York
State Department of Taxation and Finance has provided both

investigators and auditors to aid in our investigative efforts, and its cooperation with the Project has been a springboard to cooperative efforts in other areas as well.

Scholars and Experts

Acknowledgement is also due the dozens of scholars and experts who have provided us with insights, advice, and counsel in the areas of construction, labor, public policy and other related fields. Frank Anechiarico, Professor of Political Science at Hamilton College, deserves special mention for his extensive research and analysis in the area of public construction and official corruption. On the pages that follow we list, in alphabetical order, some of the many others. A few of those who assisted us have requested that their names not be disclosed.

RONALD GOLDSTOCK

December 1989

Scholars and Experts

Honorable Harold A. Ackerman, *United States District Court Judge, District of New Jersey*

Herman Benson, *Secretary-Treasurer, Association for Union Democracy, and editor of* Union Democracy Review, *Brooklyn, N.Y.*

John Bolduc, *Executive Vice President, Subcontractors Trade Association, New York City*

David Burke, *Director, Corruption Prevention and Management Review Bureau, New York City Department of Investigation*

James Chelius, *Professor, Institute of Management and Labor Relations, Rutgers University, New Brunswick, New Jersey*

Louis Coletti, *President, New York Building Congress, New York City*

Donald Cullen, *Professor, New York School of Industrial and Labor Relations, Cornell University, Ithaca, New York*

Ronald Ehrenberg, *Professor, New York School of Industrial and Labor Relations, Cornell University, Ithaca, New York*

Arthur Eisenberg, *Court-Appointed Trustee, Teamsters Local 814, New York City*

Patrick Falvey, *Counsel, Port Authority of New York and New Jersey, New York City*

Joseph J. Fater, *Managing Director, Building Contractors Association Inc., New York City*

Kevin Ford, *Inspector General, New York City Department of Environmental Protection*

Miriam Frank, *Labor Consultant, New York City*

Meyer S. Frucher, *Executive Vice President, Olympia & York and Trustee, New York City School Construction Authority, New York City*

Margaret Gates, *former Deputy Inspector General, U.S. Department of Agriculture, Washington, D.C.*

Michael Goldberg, *Professor, Widener University School of Law, Harrisburg, Pennsylvania*

John F. Grubin, *Former Chief of Commercial Litigation Division, New York City Law Department*

Casey Ichniowski, *Associate Professor, Graduate School of Business, Columbia University, New York City*

Kenneth T. Jackson, *Professor of History and Urban Planning, Columbia University, New York City*

Michael Johnston, *Professor, Department of Political Science, Colgate University, Hamilton, New York*

Brian Jones, *Professor and Head, Department of Political Science, Texas A & M University, College Station, Texas*

Richard M. Kessel, *Executive Director, New York State Consumer Protection Board, Albany, New York*

Mark A. R. Kleiman, *John F. Kennedy School of Government, Harvard University, Cambridge, Massachusetts*

James M. Kossler, *Special Agent, Federal Bureau of Investigation, New York City*

Salvatore J. LaBarbera, *Loss Prevention Consultant, Fairfax Group Ltd., Falls Church, Virginia*

Barbara Lee, *Associate Professor, Institute of Management and Labor Relations, Rutgers University, New Brunswick, New Jersey*

Robert Lemieux, *Director of Construction, Office of the Mayor, New York City*

Terry Lenzner, *Chairman, The Investigative Group Inc., Washington, D.C.*

Peter Levy, *Assistant Professor, Department of History, York College, York, Pennsylvania*

John Markle, Esq., *labor lawyer, Philadelphia, Pennsylvania*

Frank McArdle, *Managing Director, General Contractors Association, New York City*

Raymond McGuire, Esq., *Counsel, Contractors Association of Greater New York, New York City*

Joseph T. Miller, *Chief Engineer, New York City Department of Environmental Protection*

R. M. Monti, *Director of Engineering and Chief Engineer, The Port Authority of New York and New Jersey, New York City*

Mark H. Moore, *John F. Kennedy School of Government, Harvard University, Cambridge, Massachusetts*

Kurt Muellenberg, *Kroll Associates, Washington, D.C.*

Herbert Northrup, *Professor Emeritus of Management, Wharton School of Business, University of Pennsylvania, Philadelphia, Pa.*

Stewart O'Brien, *Deputy Commissioner, New York City Department of Buildings*

Tony Raiola, *Deputy Chief of Contract Division, The Port Authority of New York and New Jersey, New York City*

Peter H. Reuter, *Senior Economist, RAND Corp., Washington, D.C.*

Michael J. Reilly, Esq., *Chairman, Pennsylvania Crime Commission, Conshohocken, Pennsylvania*

Charles H. Rogovin, Esq., *Professor of Law, Temple University School of Law, Philadelphia, Pennsylvania*

Joseph Rose, *Professor of Industrial Relations, McMaster University, Hamilton, Ontario, Canada*

Jean Sexton, *Professor of Industrial Relations, Laval University, Quebec, Canada*

Peter Shawhan, *Assistant Council, New York State Department of Transportation, Albany, New York*

Arthur Smith, Esq., *labor lawyer, Murphy, Smith and Polk, Chicago, Illinois*

Thomas Spiers, *Former Executive Vice President of Construction, Battery Park City Authority, New York City*

Edwin Stier, Esq., *Court-Appointed Trustee, Teamsters Local 560, New Jersey*

Clyde W. Summers, *Fordham Professor of Law, University of Pennsylvania, Philadelphia, Pennsylvania*

Dr. Annemarie Walsh, *Former President and Trustee and Scholar-in-Residence, Institute of Public Administration, New York City*

Harold K. Walter, Jr., *construction industry executive, Washington, D.C.*

FOREWORD

by

JAMES B. JACOBS

My collaboration with the NYS Organized Crime Task Force's (OCTF) investigation of the New York City construction industry began in spring 1986 when I agreed to assume the responsibilities of chief consultant and principal draftsman of a Report associated with a comprehensive investigation of corruption and racketeering in the New York City construction industry. At that time, I knew no more about crime in the construction industry than might any casual newspaper reader, my own criminological interests having in recent years mainly focused on prisons and drunk driving. Of course, my OCTF colleagues were far more knowledgeable than I about the labor racketeering, corporate crime, and official corruption that had allegedly existed in the industry for decades. The lawyers, accountants and investigators who had been working on criminal investigations for a year before I arrived had acquired a mass of information about the construction industry and its crime problems. That information was soon augmented by the participation of consultants expert in construction, labor relations, union democracy, economics, loss prevention, and policy analysis. As the investigations and research broadened and deepened, and as we came to understand more of the industry's history, we all came to realize that our initial impressions had very considerably underestimated the extent of the problem.

What we found, and what this *Final Report* describes and documents, are systems and patterns of corrupt activities and relationships that for a century have characterized the day-to-day life of one of New York City's largest industries, or, if you will, one of its most significant economic sectors. The New York City construction industry employs more than 100,000 people and involves approximately one hundred unions and many hundreds of general and specialty contractors in addition to large numbers of architects, engineers, and materials suppliers. During any single year in the late 1980's perhaps $10 billion worth of public and private construction projects was undertaken.

There is no need to summarize the *Final Report* here; this is the task of the introductory chapter. Suffice it to say that this *Final Report* deals with labor and corporate racketeering, extortion, bribery, illegal cartels and bid rigging, in all of which Cosa Nostra organized crime families are significantly involved. In addition, this *Final Report* deals with a litany of official corruption, especially by New York City building inspectors, and with fraud, waste and abuse in the City's vast public works programs. What I want to emphasize here is that we are confronting a long established cooperative relationship between organized crime on the one hand and labor unions, contractors and suppliers on the other hand. On reflection, this relationship should not be surprising. Corruption and racketeering would not have a century-long tradition in the New York City construction industry if they had not proved advantageous for important interests in the industry.

This being so, it is not surprising that the investigation upon which this *Final Report* is based was not stimulated by an industry call for assistance in fighting racketeers. Rather, it was the consequence of a number of muckraking newspaper accounts and the responses by then Mayor Edward Koch and Governor Mario Cuomo. Law enforcement agencies and government agencies, not the participants, have been the chief constituencies for reform. Organized labor has indeed not looked kindly on this project and, with some notable exceptions, the business men and women who make up the "management" side of the construction industry have neither joined in nor applauded our efforts. The fact of the matter is that the construction industry in New York City has learned to live comfortably with pervasive corruption and racketeering. Perhaps those with strong moral qualms were long ago driven from the industry; it would have been difficult for them to have survived. "One has to go along to get along."

This *Final Report* is not cheerful reading. It paints a depressing picture of business-as-usual in the construction industry and thus offers a depressing commentary on New York City and perhaps on American society as well. It is hard, indeed painful, to contemplate (and therefore the instinct for denial is entirely understandable) that the New York City construction industry, one of the core components of the economy of the nation's largest city, is thoroughly influenced by Cosa Nostra racketeers through their roles as labor leaders, general and specialty contractors, suppliers, and as underworld powerbrokers whose tentacles reach into the economic and political corridors of power in the "upper world."

Taken as a whole this *Final Report* will sharpen our understanding of how organized crime functions. The specter of an infiltration of legitimate industry by organized crime has appeared and reappeared in Congressional hearings throughout this century. "Infiltration" conjures up an image of a cancerous organized crime organism attacking and corrupting otherwise healthy cells. What this *Final Report* shows is that organized crime does not so much attack and subvert legitimate industry as exploit opportunities to work symbiotically with "legitimate" industry so that "everybody makes money."

The nature of contemporary labor racketeering is sharply illuminated in this *Final Report*. We are not dealing with a few organized crime racketeers who are at war with the legitimate labor movement. Organized crime and other labor racketeers have been entrenched in the building trades for decades. Some local unions have experienced a succession of mob leaders, control of the union being handed down from father to son. By now, the position of these labor racketeers is supported by a large corps of union officials, business agents, and stewards, and by all the advantages and emoluments of union incumbency; it is reinforced by status conferred by other labor leaders, some political officials, and other members of the "establishment." The formation of viable opposition groups within the building trades unions is deterred by the threat of blacklisting and violence. We are not, however, just dealing with a reign of terror. Some labor racketeers are actually popular with their rank and file, at least with those who do not insist upon their federally guaranteed right to union democracy or to all the benefits promised in their collective bargaining agreements. These leaders are perceived as having obtained high wages for skilled and unskilled workers and as having the muscle to stand up to the bosses. Actually, however, organized crime does not create high union wages for the rank and file; it preys upon them and parasitically takes its cut.

There is no chorus of organized labor voices at the local, regional, or national level demanding the ouster of racketeers from New York City's "captured" building trade unions. In the early decades of the twentieth century the mainstream labor movement fought to keep itself free of labor racketeers, but the last great spokesmen were Walter Reuther and George Meany in the late 1950s. Since then organized labor seems to have concluded that it would be worse for the labor movement to try to fight organized crime than to turn a blind eye. During the early stages of this project, organized labor welcomed the Teamsters back into the AFL-CIO, despite the unprecedented federal racketeering suit that was pending against the International Brotherhood of Teamsters, charging that union with having made "a devil's pact" with organized crime and documenting several decades of organized crime racketeering in the Teamsters.

How has all this happened? How has Cosa Nostra come to play such an important role in the core economy of New York City? In part, no doubt, the answer lies in the social history of New York City and in the adjustment of immigrant groups to the economic and social conditions of the early twentieth century. As Daniel Bell pointed out thirty years ago, industrial racketeering is a kind of parody of normal business relations in certain highly competitive industries. However, an important factor facilitating industrial racketeering has been the absence, at least until recently, of an effective law enforcement effort. It is an astonishing and lamentable chapter in the history of American law enforcement that almost until the end of a half century as Director of the FBI, J. Edgar Hoover denied the existence of "Mafia" or "Cosa Nostra" and refused to devote any special intelligence or law enforcement resources to this species of American criminality. Not until the 1960s, beginning with the appointment of Robert Kennedy (who played a major role in the McClellan Committee hearings), did a serious anti-organized crime effort begin to be shaped and implemented. A key part of that effort was the establishment of the Organized Crime Strike Forces which, for twenty years, operated in cities where organized crime is a significant problem. In the 1980s these Strike Forces compiled an impressive record of successes. Ironically, as this study goes to press, the federal Organized Crime Strike Forces are being dismantled due to a series of tragically unresolved tensions and rivalries within the U.S. Department of Justice. Although the Strike Forces did not adopt the kind of systemic approach advocated in this *Final Report*, without the sustained attention and expertise of the Strike Forces, it seems inevitable that the battle against organized crime will command lower priority and fewer resources, and that the prospect of ultimate victory will have receded for this generation.

It is not only law enforcement that has failed to come to grips with organized crime. The American political system has not set itself against organized crime, in part no doubt because organized crime is active in politics through the funding of political campaigns and, in some cases, in providing union manpower for political candidates. The complex inter-relationship between organized crime, labor racketeering and mainstream politics was recently illustrated when more than two hundred Congressmen took the extraordinary step of petitioning the United States Department of Justice to drop the racketeering suit against the Teamsters.

American academics have also tended to ignore organized crime's economic and political power. For a time it was a popular sociological position that organized crime did not exist at all, but was actually a kind of "demonological myth" perpetrated by white anglo saxon protestant elites to stigmatize immigrant groups, especially Italians. There have, of course, been exceptions. A few historians, especially Harold Seidman and John Hutchinson, have provided a valuable record of labor racketeering in construction and other industries. Likewise, in the 1920s the sociologist, John Landesco, wrote with insight and great detail about organized crime in Chicago. He particularly focused on the influence of racketeers on politics and politicians. Decades later, Daniel Bell described organized crime's domination of New York City's docks and the longshoreman's union. His scholarship should have provided a hint and a model for all urbanologists who sought to describe and explain urban life and institutions. Nevertheless, since Bell there have been hardly any major academic studies of industrial racketeering. One important exception is Peter Reuter's penetrating study of Long Island's waste hauling industry, a study also generated by and prepared in collaboration with a major OCTF investigation.

This does not mean, of course, that industrial racketeering has not been a matter of public record. The Kefauver Committee hearings in 1950 paid a great deal of attention to organized crime's penetration of legitimate industries. Ten years later, the McClellan Committee focused on the Teamsters, the International Longshoreman's Association, and several other racketeer-dominated unions. The 1986 President's Commission on Organized Crime found these unions still to be dominated by organized crime and offered a somewhat more sophisticated analysis of the symbiotic relationship of organized crime, organized labor, and business in several notorious industries.

The first half of the *Final Report* is devoted to documenting and explaining corruption and racketeering in the New York City construction industry. The second half is devoted to proposals for change. Given the entrenched and intractable nature of the problem, one must conclude that only profound and radical solutions could have a chance of success, and this is what is recommended. The Organized Crime Task Force has focused again and again on the utter failure of traditional policy interventions; more of the same will simply not be adequate. For there to be hope of success, we need to be thinking in terms of long term commitments, institution building, and strategies on a scale and at a level of ambition far greater than anything that has been tried before. There is a need for completely new initiatives. Thus, many of the recommendations look toward changing the structures and processes that generate the incentives for corruption and racketeering. We hope that policymakers will not scrutinize these recommendations with an eye for finding what is wrong and impractical, but with an eye for determining how these recommendations, if impractical or misguided, could be improved, supplemented, or adapted so that they could be implemented.

Make no mistake, this *Final Report* and the criminal investigations associated with it, for better or worse, constitute this generation's major attempt at confronting organized crime racketeering in the New York City construction industry. To allow this effort to fizzle out is to postpone serious reform for at least another generation.

This *Final Report* should also be recognized as a major contribution to "institution building" in social control. It does not explain the current situation in terms of notorious criminals but in terms of the economic and social variables that create the incentives for institutional actors to reach out to racketeers and organized crime syndicates. Thus, it offers a strategy for developing a more sophisticated crime control program that involves the mobilization of all key governmental and private institutions surrounding a crime-ridden industry.

It is remarkable that an operating law enforcement agency, facing all the day to day exigencies of investigations, trials, and appeals, could have produced a study like this. That the study was carried out at all is a credit to OCTF's Director, Ronald Goldstock, who has vigorously carried on Landesco's tradition of searching for systemic solutions to systemic crime problems. The Construction Industry Project's Director, Thomas Thacher, undoubtedly the most knowledgeable person (outside the construction industry itself) on the subject of corruption and racketeering in the New York City construction industry, gave his heart and soul to this *Final Report*. OCTF's second in command, Martin Marcus was a constant and generous source of support, knowledge, and plain good sense. OCTF staffer, Wilda Hess, organized the logistical support without which this massive research project would have been a shambles. Political scientist, Frank Anechiarico, provided us powerful research assistance, especially on official corruption and on fraud, waste, and abuse in public works. The members of the Construction Industry Strike Force's investigative teams read our drafts and provided valuable suggestions and criticisms. Dozens of consultants gave their time, shared their ideas, and endured our questioning and nagging; they especially deserve our thanks.

REFERENCES

Bell, Daniel. *The End of Ideology,* New York: Free Press, 1960.

Dahl, Robert. *Who Governs?: Democracy and Power in an American City* New Haven: Yale University Press, 1961.

Goldberg, Michael J. "Cleaning Labor's House: Institutional Reform Litigation in the Labor Movement" *Duke Law Journal* (1989), 903–1011.

Hutchinson, John. *The Imperfect Union: A History of Corruption in American Trade Unions,* New York: Dutton, 1970.

Industrial & Labor Relations Review, Symposium: "Attacking Corruption in Union-Management Relations," Vol. 42, no. 4, July 1989.

Johnson, Malcolm. *Crime on the Labor Front,* New York: McGraw-Hill, 1950.

Kefauver Committee, U.S. Senate Special Committee to Investigate Organized Crime in Interstate Commerce, *Final Report,* S. Rep. No. 725, 82nd Cong, 1st Sess, 1951.

Landesco, John. *Organized Crime in Chicago* (1929). New introduction by Mark Haller, University of Chicago Press, 1968.

McClellan Committee, *Final Report of the Select Committee on Improper Activities in the Labor or Management Field,* S. Rep. No. 1139, 86th Cong., 2nd Sess., 856 (1960).

Peterson, Virgil W. *The Mob: 200 Years of Organized Crime in New York,* Ottawa, Illinois: Green Hill Publishers, 1983.

President's Commission on Organized Crime, Report to the President and Attorney General. *The Edge: Organized Crime, Business, and Labor Unions,* Washington, D.C.: GPO, 1986.

Reuter, Peter. *Racketeering in Legitimate Industries: A Study in the Economics of Intimidation.* Prepared for the National Institute of Justice, U.S. Department of Justice. Santa Monica, Cal., RAND Corporation, 1987.

Schelling, Thomas. "Economic Analysis and Organized Crime," President's Commission on Crime and the Administration of Justice, *Task Force Report on Organized Crime,* Appendix D, Washington, D.C.: GPO, 1967.

Seidman, Harold. *Labor Czars: A History of Labor Racketeering,* New York: Liveright, 1938.

INTRODUCTION

The Origins and Mandate of OCTF's Investigation

In April 1985, in the wake of allegations by the media and the State Investigation Commission of rampant corruption and racketeering in New York City's construction industry, Mayor Edward I. Koch urged Governor Mario M. Cuomo to appoint a special prosecutor. The Governor agreed that the problem was serious and needed to be addressed. In a June 25, 1985, letter to the Mayor, Governor Cuomo stated:

> [W]e must break the back of corruption in the City's massive construction industry. Price fixing, job extortion, kickbacks and organized crime infiltration and control of legitimate business cannot and will not be tolerated in the greatest City of the greatest State in America.

Rather than appoint a special prosecutor, however, the Governor requested that the New York State Organized Crime Task Force (OCTF)[1] undertake an "intensive and comprehensive investigation into allegations of corruption and racketeering in the New York City construction industry." He also requested OCTF "to determine the appropriate prosecutorial and other responses to alleged organized crime activity within the multibillion dollar construction industry" and to report its conclusions to him and to the Attorney General. OCTF responded to the Governor's request by initiating criminal investigations, designing and utilizing a computerized database on corruption and racketeering in the construction industry, undertaking a comprehensive analytical study of the nature and causes of construction-related corruption and racketeering, and embarking upon a broad-based search for strategies to attack the problem.

1

OCTF's Crime-Control Strategy

OCTF's strategy for carrying out the Governor's mandate flowed from its philosophy of organized crime control. Investigations and prosecutions are means and not ends. The ultimate goal is not to send corrupt persons to prison but to reduce industry opportunities for and susceptibility to corruption and racketeering. Many means may be appropriate and necessary to accomplish this goal, including both criminal and civil remedies, as well as legislative, administrative and structural reforms.

Four principles underlie OCTF's approach and perspective on organized crime. First, broad enforcement strategies, rather than successive but unrelated investigations and prosecutions, are needed to combat organized crime. Criminal prosecutions are an effective means to change only if coordinated with comprehensive long-term strategies for control. Such strategies must themselves evolve from broad-based analyses of particular problem areas.

Second, to design and implement effective strategies a variety of skills and disciplines are required. In addition to law enforcement specialists, such as prosecutors, investigators, accountants and analysts, there must be consultation with economists, labor relations experts, loss prevention analysts, historians and those working within the industry itself.

Third, all appropriate remedies must be employed in developing and executing the control strategy. Incarceration and criminal fines are only one type. Others include civil forfeiture of the fruits and instrumentalities of racketeering, treble damages, and equitable relief that places racketeer-controlled unions, businesses or associations in judicially supervised receiverships. Structural, technological and institutional changes may be necessary to reduce opportunities for infiltration and control by racketeers. These changes may require new legislation, agency regulation or civil litigation; alternatively, they may be voluntarily adopted by key industry participants committed to meaningful reform.

Fourth, the State has a particular role in organized crime control that is distinct from that of federal and local authorities. The State can adopt enforcement and reform strategies beyond the power of counties or municipalities to pursue strategies that reflect regional needs and concerns, and are not subject to possible shifts in federal priorities. Construction industry racketeering in the New York City metropolitan area, for example, requires the efforts of law enforcement and regulatory agencies not provided for under federal statutes and beyond the power or resources of localities to establish or support.

The Interim Report

OCTF released its *Interim Report on Racketeering and Corruption in the New York City Construction Industry* (*Interim Report*) in April 1988. The *Interim Report* defined and described the magnitude and complexity of the construction industry's crime problems, offered significant historical perspectives, illuminated Cosa Nostra's role in the New York City construction industry and attempted to explain why the industry has been so vulnerable to corruption and racketeering throughout this century. The *Interim Report* also raised a number of policy options to be explored, but refrained from making recommendations beyond recommending against appointment of a special prosecutor and proposing abolition of the Wicks Law.[2]

The *Interim Report* focused considerable attention on the New York City construction industry. Governor Cuomo said: "This opportunity [for corruption], this temptation is obviously irresistible. We have talked about the problem for years. Now it is time to do something about it."[3] In a letter to Governor Cuomo, Mayor Koch commented:

> I . . . applaud its detail, care and expanse. Clearly, the OCTF study has given New York State strong momentum. That momentum should not be lost. . . . [T]he public must have confidence that the State's response is solid, thorough and capable of attacking the persistent, vexing problem of construction industry corruption.

The Manhattan Institute invited prominent members of the building community, academics, government officials and representatives of the media to a roundtable discussion of the *Interim Report*. The *Engineering News Record*, the leading national construction trades journal, declared that:

> New York City construction is so corroded by corruption that it should be on the verge of collapse. That it isn't is testimony to the law of inertia: Something in motion remains in motion unless acted upon by some external force.

> New York Gov. Mario M. Cuomo's report on corruption in the city
> might be such a force. Unfortunately, the fact that the city's construc-
> tion industry has been blasted, plastered and tarred for so long
> means that this report probably will draw the usual yawns from
> insiders. But that won't do much to change facts, and they are
> what the city and the industry must face to deal squarely with
> the problem.[4]

After the release of the *Interim Report*, the Governor appointed
a citizens commission comprised of leaders from the building
and business communities, chaired by the Director of the Citizens Crime Commission, to analyze the construction industry's
crime problems and to advise him on possible solutions.

Creation of the Construction Industry Strike Force

Although Governor Cuomo rejected the idea of a special prosecutor's office, he recognized the need to enhance and focus the
law enforcement effort. Thus, in December 1987 he created the
Construction Industry Strike Force (CISF). Comprised of attorneys, investigators, analysts, accountants and support staff from
both OCTF and the New York County District Attorney's Office,
CISF has successfully pooled the resources, jurisdiction and
expertise of these two law enforcement offices into a concerted
attack on systematic criminality in the New York City construction industry. CISF constitutes a unique law enforcement initiative; it should serve as a model for attacking other corrupt
industries in New York City and elsewhere.

CISF has carried forward OCTF's investigations and launched
many new ones. It has obtained or significantly contributed to
the indictment and conviction of corrupt officials of construction
trade unions representing laborers, carpenters, teamsters, bricklayers and mason tenders. CISF has also successfully prosecuted
construction companies and their officers. One indictment
details pervasive corruption and racketeering by contractors,
union officials and organized crime members in the drywall
industry. Another set forth extortion, bribery and the illegal allocation of contracts in the concrete industry. Minority coalition
extortionists, building inspectors and a number of Cosa Nostra
family members and associates have also been charged and convicted.

Prosecutions directed at systemic racketeering, no matter how significant, can only provide long-term crime reduction if coupled with other remedies. Thus, in conjunction with several other prosecutorial offices, CISF is pursuing a number of civil racketeering lawsuits. These suits will seek wide-ranging judicial supervision of corrupt unions and companies.

With each investigation and prosecution, CISF has grown more sophisticated in its understanding of the intricacies of how racketeers exploit the construction industry, which trades are most corrupt, which companies have formed cartels, and which unions are mob dominated or are on the verge of becoming so. No other agency has the depth and breadth of knowledge about corruption and racketeering in the New York City construction industry.

CISF has increasingly used this knowledge to assist other public agencies, including the New York City School Construction Authority and the Port Authority of New York and New Jersey, to detect and deter criminality in their capital construction programs. For example, CISF has agreed to assign two teams of attorneys and investigators to conduct investigations relating to School Construction Authority projects, and the Port Authority has asked CISF to assign another team to focus on construction at JFK International Airport.

In addition to the joint criminal investigations and prosecutions begun under the CISF umbrella, OCTF's Construction Industry Project has continued its study of the construction industry. We have held workshops on the characteristics of and problems in the construction industry that give rise to corruption and racketeering, and on the effectiveness and viability of proposed reforms. Our involvement with the School Construction Authority and the Port Authority has also increased our awareness of the difficulties that public agencies face in making their operations crime resistant.

Based on our criminal investigations, consultations and workshops, and our review and analysis of the scholarly literature, we have come to understand the mechanisms of corruption and racketeering in the New York City construction industry. With that understanding, we have sought out, developed, considered and analyzed a wide variety of proposals for change. This *Final Report* is the result.[5]

The Final Report

The *Final Report* is divided into two parts. Part I, comprised of Chapters 1 through 5, presents the "Nature of the Problem," and sets forth a comprehensive description and analysis of the crime problems affecting the New York City construction industry. Chapter 1 provides examples of the types of crimes that regularly occur in New York City's construction industry. Chapter 2 presents an analysis of the economic, legal and social factors that provide incentives for corruption and racketeering. It introduces the key concepts of "racketeering susceptibility" and "racketeering potential" and links them to the industry's crime problems. Chapter 3 documents how racketeers and crime syndicates, since the early twentieth century, have taken advantage of the industry's high levels of racketeering susceptibility and potential to achieve influence and power in the building trades and construction firms. This chapter also documents that Cosa Nostra crime families have been the dominant racketeering force in the industry since the 1930s. Chapter 4 is devoted to official corruption in the construction industry, including the corrupt activities of land use and construction regulators, public works administrators and powerbrokers who exert influence over both regulators and administrators. Chapter 5 focuses on fraud in public construction, demonstrating the many ways that corrupt contractors can siphon money out of the City's vast public works projects. Part II, "Paths to Reform: A Comprehensive Crime-Control Strategy," which includes Chapters 6 through 10, builds directly on the documentation and analysis provided in Part I.

No "knockout punch" exists that can instantly remove pervasive and entrenched corruption and racketeering from the New York City construction industry. Instead, the City's goal must be to institutionalize a *process of change* by making a long-term commitment to reform that includes, most importantly, a continuing effort to understand the underlying causes of racketeering susceptibility and potential and to develop creative initiatives to neutralize or, at least, reduce them. This long-term commitment must also include the design and implementation of a comprehensive crime-control strategy.

Chapter 6 sets out the general organizational framework necessary to put the comprehensive crime-control strategy in place and provides the general principles upon which such a strategy should be based. We have not recommended a new super-regulatory agency, because one of the main impediments to change has been the tendency of the relevant government agencies to define corruption and racketeering in the construction industry as "somebody else's problem." The better course lies in integrating the efforts of the several law enforcement agencies with jurisdiction over crime in the industry, and in mobilizing the energies of those agencies directly or indirectly involved in regulating the construction industry and in implementing public works. While we primarily rely on the synergism that will result from more effective integration and utilization of existing resources, and recommend against the establishment of new bureaucracies, we also call for the creation of two new agencies, an Office of Construction Corruption Prevention (OCCP) and an Office of Union Members Advocacy (OUMA). We also call for implementation of a Certified Investigative Auditing Firm (CIAF) program, which would result in private sector support for the design, implementation and monitoring of reform initiatives.

Chapter 7 deals with labor racketeering, the most serious crime problem in the construction industry. It identifies union democracy as the most promising antidote to labor racketeering, and offers several strategies to increase democracy in the building trades. Among these are recommendations for making enforcement of the federal Landrum-Griffin law more effective, and strengthening court-ordered trusteeships over racketeer-ridden unions.

Chapter 8 takes up the problem of corporate racketeering, which involves businessmen who conspire with corrupt labor officials to sell out the rights of union members, and who engage in systematic criminality that includes antitrust violations, tax frauds, bribery of public officials and fraud on public construction projects. Ways must be found to stimulate competition in those areas of the construction industry currently under the domination of corrupt cartels and monopolies. We recommend much more vigorous use of antitrust and tax laws to eliminate the "edge" which corrupt contractors enjoy over honest businessmen and women. In addition, we recommend amending several criminal law statutes and adopting procedural reforms that

would make the investigation and prosecution of corporate racketeering more productive.

Chapter 9 presents recommendations for preventing official
corruption, including increased privatizing of inspections,
improved agency accountability, and better ethics and campaign
finance laws. Chapter 10 is devoted to recommendations for
reducing fraud in public construction. This is especially timely
because of the public sector's one hundred billion dollar, ten-year
plan to rebuild the City's infrastructure for the twenty-first century. Our recommendations on this subject deal with improving
auditing procedures and strengthening the administration of
public works.

FOOTNOTES

1. The legislature established OCTF in 1970 (Executive Law § 70-a). The director is appointed jointly by the Governor and Attorney General. OCTF's mandate is to investigate and prosecute multi-county organized criminal activity and to assist local law enforcement agencies in their efforts against organized crime.

2. The Wicks Law, which requires public works projects to hire four prime contractors rather than one general contractor, is discussed in Chapters 5 and 10.

3. "Cuomo to Unleash Strike Force to Combat New York Corruption," *Engineering News Record* 220 (26 May 1988): 11.

4. Editorial, *Engineering News Record* 220 (26 May 1988): 74.

5. This Report was substantially completed in December 1989 and a copy given to Governor Cuomo. Thereafter, stylistic changes were made, and the Report was readied for publication. Minor substantive changes have also been made to reflect events in the intervening months and to assure accuracy as of April 1990.

PART I

The Nature of the Problem

CHAPTER 1

A catalog of corruption and racketeering in the construction industry

Introduction

A previous commission studying corruption in New York City's building trades described criminal activity in all phases of the industry, engaged in by participants at every level. It found extensive union extortion of builders and contractors, expressed amazement at the extent of collusive agreements among contractors and suppliers, and documented racketeers using their control over construction unions to extort large "tribute" payments from builders and contractors by threatening to withhold labor unless the payments were made. It also reported that contractors and suppliers had substantially eliminated competition by forming cartels or "combinations":

> In almost every branch of the many activities that enter into building construction we found these combinations rampant and unchecked and competition completely throttled. The result was accomplished by all manner of devices, from the flagrant matching of bids and illegal combinations between employers and employees associations, to the surreptitious agency of the apparently innocuous Luncheon Club, under cover of which production was regulated, territory apportioned and prices fixed between ostensible competitors.

These findings were not made in the 1980s, but in a 1922 report of the New York State Joint Legislative Committee on Housing (the "Lockwood Commission").[1] The similarity between the scandalous conditions in 1922 and those that exist today underscores how deeply rooted the construction industry's crime problems are, and cautions against promising "quick fixes" and instant solutions.

To appreciate the extent and complexity of the construction industry's interrelated and multifaceted crime problems, an understanding of the industry's organization and operation is necessary. Thus, we turn first to a description of the New York City construction industry, and then to a catalog of criminality that occurs throughout the construction process.

Putting the New York City Construction Industry in Perspective

New York City's construction industry is not a single, vertically or horizontally organized industry dominated by a small number of national or multinational corporations. It is a huge, fragmented, decentralized industry characterized by thousands of small and medium sized construction companies and materials suppliers. In fact, economists often prefer to speak of construction as a sector of the economy rather than as a single industry.

New York City's construction industry includes more than one hundred thousand workers, many hundreds of specialty subcontractors, hundreds of general contractors, dozens of major developers and many one-time or infrequent builders ranging from large corporations to small entrepreneurs. Architects, engineers, bankers, insurance brokers, lawyers, accountants, public administrators, and government inspectors and contracting personnel also play significant roles.[2]

One way to classify construction is to distinguish between public works and private projects. Public work projects include bridges, roads, tunnels, mass transit, parks, schools, housing projects, airports, water supply and waste disposal systems, courts, jails and government office complexes. New York City's public works projects are some of the country's largest. The North River Water Pollution Control Plant, which has been under construction along the Hudson River in upper Manhattan since 1970 and began operating in 1986, is expected to cost $1.1 billion. The Third Water Tunnel (the first phase of which is being constructed from the Bronx/Westchester border, through mid-Manhattan, east to Roosevelt Island, and ending in Astoria, Queens) is the most expensive public works project ever undertaken by the City of New York. It is estimated that the entire project will cost $5 billion. The City's Executive Budget calls for expending more than $5 billion on capital projects in Fiscal Year 1989 (see Table 1)[3] and a total of $57.3 billion for Fiscal Years 1989 through 1998.[4] This figure does not include the projects undertaken by such major public builders as the Port Authority (builder of the World Trade Center), the Metropolitan Transit Authority and the Battery Park City Authority. Total public works spending over the next ten years could well amount to more than $100 billion.

Private construction ranges from single family homes to retail stores, shopping centers, factories, utilities and high-rise residential and commercial buildings. Although occurring throughout the City, high-rise construction is concentrated in Manhattan. Many of these buildings or multibuilding projects are awesome architectural and engineering feats, with extraordinary costs and construction histories. The per-square-foot construction costs of these projects are the highest in the United States; not surprisingly, so are the rental and purchase costs.

At any time, New York City has hundreds of projects at different stages of completion. In Fiscal Year 1989, builders filed 45,288 plans with the Buildings Department; the Department performed over 120,000 inspections and issued 10,335 certificates of occupancy.[5] Between 1981 and 1987, fifty-two million square feet of office space (the equivalent of twenty Empire State Buildings) were constructed.[6]

All major New York City construction projects, public and private, are carried out by workers, many of whom are organized into approximately one hundred building trades local unions. These unions can be roughly divided into four groups. The first includes the skilled mechanical tradespeople, such as electricians, iron workers, sheet metal workers, plumbers, steamfitters, elevator constructors and operating engineers. The second group is comprised of skilled nonmechanical tradespeople such as carpenters, bricklayers, painters and roofers. The third group includes unskilled laborers who carry out such tasks as pouring and spreading concrete, carrying and moving materials, and assisting the skilled trades. The fourth group is comprised of those who support, but are not actually involved in, the physical construction process. Truck drivers who deliver materials to, and remove debris from, construction sites are the largest compo-

nent in this group. Organized by the International Brotherhood
of Teamsters, they constitute one of the most vital and powerful
unions in the industry.

Construction unions rarely negotiate labor contracts directly
with individual employers; rather, they negotiate with employer
associations formed by contractors involved in the same type of
construction work. There are approximately fifty such contractor
associations in New York City. Because an individual contractor
may perform several types of construction work, it is not unu-
sual for a company to be a member of several associations.
General contractors, for example, have their own employer
associations. Three principal associations are the General Contractors Association (GCA), representing heavy construction,
excavation and road contractors; the Building Contractors
Association (BCA), representing alteration and high-rise
builders; and the Contractors Association of Greater New York
(CAGNY), another group that includes some of the major high-
rise builders.

This structure of unions and contractors creates a very complex system of collective bargaining.[7] A single contractor may
have several employer associations negotiating on his behalf
with a single union. Conversely, a union may be involved in collective bargaining with as many as a dozen contractor associations. For example, the Carpenters Union has contracts with the
GCA, BCA, CAGNY, the Metropolitan Drywall Association, the
Manufacturing Woodworkers Association and other specialty
contractor associations.

Much of this report deals with high-rise construction projects.
A description, even if abbreviated, of how such projects are built
is therefore useful. The first steps rely heavily on complementary
service sector industries. Sources of finance must be found to
provide the working capital. Lawyers and consultants are
needed to obtain zoning approvals and permits as the often time-
consuming process of land assemblage takes place. Architects
and engineers develop plans that must meet the numerous building and safety standards as interpreted by the various City agencies with authority over construction. (See Table 2.)

The next steps are demolition, site clearance and site excavation. Foundations containing huge quantities of concrete are

then laid. The superstructure is then built, using steel, reinforced concrete, brick or some combination of these materials. Where concrete is the dominant ingredient, it may account for as much as twenty percent of the project's total cost.[8]

After the superstructure is in place, the interior work begins. Elevators, stairs, plumbing, electrical systems, drywall, and heating and cooling systems are installed. The last stages include such finishing work as carpentry, painting, and the installation of doors, windows, and fixtures. Large projects, which can take years from planning to tenant occupancy, include the participation of thousands of workers and scores of contractors.

The owner or developer is represented on a construction site by a construction management company or a general contractor whose responsibilities include selecting and supervising the many contractors. Most contractors are required to maintain on their payrolls on-site representatives of unions with jurisdiction over the contractors' workforce. These union representatives are known variously as shop stewards, working teamster foremen or master mechanics and, although paid by the contractor, do little or no construction work; often their only responsibility is to assure compliance with collective bargaining agreements.

Large construction sites are enclosed by fences with security guards monitoring ingress and egress of workers and materials. "Working teamster foremen" are posted in trailers near the gates to verify the union membership of all drivers who deliver materials to the site. The enclosed site is dotted with trailers or shacks that serve as the contractors' field offices.

The presence of so many parties, engaged in so many disparate activities with multiple layers of responsibilities and often conflicting commands on loyalties, makes coordination of the construction process an extraordinary challenge. New Yorkers can be justly proud of the world famous accomplishments of their city's construction industry, which operates under some of the most difficult conditions in the world. They should also be profoundly disturbed by the pervasive corruption and racketeering that have plagued this industry throughout the twentieth century.

Description of Pervasive Corruption and Racketeering

Because of the size, diversity and complexity of New York City's construction industry, a comprehensive audit of the corrupt activities within it is impossible. Construction is project oriented. Each project has a unique life with a different constellation of builders, general and specialty contractors, and workers. However, the same unions (albeit through different locals) are involved in almost all construction projects throughout the New York City metropolitan area.

Construction projects are not easily subject to generalization and do not hold still for "snapshot" descriptions. Thus, it can always be argued that yesterday's information is outdated or that conclusions based upon a particular project, contractor, union or supplier cannot be applied to others. Those who wish to minimize or paper over problems, or throw cold water on proposals for reform, may claim that problems revealed by one investigation or prosecution are aberrational and not necessarily typical of the industry as a whole. Such criticisms are not persuasive. While recognizing the hazards of generalizing from limited data, we believe that historical and contemporary evidence, including our own criminal investigations, establish beyond any doubt that corruption and racketeering pervade New York City's construction industry and provide an ample factual basis for developing proposals for reform.

We use the term "racketeering" to refer to the activities of professional criminals—those who engage in crime as a business. They may be full-time criminals and members of criminal syndicates, or they may operate as businessmen, union officers, or government officials who systematically use their legitimate positions for illegitimate ends. Racketeers span the gamut from unskilled hustlers to sophisticated leaders of large legitimate or illegitimate organizations. New York City's construction industry has many types of racketeers. By far the most important are members and associates of New York City's five Cosa Nostra organized crime families. They have been involved in the City's construction industry for decades, utilizing their organizational expertise, underworld networks, and reputation and capacity for violence. Cosa Nostra's entrenchment in construction companies and unions makes the industry's "crime problem" all the more serious and the need to address it all the more imperative.

This chapter as well as Chapters 4 and 5 describe the most common forms of corruption and racketeering. They demonstrate the extent and magnitude of the challenge which the political system, law enforcement, and the industry itself face in formulating and implementing strategies for change. The examples are drawn mostly from criminal prosecutions that are now matters of public record. We have also drawn upon the insights and information gained from the many construction investigations conducted by the Construction Industry Strike Force (CISF). We are, however, constrained by statutory prohibitions and the investigative need for confidentiality not to disclose details of on-going investigations and prosecutions, since they include secret grand jury information or involve yet undisclosed electronic surveillance, confidential informants and undercover operations.

Extortion[9]

In the construction industry, only a thin line separates extortion and bribery. Illegal payments flow from contractors to union officers and public officials. Sometimes money is paid to avoid an explicit or implicit threat; this is extortion. Sometimes money is paid to buy favors; this is bribery. Sometimes contractors claim not to know exactly why they pay; experience tells them that payoffs are necessary to assure that "things will run smoothly."

Many different types of extortion are commonplace in the construction industry. All involve the use of threats to obtain money, services or other things of value. Perhaps the most common form of extortion involves union officials "shaking down" contractors by threatening labor problems.[10] Unless the contractor pays off, he will be subjected to work slowdowns, disruption, sabotage or physical harm. Consider the following examples:

- John O'Connor, business agent of Carpenters Local 608, the largest Carpenters' local in the country, was indicted in 1987 on 127 counts alleging bribery, extortion, and taking unlawful gifts from seventeen contractors. The indictment alleges that O'Connor threatened contractors with labor unrest or insufficient workers for a project unless they paid him sums of money up to $4,000.[11] In a companion indictment, Local 608 Business Agent Martin Forde was charged with extortion and related offenses.[12]

- Attilio Bitondo and Gene Hanley, business agents for Carpenters Local 257, were indicted in 1987 on multiple counts of extortion over a ten-year period. They allegedly received as much as $7,500 per bribe from contractors by threatening to withhold assignment of skilled labor. [13]

- Laborers Local 66 vice-president Peter Vario was convicted after trial, and Michael LaBarbara, Jr. (business manager) and James Abbatiello (assistant business manager) pleaded guilty to accepting multiple payoffs involving eight Long Island construction companies. In exchange for these payments, the contractors were permitted to pay workers below union scale; to avoid hiring shop stewards; did not have to contribute money to union welfare and benefit funds; and were allowed to use nonunion workers. [14]

- George Boylan, business manager of Local 5 of the International Brotherhood of Boilermakers, was convicted of extorting more than $1 million over a fifteen year period from six construction companies working on electrical power plants. Boylan threatened a strike if the payments were not made. His demands were allegedly supported by Pittsburgh organized crime figures. [15]

- Gaetano "Corky" Vastola, a member of the DeCavalcante Crime Family of New Jersey, was indicted in May 1969 for allegedly extorting more than $500,000 from one of the country's largest carpet manufacturers. Vastola extorted the money by threatening to organize a union in the company's Georgia plant and to prevent the company's carpets from being laid in the metropolitan area. The indictment also named as criminal participants Jesse Smith, an assistant to the president of Local 2241 of the Carpenters Union, and Ronald Annunziata, president of the Greater New York Floor Covering Association. Upon his conviction in 1970, Vastola was sentenced to three to five years imprisonment. [16]

- During his U.S. Senate Confirmation Hearings, former Secretary of Labor Raymond Donovan testified about labor problems encountered by his company, Schiavone Construction Company, on the 63rd Street Subway Tunnel Project. Donovan stated that Teamsters Local 282 business agent Harry Gross personally threatened him with labor shutdowns. Following settlement of a work stoppage, Schiavone hired a non-working teamster foreman, whose duties were to provide chauffeuring services to Gross. [17]

- Teamster Local 282 business agent Harry Gross pleaded guilty to extorting $2,500 from Vacar Construction Corp. by threatening illegal work stoppages. [18]

- A federal investigation of the drywall industry (code name LILREX) led to the indictment of the president of the New York City and Vicinity District Council of Carpenters and five other union officials connected to organized crime families for extorting more than $100,000 from a drywall contractor. [19] The District Council president disappeared and was presumed murdered on the eve of trial.

- The federal government brought a civil RICO suit against Cement and Concrete Workers Local 6A of the Laborers' International Union, alleging that the union local and its district council, their officers and certain organized crime figures extorted one percent of the contract price from ready-mix concrete contractors by threatening "labor problems." The settlement of the action included the resignation of more than a dozen union officers and the installation of a court-appointed trustee to oversee the running of the union.[20]

- The president and other officers of Housewreckers Local 95 of the Laborers Union were convicted of extorting $20,000 from Schiavone-Chase Corporation by threatening labor delays on a Westway Highway demolition contract.[21]

- On August 26, 1986, two former building inspectors were charged with extorting more than $40,000 in bribes and kickbacks from contractors doing approximately $2 million of masonry work at Co-op City in the Bronx. The inspectors threatened "on the job harassment." After being convicted of extortion under the "Hobbs Act" (Title 18 U.S.C. § 1951) and tax fraud, one was sentenced to a prison term of five years and a fine of $100,000. His co-defendant was sentenced to two years in prison and fined $10,000.[22]

- In August 1988, officials of three Bricklayers locals were charged with, *inter alia*, racketeering and extortion. Jack Argila, the business manager of Bricklayers Local 30, was convicted of accepting an illegal cash payment from a subcontractor. Sebastian "Barney" Scola, ex-business agent for Bricklayers Local 9, in pleading guilty to a violation of the Taft-Hartley Act, admitted accepting a labor peace payoff. Frank Alessi, business agent of Bricklayers Local 41, pleaded guilty to accepting five separate payoffs from contractors in violation of the Taft-Hartley Law.[23]

- Edward Annino, a working teamster foreman for Teamsters Local 282, was convicted in January 1989 of conspiracy to extort and extortion of money from a nonunion contractor who was performing scaffolding work during the construction of the International Design Center of New York in Queens in 1985.[24]

New forms of extortion continue to appear. Persons operating under the guise of groups advocating increased minority workforce representation extort payments by threatening to disrupt operations unless payoffs are made. For example:

- Leaders of Link Community Construction Works, Inc., FAIR, South Brooklyn Construction Workers, Inc., and Brooklyn Fight Back claimed they were putting pressure on contractors to hire minorities but, in fact, were perpetrating a cynical scheme to line their own pockets. These groups, located in Brooklyn, intimidated, harassed and threatened to stop the work of contractors who refused to make payoffs to them. They demanded salaries for no-show jobs, cash payoffs, and work for companies they owned. Three defendants, who eventually pleaded guilty, netted more than $100,000 from 1981 to 1984.[25] Four other defendants were convicted after trial in 1989.

• Four men, using their association with a labor organization known as United Tremont Trades (UTT), were indicted in February 1989 for extorting more than $16,000 from contractors at ten building sites by threatening violence, property damage and work stoppages. The payoffs were disguised by placing the extorters on the contractors' payroll in nonexistent positions as "equal employment officers" and "coordinators" for UTT.[26]

Bribery[27]

Bribes, "grease" payments and tips are a way of life in New York City's construction industry. Bribes are frequently paid by contractors to obtain contracts, favors and services to which they are not entitled. Bribes have frequently been solicited by government officials who control contract letting or building permits, or by union officials who can offer sweetheart contracts (contracts that omit significant and customary benefits and rights for employees in order to reduce the employer's labor costs, arrived at without the approval—or even the knowledge—of union members) or nonenforcement of costly collective bargaining provisions. Grease payments and tips are often paid to assure delivery of goods or performance of services to which the payor is legally and contractually entitled.

Extortion and bribery often go hand in hand. The Second Circuit Court of Appeals described the corrupt activity of some Long Island construction engineers:

> Over a 12-year period ending in 1979 appellants engaged in an audacious pattern of corrupt and illegal activities in New York, New Jersey and Connecticut. As consulting engineers on a number of major sewer construction projects in the tri-state area, and with the connivance of others, appellants extorted money from the project contractors under their control and fraudulently overstated payment claims. Equally outrageous, appellants then used the proceeds of these illegal actions to bribe public officials in order to obtain additional contracts and other forms of preferential treatment from the municipalities they were ostensibly serving.[28]

There have been periodic revelations of corruption among City building inspectors who solicit and accept bribes to provide necessary permits and certificates of occupancy:

- In 1986, a civil RICO action was filed to recover $35 million from plumbing and excavating contractors and $2.4 million from four building inspectors in connection with a scheme from 1975 to 1984 in which bribes were paid to insure issuance of certificates of inspection in the Bronx, Queens, and Manhattan; as a result, improper sewer connections and repairs caused substantial structural problems in the City's sewer system. The four inspectors had previously been convicted of federal mail fraud and Hobbs Act violations.[29]
- The Brooklyn manager of electrical inspections and a field-level inspector were convicted of taking bribes from private electrical contractors to facilitate departmental paperwork and overlook code violations.[30]
- In 1986, the Kings County District Attorney's Office indicted twenty-six building maintenance inspectors employed by the New York City Board of Education for conspiracy to solicit money from contractors undertaking construction for the Board of Education. The indictments allege that the inspectors received over $100,000 from contractors in return for assistance in obtaining inspection approvals.[31]
- In July 1985, thirteen building owners and contractors were arrested for offering bribes to a city building inspector engaged in undercover work for the City's Department of Investigation. During the three month undercover investigation, the inspector made routine inspections at building sites in Brooklyn and was offered money by twenty-eight owners or contractors in exchange for specific favors or future cooperation.[32]
- In January 1987, the manager of Matthews Industrial Piping Company testified that between 1979 and 1983 he had paid $126,000 to Milton Fishkin, a City fire prevention inspector, in order to obtain expedited processing of certificates of compliance with fire safety standards. He also testified that Fishkin had recommended to Mobil Oil that the Matthews Company be awarded the Port Mobil contract.[33]

Another common form of bribery is contractor payoffs to union officials to obtain "waivers" of such collective bargaining provisions as hiring hall and union shop agreements, contributions to employee benefit funds, overtime pay, and mandated ratios of union stewards to workers at the site. For example:

- The LILREX investigation of the drywall industry revealed that two large carpentry firms bribed officials of the Carpenters Union to permit the hiring of nonunion workers who were paid on a "piecework" or "lumping" basis (that is, by the number of drywall sheets installed rather than by the hour). The bribe also assured avoidance of required overtime and fringe benefit payments.[34]

- John Cody, president of Teamsters Local 282 from 1976 to 1984, had the ability to paralyze the construction industry (as evidenced by the three-month strike in 1982). Because of this power, Cody was able to solicit payoffs from employers who depended on his union members for delivery of necessary building materials. He took bribes in the form of free labor and building materials for his summer home from a company employing Local 282 workers. He was also convicted of accepting chauffeur services provided by another construction company.[35]
- Attilio Bitondo and Gene Hanley, business agents for Carpenters Local 257, have been charged with extorting tens of thousands of dollars from contractors over a period of ten years. This money was allegedly obtained under threat of refusing to refer a sufficient number of skilled carpenters to meet the companies' needs. According to the indictment, one contractor was forced to construct a portion of Hanley's home at a price $5,000 below full-market value.[36]

Under Federal law, employees who work on federal construction projects are entitled to the prevailing wage rate for workers on nongovernment projects. Contractors have not only violated this law by underpaying their employees, but have bribed officials in order to avoid paying the penalties in the form of wages determined to be owed to the employees for previous work.

- In February 1989, five contractors were charged with paying bribes of up to $10,000 to a U.S. Department of Labor official in connection with construction of a federally-subsidized nursing home on Long Island and with filing false reports with the U.S. Department of Labor and the U.S. Department of Housing and Urban Development. One contractor, upon pleading guilty to a mail fraud violation, was sentenced to five years probation and ordered to make restitution of $271,000 to his employees.[37]

Construction workers themselves are sometimes in a position to solicit bribes; for example, a worker in a critical position can demand a payoff from contractors before performing his assigned task. It is common for "working teamster foremen" to seek money for granting access to a site and for hoist and crane operators to demand cash for taking supplies and workers up and down the elevators. In an electronically intercepted conversation presented at the trial of Teamsters Local 282 Shop Steward Edward Annino, Annino explained to a contractor that bribes for persons holding certain positions on the job site should be calculated as part of the cost of doing business:

> ANNINO: See, when you figure a job, you gotta figure a master
>   mechanic, the elevator. You gotta figure all that in
>   there.[38]

Theft

Newspapers have reported, and OCTF sources have confirmed, that theft is rampant on some construction projects. For example, a *New York Times* investigative report described systematic theft in the 1970s renovation of the Chrysler building:

> Building supplies disappeared from the site. Wiring was installed during the day and vanished at night.... In addition, construction workers carried off cartloads of scrap metal from the interior of the building. This practice of keeping scrap, known in the trade as mungo, is widely viewed by demolition workers as a perquisite of the job.[39]

According to a national survey of contractors by the Associated General Contractors, losses by theft have amounted to $1 billion annually.[40] The largest losses are of equipment and materials. One contractor explained the general practice of incorporating the cost of anticipated employee pilferage into bids. He also asserted that it was sometimes cheaper and more efficient to repurchase his own stolen property from employee thieves than to replace it.[41] As another example:

> • On June 4, 1987, two operators of a Long Island pipe supply company pleaded guilty to stealing $1 million worth of pipes from New York City's pipeyards in four of the five boroughs. The scheme involved payments of $250,000 in cash bribes to employees of the City's Department of Environmental Protection to obtain their assistance in stealing the pipes and pipe fittings. The defendants sold the stolen pipes to contractors working on the City's sewer and water mains. In effect, the defendants thus stole the pipes from the City and then sold them back to the City.[42]

Frauds

Fraud is the offense of obtaining property through deceit or trickery. Four basic types of fraud exist in New York City's construction industry: (1) fraudulent billing for work not performed or materials not used; (2) defrauding union pension and welfare funds by avoiding required payments; (3) defrauding the government by failing to report taxable income or by falsely reporting business expenses; and (4) fraudulent performance bonds.[43]

Fraudulent Billing

Unscrupulous contractors can defraud owners and developers by submitting claims for work not performed and building materials not used. This is an especially serious problem in public construction, where supervision and monitoring are notoriously lax and where, by law, public agencies must supervise construction projects themselves rather than delegate supervision to a general contractor, which is standard practice for private builders.

- In 1987, officers of an electrical contracting firm, Federal Chandros, Inc., were indicted for submitting false and fraudulently altered payment claims and invoices to City agencies. The defendants allegedly photocopied the original invoices paid by Federal Chandros, altered the dollar amounts and delivery information, rephotocopied the altered invoices to disguise tampering and billed the City for the altered amounts. According to the indictment, Federal Chandros defrauded the City and its agencies of $6 million on a variety of construction projects, including the Owls Head Water Pollution Control Plant, Transit Authority subway power substations, New York County State Supreme Court building, New York City Police Headquarters, offices of the New York City Planning Commission, and the Metropolitan Museum of Art.[44]
- In the 1987 Tag Pipe case, the company, a major supplier of pipes and pipe fittings in the metropolitan area, admitted to the "creation of millions of dollars of fictitious and inflated invoices" for numerous City contractors, who used these phony invoices to defraud the City.[45]
- Also in 1987, Durante Bros. Construction Corporation and its president were indicted for stealing $342,000 from New York City agencies by overstating the amount of asphalt delivered to City construction sites. The contractor was charged with submitting false and/or inflated delivery tickets to a number of City agencies.[46]

Public agencies are highly vulnerable to fraud for many reasons. Perhaps the most important is that they lack knowledge about the performance record of the contractors with whom they deal. A public agency today has no adequate means to find out whether a particular contracting company's officers have previously been convicted of, charged with, or linked to fraud. The Third Water Tunnel Project illustrates the problem. *Newsday* reported that the Omaha-based Peter Kiewit firm is part of a consortium that has won six of the nine Water Tunnel contracts.[47] Since 1973, this firm and its subsidiaries have been charged with bid rigging on six American contracts and one Canadian contract. The Kiewit companies have been found guilty or pleaded no contest in five of these cases. Similarly, until recently, New York City purchased concrete for the Water Tunnel Project from two firms, Transit Mix and Certified Industries, which at the time were under indictment in federal and state courts.[48]

Pension and Welfare Fund Fraud
Of the two major types of frauds involving union pension and welfare funds, one is perpetrated by contractors and the other by fund trustees. Contractors defraud the workers' funds by bribing union officials to permit double-breasted shops[49] and off-the-books payrolls under which contributions to the employee benefit funds are avoided. Workers are sometimes willing to forgo fringe benefits in return for unreported cash wages that can be shielded from federal, state and local taxes. Indeed, workers may have little financial incentive to object, especially if pension benefits vest after a minimum number of hours of work per year. In any event, workers who complain are vulnerable to reprisals, including physical violence or blacklisting.

  • The LILREX investigation revealed corrupt carpentry contractors
    defrauding union pension and welfare funds by paying employees
    in cash "off-the-books." Each company went further by fraudu-
    lently certifying its off-the-books employees as unemployed, so
    that they could collect unemployment insurance—yet another
    fraud.[50]

A recent example of how to maximize profits at the expense of employees was revealed through OCTF's analysis of records seized, pursuant to a search warrant, from a Long Island-based concrete contractor. The contractor reported and paid benefits on a weekly maximum of thirty-five hours per employee. Overtime hours—those over thirty-five hours per week—were paid by check through a shell corporation (by which means overtime rates were avoided while federal and state taxes were withheld) or in cash (by which means overtime rates, contributions to benefit funds, and taxes were avoided). Over a six-month period in 1985, the contractor underreported and paid no benefits on 3,470 hours. Since the required benefit contribution was $5.42 per hour, the contractor defrauded Laborers Local 66 benefit funds of at least $18,800. In addition, because overtime hours were paid at straight time, and not at the required time and one half, the contractor was spared $25,573 in overtime wages. Thus, this contractor saved at least $44,380 in contributions and wages over a six-month period. The annual fraud can therefore be estimated at $88,700. Although no admissions were made for 1985, the principal of this concrete company admitted making illegal payments totaling $13,000 to Local 66 union officials during the preceding five years—an average of $3,250 per year. From this data it could be inferred that it is possible this contractor saved at least $85,500 annually by violating certain terms of the collective bargaining agreement and filing false tax returns.[51]

Moreover, these calculations reflect only the contractor's savings on wages and benefits. By employing a cash payroll, the contractor (and his employees) also avoided paying federal and state taxes, thereby realizing an additional savings.[52] Furthermore, this analysis looked only at the most costly expense to a concrete contractor—labor—and only at one union trade—Laborers Local 66. According to the principal of the company, that trade comprised only eighty-five percent of his workforce. The fraud estimates would be substantially higher if, as seems likely, the contractor made similar arrangements with other trades necessary to concrete pouring, such as carpenters, cement masons and wire lathers. Although they comprised a much smaller percent of his workforce, their hourly wages are double that of the laborers. This could have raised his illegal profits on unpaid wages and benefits alone to more than $100,000.

Trustees and/or consultants use a variety of schemes to exploit opportunities to bilk the pension and welfare funds of which they are fiduciaries.[53] Corrupt trustees embezzle funds by simply withdrawing money in their own or fictitious names. They make "loans" to themselves, friends, and organized crime associates, without expectation of repayment. They fraudulently pay for nonexistent goods and services, or pay money to ineligible "beneficiaries." They steer contracts for benefit plan services (for example, medical, dental and legal benefits) to companies controlled by fellow racketeers or to legitimate companies willing to pay kickbacks to obtain these lucrative contracts.

• The president and other officials of Local 101 of the International

Brotherhood of Craftsmen, Professionals and Allied Trades embezzled medical and pension fund assets by falsely charging the funds for fictitious work. Even after the trustees were successfully prosecuted, the fund's new trustees did not seek restitution from those who had been convicted.[54]

- In 1982, John Cody, president of Teamsters Local 282, was convicted of using the union and its pension fund to support a pattern of racketeering that spanned a fourteen-year period. Among the several instances of fraud involving the union's pension fund was a $100,000 kickback from a commission on the sale of three parcels of land to the fund.[55]
- Mario Renda, owner and president of an investment firm, and Martin Schwimmer, an agent of the firm and a fiduciary of Teamsters Local 810 and Sheetmetal Workers Local 38 benefit plans, were convicted in 1988 of skimming $14 million in pension assets which they had invested for the two unions. They placed the union funds in financially troubled banking institutions from which they illegally extracted large commissions. These commissions were then funneled into secret bank accounts.[56] In 1989, Schwimmer was held in contempt for refusing to testify before a grand jury investigating whether this scheme also included kickbacks to officials of the two unions.[57]

Tax Fraud and Falsification of Business Records

Almost all forms of construction-related corruption and racketeering involve some form of tax fraud. A contractor making illegal payments invariably conceals the true nature of these payments by fabricating expenditures that can be deducted as legitimate business expenses. Not only do such actions constitute tax fraud against federal, state and local governments, but the falsification of the business records to conceal such frauds is itself a separate state crime.[58] Recipients of illegal payments also know that they may be prosecuted for tax evasion (whether or not their bribe receiving can be proven), if they cannot legitimately explain their criminal income. Thus they, too, often launder their bribes by falsifying business records or engaging in artificial transactions.[59]

There are so many fraudulent schemes by which construction contractors generate cash and conceal payments to racketeers, or merely disguise personal expenditures as business expenses, that they are too numerous to catalog. Among the most common forms are false or inflated invoicing, purported payments to "ghost" or fictitious employees or suppliers and actual payments to no-show employees.

The use of false or inflated invoicing produces cash while creating a business expense record for tax audits. False invoices can be concocted by contractors or can be purchased from others.[60] Indeed, one investigation exposed two companies whose principal business was the supplying of false invoices. Typically these companies "kicked back" in cash ninety percent or more of the amount paid, keeping a percentage as an "administrative" or "handling" fee.[61]

Cash may also be generated by including fictitious employees on payrolls and retaining the money purportedly paid to such employees.

- One prosecution disclosed a scheme by which contractors concealed bribes to officials of Blasters Local 29 of the Laborers Union by writing checks made out to fictitious members of that union. The union officials cashed the checks with forged endorsements, and the contractors used the cancelled checks as documentation of employee business expenses.[62]
- Basil Cervone, business manager of Mason Tenders Local 13 of the Laborers Union, gave large contracting companies, or those which had repeated business within the local's jurisdiction, names to use as "ghost" laborers on the company's payroll. The checks for the "ghosts" were either delivered to Cervone at the union office or picked up from the contractors by Basil's son, Joseph Cervone (president of Local 13), or by another of his associates.[63]

Under another scheme, contractors set up shell corporations that are no more than named bank accounts, write checks to these "corporations," record them on their books as legitimate business transactions (such as payments to subcontractors) and use the cash for bribery, off-the-books wages or personal living expenses.[64]

- In the 1987 Tag Pipe case, the defendants created a shell corporation "for purposes of generating the cash to pay bribes to City employees and for disguising and laundering the proceeds of this fraudulent scheme."[65]
- In 1987, federal prosecutors charged Carl Capasso, president of Nanco Construction, with a series of federal tax violations alleging that Capasso generated approximately $1.5 million by "settling" nonexistent liability claims against Nanco, which were purportedly filed by persons living near Nanco construction sites. Capasso allegedly claimed a business deduction on his taxes and pocketed the money. After pleading guilty to filing a false return, defrauding

the government and conspiracy to defraud, he received a four-year sentence.[66]

- Joseph Mavielli, an owner and operator of American Transit Mix, was convicted of five counts of tax evasion for diverting $70,000 from the corporation to himself and others.[67]

Performance Bond Fraud

Both public and private builders require their contractors and subcontractors to provide bonds guaranteeing that they will carry out their work satisfactorily and that they will pay their workers and suppliers. In the event that a contractor does not or cannot perform, the builder can recover damages from the insurer. These bonds may cost anywhere from one-half to two percent of a contract, depending upon the insured's performance history. The *New York Times* reported that this insurance system is "permeated with fraud," including phony or unscrupulous companies issuing worthless bonds on which they have no ability or intent to perform.[68]

> - A scheme involving fraudulent payment and performance bonds was uncovered in 1988, when a subcontractor inquired about the validity of a bond submitted by the Apollon Waterproofing & Restoration Corporation of Astoria, Queens, for a City funded project involving One Police Plaza (NYPD Headquarters). The Department of Investigation eventually discovered a total of fifty-four phony bonds submitted by the same company to cover twenty-one City contracts valued in excess of $26 million.
>
> While the investigation was underway, and after Apollon learned that it was a target, the City required the company to submit new bonds to replace the bogus ones. The new bonds were later discovered to be phony as well. In all, the bogus bonds involved premiums in excess of $700,000. An employee of Apollon was arrested in January 1990 in connection with the bond scheme. The investigation is continuing.

Intimidation and Violence

Corruption is supported by intimidation and violence. The presence of so many known organized crime figures in the industry makes the explicit threat of violence credible and the implicit threat of violence sufficient. Actual violence is only rarely necessary; but it materializes from time to time to punish uncooperative contractors,[69] union "reformers," or rival racketeers. Dissident union members who challenge the leadership of mob-dominated unions have perhaps been the most frequent victims. For example, when Bruno Bauer, a Teamsters Union dissident, was murdered on Long Island, shock waves reverberated throughout the Teamsters and other unions.[70] By such means, racketeers create the perception that complaints about union management policies or practices invite severe reprisals.

Internal struggles for control of the New York City Carpenters union has left a trail of murders over three decades, as was recounted in *Union Democracy Review*:

> In 1957, Ed Murtha, a prominent leader of the Carpenters union in Long Island reputed to be an honest officer trying to buck the system, was murdered. In the early 60's a reform movement based in Long Island Local 1837, took up the cause and continued the battle until its leaders were starved out. In 1975, Willie Nordstrom ran as an insurgent for business manager of Carpenters Local 488 in the Bronx. His car was burned; he was threatened; but he refused to give up and finally ousted the old regime and took over as business manager, winning a reputation as a fine, effective, honest union leader. In 1978, he was shot to death. In 1981, a group of delegates from California came to the Carpenters convention prepared to nominate an opposition candidate for international president, but they changed their mind only after they were physically threatened. Ted Maritas, president of the New York Carpenters [District] Council, no reformer, disappeared, presumably murdered, while on trial on racketeering charges in 1982.[71]

Judge Harold Ackerman, in instituting a RICO receivership for Teamsters Local 560, described in chilling terms the atmosphere that Cosa Nostra labor racketeers had created over a period of several decades:

> It is not a pretty story. Beneath the relatively sterile language of a dry legal opinion is a harrowing tale of how evil men, sponsored by and part of organized criminal elements, infiltrated and ultimately captured Local 560 of the International Brotherhood of Teamsters, one of the largest local unions in the largest union in this country.

> This group of gangsters, aided and abetted by their relatives and sycophants, engaged in a multifaceted orgy of criminal activity. For those that enthusiastically followed these arrogant mobsters in their morally debased activity there were material rewards. For those who accepted the side benefits of this perverted interpretation of business unionism, there was presumably the rationalization of "I've got mine, why shouldn't he get his." For those who attempted to fight, the message was clear. Murder and other forms of intimidation would be utilized to insure silence. To get along, one had to go along, or else.[72]

Violence can also be a tool used by racketeers to discipline uncooperative contractors. In an intercepted conversation played in the prosecution of Colombo Family Boss Carmine Persico, Ralph Scopo explained to James Costigan, a contractor, how Cosa Nostra protects favored contractors and disciplines those who are uncooperative.

SCOPO: ... If I tell you stories about contractors that you know, that's supposed to get hurt, that I protected ...

COSTIGAN: Why would any, they get hurt?

SCOPO: Well, we ... for doin' what they're not supposed to be doin'.[73]

Violence may also be a tool for a mob family to reassert its authority and control. Wiretap conversations and the disclosures of co-conspirators revealed that a Carpenters' Union official was shot in retaliation for his having picketed and trashed a racketeer-controlled restaurant then under construction by nonunion workers.

Sabotage

In the construction industry, sabotage takes the form of the purposeful destruction of materials, fixtures or structures. Examples include cutting electrical wires and cables and rendering plumbing inoperable. Such sabotage, known as "trashing," is carried out by disaffected workers in order to punish a contractor or developer, or to discourage the contractor from dealing with a rival union or using nonunion workers. It also can serve as a means for creating additional work.

- In one case jointly prosecuted by OCTF and the New York County District Attorney's Office, John O'Connor, business agent of Carpenters Local 608, was charged with directing the destruction of the Bankers and Brokers Restaurant during its construction in Battery Park City. The sabotage is alleged to have been undertaken in retaliation for the use of nonunion carpenters.[74]
- Sidney Glasser and two other officials of Local 1087 of the Painters Union responded to reports that certain contractors were using nonunion-installed window glass by destroying the glass with acid. Afterwards, Glasser was able to steer the glass repair work to a company owned by one of his relatives.[75]

In May 1986, the *Wall Street Journal* reported a series of incidents involving sabotage and vandalism in the construction of
several multimillion dollar projects.[76] The article listed the following examples:

- As the Marriott Marquis Hotel neared completion, "work kept getting done and undone, electrical work was put in and pulled out,
  and cement was poured down toilets."
- One week before the opening of the South Street Seaport in 1983,
  all wiring on Schermerhorn Row was cut. Workers were then paid
  overtime to repair the damages.
- When construction slowed down at the World Financial Center in
  Battery Park City and several electricians were laid off, extensive
  vandalism included the cutting of wires. The vandalism at the Dow
  Jones Building alone amounted to $500,000.
- Just prior to the opening of the $496 million Jacob Javits Convention
  Center, glass panels were broken, electrical cables were severed,
  automatic controls were damaged, and pumps were tampered
  with. The Convention Center Development Corporation was
  forced to hire twelve undercover security guards to monitor each
  work shift in order to prevent further vandalism.

A great deal of sabotage has been carried out against electrical
contractors who have signed representational agreements with
Teamsters Local 363. The saboteurs were members of the International Brotherhood of Electrical Workers (IBEW) Local 3, who
organized into clandestine squads called "minute men."[77]

- In SIC hearings on September 15, 1982, a Special Agent of the
  Bureau of Alcohol, Tobacco, and Firearms testified about incidents
  of bombings and arson perpetrated against individuals who were
  Teamsters Local 363 members or contractors who employed Local
  363 members. The special agent attributed these acts to Local 3
  IBEW's efforts to gain exclusive control of the electrical industry.[78]
- Anthony Cardillo, president of United Construction Contractors'
  Association, also identified acts of violence perpetrated from September 1971 to June 1982 against contractors who utilized Local 363
  workers. Many of these acts were preceded by Local 3 members'
  threats against contractors if they failed to leave certain job sites.[79]

Collusive Bidding/Bid Rigging[80]
There are four types of collusive bidding practices that are carried out in the construction industry:

1. predatory bidding, in which firms collusively agree to bid below
   prevailing market rates in order to drive out the competition; once
   this is accomplished, the firms typically inflate prices;

2. identical bidding, in which firms agree not to bid competitively;

3. territorial bidding, in which firms agree not to submit competitive bids in each others' territories (established by geography or customers); and

4. rotational bidding, in which firms agree to take turns in obtaining contracts through low bidding; this practice is usually concealed through the use of complementary inflated bids submitted by other "club" members.[81]

Public construction is more vulnerable to bid rigging than private construction, because state and local governments are required to let their construction projects via competitive bids with no opportunity for negotiation. Because the governmental agency must award the contract to the lowest responsible bidder, "competing" contractors can easily collusively predetermine who the successful low bidder will be. Contractors have not been reluctant to seize these opportunities, as road construction prosecutions in New York State and elsewhere amply demonstrate.[82]

Bid rigging conspiracies may founder because the conspirators are unable to police their cartels effectively. Cartels are weakened when participants compete for more than their share, or when outside competitors take business away from the cartel. Historically, corrupt union officials, often members or associates of organized crime groups, have established the building trades cartels and enforced their rules. They keep members in line, and nonmembers from competing, by denying them a reliable labor force or by threatening them with labor unrest, violence, and sabotage.

- A recent OCTF investigation revealed the existence of a concrete contractors "club" on Long Island. This collusive bidding scheme was coordinated by Peter Vario, vice-president of Laborers Local 66. One percent of these contracts was paid to Vario, who then funneled a portion of the money to the Lucchese, Genovese and Gambino Crime Families. In addition to receiving greater profits through inflated contract prices, they were able, through Vario, to avoid strict enforcement of the terms of the collective bargaining agreement.[83]

- Painting contractors engaged in a bid-rigging conspiracy by agreeing in advance on who would submit the lowest bid on New York City Housing Authority contracts. The conspirators paid an official of the Painters Union to harass any member of the cartel who violated cartel rules and to cause union trouble for any nonmember who tried to obtain a contract from the Authority. If a nonmember

did obtain a contract, union officials would insist on strict compliance with all collective bargaining provisions, and union stewards
assured low worker productivity. For these services, the union official received two percent of the contract.[84]

- The LILREX investigation revealed a cartel of dry-wall contractors
  who collusively rigged bids on renovation projects. Evidence introduced at one of the ensuing trials revealed that the president of the
  New York City and Vicinity District Council of Carpenters, Theodore Maritas, and Genovese Crime Family member Vincent DiNapoli policed the cartel.[85]

- More recent federal prosecutions proved the existence of a concrete contractors club which conspired to rig bids and allocate markets for all poured concrete used in New York City construction.
  Nonclub members were prevented from submitting bids on concrete contracts totaling more than $2 million through union threats
  of labor problems, concrete supply difficulties and physical harm.
  The conspiracy was policed by Ralph Scopo, a member of the
  Colombo Crime Family and president of the District Council of
  Cement and Concrete Workers, and by three other New York City
  organized crime families. The four families divided equally approximately two percent of the price of every contract.[86]

- Three Long Island highway construction firms and their officers
  were indicted for conspiracy to fix bids let by the New York State
  Department of Transportation. The conspirators allegedly paid
  officials of the roadworkers union one percent of the contract price
  to create labor problems for any outside firms.[87] The threats were
  apparently successful. New York State's Attorney General has
  asserted that "[f]rom 1975 to 1984, virtually no construction firms
  from outside Nassau and Suffolk [Counties] bid on Long Island
  highway construction contracts," while in other regions of the
  state, construction firms successfully bid on projects one hundred
  miles or more from their home base.[88]

Implications of Corruption and Racketeering

Corruption affects the cost of every type of construction. Consider the cost of concrete. During the reign of the "concrete conspiracy" documented in the "Commission Case" brought against
Cosa Nostra, it was higher in New York City than anywhere else
in the country. There is substantial reason to believe that this
could be directly explained by: (1) the Cosa Nostra sponsored
cartel among the concrete contractors; (2) the Cosa Nostra sponsored monopoly in the production of ready-mix concrete in
Manhattan; and (3) the Cosa Nostra controlled Cement and Concrete Workers Union. Organized crime's stranglehold on the concrete industry made all projects, public and private, far more

expensive in New York City. Corruption on residential projects means less middle-and low-income housing, where profits cannot so easily absorb the costs of corruption. Corruption on industrial and commercial projects means higher commercial rents and, therefore, higher costs for goods and services. Ultimately, the high cost of construction affects the likelihood of attracting and retaining businesses in New York City and of providing New Yorkers with the public services (roads, subways, hospitals, libraries, schools, etc.) necessary for a satisfactory quality of life in an urban metropolis.

Corruption affects health and welfare when it touches the quality of construction—as, for example, when buildings fail to meet safety requirements and specifications due to fraud in building materials and workmanship or to bribery of public inspectors.

The corruption of labor unions is especially tragic. Workers have a right to open and democratic unions, and to the legitimate benefits of their collective bargaining agreements. They are victimized when threatened by violence, when blacklisted for dissent and disagreement, and when their union officers seek payoffs to permit contractors to avoid payments to employee benefit funds or to otherwise ignore contract provisions designed to protect workers' safety and welfare.

The types of corruption and racketeering cataloged above breed cynicism and disrespect for honest dealings and ethical behavior. Corruption in New York City's construction industry is so pervasive and open that it inevitably contributes to a general impression that "the only crime is getting caught."

The power, influence and criminal activities of New York City's racketeers affect all who participate in the construction industry, creating an environment in which many suppliers, contractors, craftsmen and laborers are deterred from performing an honest day's work for an honest day's pay. When some do business through extortion, bribery, sweetheart contracts and off-the-books payrolls, the reality of economic competition pressures others to do the same.

The patterns of corruption and racketeering which so plague New York City's construction industry deter contractors in other cities from bidding on New York City projects. The industry's reputation for being mob dominated also frustrates law enforcement. Victims have historically been hesitant to cooperate with criminal investigations because they fear reprisals and believe that, in any event, law enforcement cannot make a meaningful difference.

FOOTNOTES

1. State of New York, *Intermediate Report of the Joint Legislative Committee on Housing* (Albany: J. B. Lyon, 1922) 65.

2. In October 1989, a total of 127,300 persons were employed in the New York City construction industry. State of New York, Department of Labor, Division of Research and Statistics, *Labor Area Summary, Monthly Statistical Report*, Vol. 1, No. 10, Table 1, "New York City" (December 1989).

3. Source: New York City Executive Budget, Fiscal Year 1989; quoted in New York Building Congress, *Building New York City for the 21st Century* (April 1990) 6; reprinted by permission of the New York Building Congress.

4. City of New York, Office of Management and Budget, *Overview—Ten-Year Capital Plan, Fiscal Years 1989-1998* (New York: City of New York, May 1988).

5. City of New York, *Mayor's Management Report* (New York: City of New York, September 17, 1989) 303, 311.

6. Albert Scardino, "Changing Era for New York's Economy," *New York Times*, 18 May 1987, late ed.: B1.

7. See Jan Stiglitz, "Union Representation in Construction: Who Makes the Choice?" *San Diego Law Review* 18 (1981): 583.

8. Selwyn Raab, "Experts Say Irregularities in Concrete Industry Inflate Costs of Construction," *New York Times*, 26 April 1982, late ed.: A1.

9. Under the New York State Penal Law a person commits extortion when he compels or induces another person to deliver property to himself or to a third person by instilling in him fear that, if the property is not delivered, the actor or another will, among other acts specified in the statute, (i) cause physical injury to some person in the future, (ii) cause damage to property, (iii) cause a strike, boycott or other collective labor group action injurious to some person's business (except if the property is demanded for the benefit of a group in whose interest the actor purports to act), (iv) perform any other act that would not materially benefit the actor but which is calculated to harm another person materially with respect to his health, safety, business, calling, career, financial condition, reputation or personal relationships. N.Y. Penal Law § 155.05(2)(e) (McKinney 1988).

10. There are also many examples of extortions by persons other than union officials, e.g., *United States v. DeSapio*, 456 F.2d 64 (2d Cir. 1972) (defendant, Manhattan Democratic Party Chairman, was convicted of extorting Consolidated Edison Company by threatening to withhold permits until the utility awarded certain construction contracts to a designated contractor); *United States v. Langella*, 804 F.2d 185 (2d Cir. 1986) (defendant Cosa Nostra Family members were charged with extortion in relation to concrete pouring jobs valued at more than two million dollars; contractors were required to pay two percent of the contract price to the defendants in order to obtain the contracts); *United States v. Walsh*, 700 F.2d 846 (2d Cir. 1983) (defendant consulting engineers were convicted of conspiracy and violation of the Hobbs Act, Travel Act, and RICO for extorting money from project contractors under their control on a number of major sewer construction projects in the tri-state area).

11. *People v. O'Connor*, Ind. No. 7953/87 (N.Y. County 1987).

12. *People v. Forde*, Ind. No. 6974/86 (N.Y. County 1986).

13. *People v. Bitondo*, Ind. No. 7952/87 (N.Y. County 1987).

14. *United States v. Vario*, 88 CR 719 (E.D.N.Y. 1988).

15. *United States v. Boylan*, 620 F.2d 359 (2d Cir. 1980). See also Thomas Cook, "The Invisible Enterprise, Part 5: The Mob's Legitimate Connections," *Forbes*, 24 November 1980: 145.

16. *United States v. Vastola*, 69 CR 457 (S.D.N.Y. 1969); "2 Are Indicted Here as Labor Extorters," *New York Times*, 28 May 1969, late city ed.: 40.

17. United States, Senate, Committee on Labor and Human Resources, *Hearings on Raymond J. Donovan of New Jersey, to be Secretary of Labor*, 97th Cong., 1st sess., January 12 and 27, 1981 (Washington, D.C.: GPO, 1981), 26.

18. *United States v. Gross*, 84 CR 252 (E.D.N.Y. 1984).

19. *United States v. Maritas*, 81 CR 122 (E.D.N.Y. 1981).

20. *United States v. Local 6A, Cement and Concrete Workers*, 86 Civ. 4819 (S.D.N.Y. 1986).

21. *United States v. Sherman*, 84 CR 205 (S.D.N.Y. 1984).

22. See *United States v. DeMeo*, 86 CR 703 (S.D.N.Y. 1986).

23. *United States v. Argila*, 88 CR 463 (E.D.N.Y. 1988); *United States v. Scola*, 88 CR 464 (E.D.N.Y. 1988); *United States v. Alessi*, 88 CR 465 (E.D.N.Y. 1988).

24. *United States v. Annino*, 88 CR 466 (E.D.N.Y. 1988).

25. See *United States v. Jones*, 87 CR 796 (E.D.N.Y. 1987). Nine defendants were indicted on December 10, 1987; seven were convicted, one was acquitted, and charges against one were dismissed.

26. *People v. Thomas*, 89 CR 999 (N.Y. County 1989). Three of the defendants pleaded guilty to grand larceny and were given prison terms; the fourth pleaded guilty to a lesser offense and was sentenced to probation.

27. New York law criminalizes both traditional bribery of a public official and commercial bribery. In addition, it defines bribery of a labor official as a separate felony offense. N.Y. Penal Law §§ 180.00, 180.03, 180.15, 200.03, 200.04 (McKinney 1988). It is also an offense for a public official, labor official or businessman to solicit, receive, or agree to receive a bribe.

28. *United States v. Walsh*, 700 F.2d 846, 849 (2d Cir. 1983).

29. *New York v. Joseph Balkan Inc.*, 86 Civ. 1428 (E.D.N.Y. 1986). As of December 1989, the City had settled with eight of the contractor groups involved. The City will receive several hundred thousand dollars in damages, all work needed to correct the problems, and a guarantee that the work is satisfactorily completed. Video inspections of sewer lines will confirm that all repairs have been made. The City has yet to settle with three contractor groups, two excavators, and four former sewer inspectors.

30. *United States v. Riccardelli*, 794 F.2d 829 (2d Cir. 1986); *People v. Zelkowitz*, 84 Misc.2d 746, 375 N.Y.S.2d 1005 (N.Y. County 1975) (contractor convicted of attempting to bribe a City construction inspector).

31. *People v. Andros*, Ind. No. 4114/86 (Kings County 1986). As of August 1989, nineteen defendants had pleaded guilty, two had been tried and found guilty, and the remaining five cases were pending.

32. "13 Seized on Charge of Bribing Inspector in Undercover Role," *New York Times*, 25 July 1985, late ed.: B5.

33. Leonard Buder, "A Contractor Says He Paid Bribes to New York City Fire Inspectors," *New York Times*, 31 January 1987, late ed.: A1.

34. *United States v. Prince Carpentry*, 84 CR 188 (E.D.N.Y. 1984); *United States v. Standard Drywall Corp.*, 617 F.Supp. 1283 (E.D.N.Y. 1985).

35. *United States v. Cody*, 722 F.2d 1052 (2d Cir. 1983), *cert. denied*, 467 U.S. 1226 (1984).

36. *People v. Bitondo*, Ind. No. 7952/87 (N.Y. County 1987).

37. *United States v. Becker*, 89 CR 278 (E.D.N.Y. 1989). Two other contractors have pleaded guilty to selected counts and are awaiting sentencing; see *United States v. Wehrlin*, 89 CR 279 (E.D.N.Y. 1989) and *United States v. Favale*, 89 CR 614 (E.D.N.Y. 1989). Two more contractors are awaiting trial: *United States v. Biddle*, 90 CR 174 (E.D.N.Y. 1990) and *United States v. Millman*, 90 CR 173 (E.D.N.Y. 1990).

38. *United States v. Annino*, 88 CR 466 (E.D.N.Y. 1988).

39. "The Costs of Corruption," *New York Times*, 25 April 1982, late ed.: A52.

40. *Engineering News Record* 208 (27 May 1982): 63.

41. See also Ralph C. Thomas III, "Organized Crime in the Construction Industry," *Crime and Delinquency* 3 (July 1977): 304.

42. *United States v. Galucci*, 87 CR 490 (S.D.N.Y. 1987); *United States v. Spring*, 87 CR 491 (S.D.N.Y. 1987). See also, Arnold H. Lubusch, "L.I. Executives Plead Guilty to Stealing Pipes from City," *New York Times*, 5 June 1987, late ed.: B3.

43. Fraud in connection with affirmative action programs requiring minority business enterprise ("MBE") participation is a fifth basic fraud. Because it is found exclusively in connection with public construction projects, it is described in Chapter 5.

44. *United States v. Gelb*, 87 CR 104 (S.D.N.Y. 1987).

45. See footnote 42, *supra*.

46. *People v. Durante*, Ind. No. 7098/87 (N.Y. County 1987).

47. Leonard Levitt and Michael Arena, "Firm Got Contracts Despite Convictions" *Newsday*, 25 March 1986, New York ed.: 5.

48. Unfortunately, there were, for a long period of time, no other concrete producers with whom to contract, since the two corrupt companies had a virtual monopoly on the production of ready-mix concrete.

49. "Double-breasted shop" is the term used to describe the operation of a company that employs both union and nonunion construction workers. Construction unions in New York City universally negotiate contract clauses prohibiting contractors from operating a double-breasted shop.

50. *United States v. Prince Carpentry*, 84 CR 188 (E.D.N.Y. 1984); *United States v. Standard Drywall Corp.*, 617 F.Supp. 1283 (E.D.N.Y. 1985). See also, "Carpenters Sue for $$Millions in Un-Paid Fringe Benefits," *On the Level* (Summer 1985), published by Carpenters for a Stronger Union. When the fund trustees refused to seek restitution from those companies, rank and file members attempted to institute their own action; they were ultimately forced to discontinue their lawsuit due to lack of resources.

51. The contractor in the above case has pleaded guilty to one count of federal income tax evasion and has made restitution of more than $100,000 to state and federal tax authorities.

52. Taxes not paid included both employer and employee social security contri-

butions; both federal and state employee income taxes; and the employer's contribution to the New York State Workman's Compensation Fund.

53. If, as is often the case, "management" trustees of these funds are handpicked by union officials and play no active role in fund administration, there is no check on corrupt union trustees.

54. *United States v. Koenig*, 81 CR 398 (E.D.N.Y. 1981). Local 101 President William Koenig was convicted of racketeering, extortion, embezzlement and violations of the Taft-Hartley Act.

55. *United States v. Cody*, 722 F.2d 1052 (2d Cir. 1983).

56. *United States v. Schwimmer*, 692 F.Supp 119 (E.D.N.Y. 1988).

57. *United States v. Schwimmer*, 882 F.2d 22 (2d Cir. 1989).

58. N.Y. Penal Law §§ 175.05, 175.10 (McKinney 1988).

59. The conversion of checks (falsely recorded as business expenses) to cash in order to conceal the receipt of bribes constitutes the new crime of money laundering. N.Y. Penal Law §§ 470.00-470.20 (McKinney 1989).

60. See *United States v. Persico*, 621 F.Supp. 842 (S.D.N.Y. 1985).

61. *United States v. Galucci*, 87 CR 490 (S.D.N.Y. 1987); *United States v. Spring*, 87 CR 491 (S.D.N.Y. 1987).

62. *United States v. Sanzo*, 81 CR 151 (E.D.N.Y. 1981).

63. *United States v. Cervone*, 87 CR 579 (E.D.N.Y. 1987).

64. *United States v. Prince Carpentry*, 84 CR 188 (E.D.N.Y. 1984); *United States v. Standard Drywall Corp.*, 617 F.Supp. 1283 (E.D.N.Y. 1985).

65. See footnote 42, *supra*.

66. *United States v. Capasso*, 87 CR 041 (S.D.N.Y. 1987).

67. *United States v. Mavielli*, 85 CR 307 (E.D.N.Y. 1985).

68. Michael Oreskes, "Corruption is Called a Way of Life in New York Construction Industry," *New York Times*, 25 April 1982, late ed.: A10.

69. See *People v. Wheatman*, 31 N.Y.2d 12, 334 N.Y.S.2d 842 (1972). A contractor who refused to participate in the cartel testified that he was harassed and assaulted as part of a conspiracy to control the bidding on Housing Authority proposals.

70. "Gang-Style Murder at Truck Depot," *Union Democracy Review* 56 (January 1987): 1.

71. Herman Benson, "The Real Victims of Construction Corruption," *Union Democracy Review* 48 (September 1985): 2.

72. *United States v. Local 560, International Brotherhood of Teamsters*, 581 F.Supp. 279, 282 (D.N.J. 1984), aff'd, 780 F.2d 267 (3d Cir. 1985), *cert. denied*, 476 U.S. 1140 (1986).

73. *United States v. Persico*, 84 CR 809 (S.D.N.Y. 1984).

74. *People v. O'Connor*, Ind. No. 7953/87 (N.Y. County 1987).

75. *United States v. Glasser*, 443 F.2d 994 (2d Cir. 1971).

76. Robert Guenther and Joanne Lipman, "Building Distrust: Construction Industry in New York Is Hotbed of Extortion, Bribery," *Wall Street Journal*, 7 May 1986: A1.

77. State of New York, Commission of Investigation (SIC), *Annual Report* (1982) 6-7; see also, Selwyn Raab, "State Panel Told about Violence in Construction," *New York Times*, 16 September 1985, late ed.: B3.

78. SIC, *Annual Report* (1982), 7.

79. *Id.*, 7.

80. Any departure from a completely independent decision to refrain from bidding, submitting a bid, or bidding a certain price constitutes bid rigging. Rigging bids is a criminal violation of state and federal antitrust laws. Donnelly Antitrust Act, N.Y. Gen. Bus. Law § 341 (McKinney 1988); Sherman Antitrust Act, 15 U.S.C.A. § 1 (1973). See also N.Y. State Fin. Law § 144(2) (McKinney 1989).

81.

> When competitors allocate markets they collectively pre-determine which company will serve a particular customer or geographical area or control the sale of a particular item or service. If all or part of their market involves contracts awarded after competitive bidding, they will collusively formulate bids to preserve the pre-ordained market allocation....
>
> A bid rotation involves companies who, by agreement, take turns winning a specific contract or set of contracts. Complementary bids, intentionally submitted above the price bid by the collusively pre-determined low bidder, attempt to convey the impression that the competitive process and bidding laws are working well.

Attorney General Robert Abrams, *Bid-Rigging in the Competitive Process: A Report to the Legislature* (Albany, N.Y.: New York State Department of Law, 1985) 3-4.

82. Since 1980, the U.S. Department of Justice's antitrust division has indicted 378 road contractors for price fixing. See *United States v. Oswego Asphalt Corp.*, 86 CR 1987 (N.D.N.Y. 1986); *United States v. All State Asphalt*, 86 CR 1986 (N.D.N.Y. 1986); *United States v. Penn-Can Road Materials*, 86 CR 185 (N.D.N.Y. 1986).

83. See *United States v. Vario*, 88 CR 719 (E.D.N.Y. 1988).

84. *People v. Wheatman*, 31 N.Y.2d 12, 334 N.Y.S.2d 842 (1972).

85. *United States v. Maritas*, 81 CR 122 (E.D.N.Y. 1981).

86. *United States v. Salerno*, 85 CR 139 (S.D.N.Y. 1985); *United States v. Persico*, 621 F.Supp. 842 (S.D.N.Y. 1985); *United States v. Salerno*, 86 CR 245 (S.D.N.Y. 1986).

87. In *United States v. Ambrosio*, 83 CR 159 (E.D.N.Y. 1983), prosecutors alleged a conspiracy to allocate via bid rigging virtually every major highway and sewer project on Long Island. However, defendants Lizza Industries, Inc., and its president Herbert Hochreiter were the only defendants convicted on racketeering charges. Lizza was fined $52,000 and agreed to forfeit the $1 million profit made on the rigged contracts; Hochreiter was imprisoned for two years, fined $62,000 and forfeited his $40,000 profit share and his 30 percent interest in Lizza. In *State of New York v. Amfar Contracting Corporation*, 83 Civ 2598 (S.D.N.Y. 1983), a civil antitrust suit brought against the defendants in *Ambrosio*, the state won a judgment of $7.8 million against all of the civil defendants. See also, *People v. DiNapoli*, 27 N.Y.2d 229, 316 N.Y.S.2d 622 (1970) (bid rigging on contracts let by Consolidated Edison and other utilities).

88. Abrams, 12.

Analysis of why racketeering and corruption have been so persistent and pervasive in the construction industry

Introduction

Our goal is to reduce corruption and racketeering in New York City's construction industry. To formulate realistic remedial strategies requires an understanding of why these problems have plagued the industry for so long. With such an understanding, we can develop strategies for change through law enforcement initiatives and through structural and organizational reforms designed to block opportunities and incentives for this systemic criminality.

The first step is to identify those industry characteristics that generate opportunities and incentives for profitable racketeering. Our analysis of such opportunities and incentives is based on the concepts of "racketeering susceptibility" and "racketeering potential." Racketeering susceptibility reflects the degree to which an industry's structure and organization (1) create incentives for industry participants to engage in racketeering or (2) provide the means and opportunity for racketeers both inside and outside the industry to control or influence critical industry components.[1] With control or influence over an industry's critical components, racketeers can extract payments by (1) providing "services" (e.g., harming competitors, enforcing cartels, insuring labor peace, facilitating avoidance of collective bargaining agreements) or (2) threatening injury (e.g., labor problems, disruption of supplies, property damage, physical injury or loss of employment). Thus, racketeering susceptibility focuses on the vulnerability of an industry to racketeering exploitation.

Racketeering potential reflects the profits racketeers may reap from exploitation of an industry's susceptibility. Assessing racketeering potential requires analysis of industry operations to identify such factors as the amount of money that industry participants can generate and make available to racketeers, and the ability to hide corrupt payments from regulatory and law enforcement agencies. The profitability of racketeering, however, cannot be measured by monetary rewards alone. For example, the availability of jobs which provide legitimate status and income to racketeers or to their associates and friends enhances an industry's racketeering potential. To take another example, the control of a construction company has a value to racketeers beyond the illicit profits which can be extracted from it. The company can be used to launder dirty money or to generate phony business transactions necessary to disguise illicit payments and tax frauds.

The analysis that follows demonstrates that the structural and organizational characteristics of New York City's construction industry create a high level of racketeering susceptibility and potential. It is thus not surprising to find that pervasive corruption and racketeering have existed in the City's construction industry throughout the twentieth century. Given these characteristics, the pathology of the industry cannot be addressed successfully without a coordinated long-term law enforcement commitment and significant structural and organizational reform.

Racketeering Susceptibility in the Industry

Many features of New York City's construction industry contribute to its racketeering susceptibility. We have grouped them into five categories: the labor market; the collective bargaining structure; the competitive business environment; the high costs of delay; and the fragility of the construction process.

Characteristics of the Labor Market Contributing to Racketeering Susceptibility

One critical component of the industry which racketeers have historically used to create and maintain their influence has been the construction unions. Thus it is important to understand why New York City's construction unions are so powerful and why they are so vulnerable to racketeer influence and control.

Why Construction Unions Are Powerful

Traditionally, unions have had a great deal of leverage in high-rise construction because of their monopoly over the skilled and unskilled workers required for this highly complex type of building. Construction unions have been much less successful in establishing dominance over construction of single family homes, small commercial buildings and renovations. Nationally, this type of construction is dominated by nonunion contractors.[2]

At least three factors account for the strength of the City's construction trade unions. First, construction unions control apprentice training for the skilled trades, which is the principal means through which these trades can be learned. In the 1980s, a number of large open shop contractors began their own apprenticeship programs, but so far these have achieved only modest success.[3] Thus, New York City does not have a large pool of skilled nonunion workers.

Second, in New York City, as in most major cities (especially in the northeast and midwest), political support for organized labor has traditionally been strong. Prevailing wage laws and other public policies blunt whatever competition nonunion contractors might offer by requiring public agencies to pay "prevailing wages" (equated with union wages) to nonunion employees. Obviously, if nonunion workers must be paid according to union scale, any economic advantage of nonunion labor is substantially reduced.[4]

Third, unique characteristics of the construction labor market strongly influence workers to join and maintain membership in a union. All large construction projects in New York City are carried out by unionized labor. One reason is the special treatment given to the construction industry under the National Labor Relations Act.[5] Section 8(f) of the Act permits contractors and unions to enter into "prehire agreements" which commit a contractor to a particular union before a project has begun, even before the contractor has hired any workers. To work in New York City's construction industry, contractors must as a practical matter either individually or through their associations sign such prehire contracts.[6] These contracts often commit employers to obtain some or all of their employees through union referrals. Some prehire contracts contain clauses requiring contractors to hire all or part of their employees from union hiring halls.[7] Even where there is no hiring hall provision, the union's designation as exclusive bargaining agent gives its officials effective control over who works for that contractor. Because union business agents control the union hiring hall or referral systems as well as the stewards who represent the union on work sites, it is generally the business agents who determine where and for whom most workers will be employed. While an employer has the theoretical option of rejecting undesirable or unqualified employees sent by the union, in practice this is rarely a realistic option for an employer without a close relationship with the affected union. A vindictive business agent could easily punish the troublemaking contractor by replacing the rejected employee with an even less qualified or less desirable worker.[8]

Unlike workers in other industries, the construction worker's employment is in the hands of his union, not his employer. In most industries a worker's attachment is principally to an employer who has the power to hire and fire, to determine qualifications and eligibility for promotion, and with whom the worker may have a long-term employment relationship. By contrast, in the construction industry most workers owe little fealty to the contractor/employer who signs their paychecks. In a real sense, construction workers are "employed" by their unions.

This weak tie between employer and employee is further strained by the short duration of many construction jobs. A construction worker must always be concerned about where and for whom he or she will next work. Particularly during the "off-season," or during a period of slow construction activity, obtaining work often depends more on a worker's status in the union and relationship with the business agents than on past job performance.

Why Construction Unions Are Susceptible to Racketeer Domination
Control over construction labor unions gives racketeers power to confer critical benefits or impose prohibitive costs on contrac-

tors. This is true because construction depends on the availability, reliability and competency of labor, all of which are within the direct control of construction unions. Given the importance of these unions, it is not surprising that racketeers have long sought to control and exploit their strategic leverage to solicit bribes, extort payoffs or obtain other criminal benefits.

Construction unions have been all too easy for racketeers to control and exploit, in part because there is no effective mechanism for policing internal union affairs. The Landrum-Griffin Act[9] was passed in an attempt to assure that workers would be represented by democratic unions. Title I, entitled a Bill of Rights of Members of Labor Organizations, sets out mechanisms for lodging complaints with the U.S. Department of Labor. Unfortunately, the expectations of its sponsors have not been fulfilled. Courts have interpreted the law narrowly and have shown a strong disinclination to use Landrum-Griffin as a vehicle to "interfere" with internal union affairs.

In reality, therefore, protecting unions and union members from racketeering is, by default, left to the unions themselves. The history of labor racketeering demonstrates organized labor's unwillingness or inability to keep its own house clean, at least insofar as construction unions have been concerned. Indeed, the AFL-CIO Ethical Practices Committee, created in the 1950s in response to the McClellan Senate Hearings' exposure of extensive labor racketeering, has not met in more than twenty years.

Most large labor unions are organized hierarchically; the international unions charter locals, which are often affiliated with regional district councils. In some industries, these internationals actively monitor and police the operations of their locals, thereby providing some protection against attempts at domination or exploitation by racketeers. In the construction industry, however, union internationals typically delegate to union locals autonomy over their internal affairs. Historically, racketeers who control construction locals have not needed to worry about interference from the parent organization.

The Carpenters Union is a good example. In spite of the numerous revelations of corruption within the New York City and Vicinity District Council and locals in the New York metropolitan area, the United Brotherhood of Carpenters and Joiners of America has all but ignored its responsibilities. It has intervened only once, and that was only occasioned by the widespread publicity surrounding the 1982 "disappearance" of District Council President Theodore Maritas, who was then awaiting trial on charges that he ran the District Council as a racketeering enterprise.

Over the last three years, there has been a continuing stream of investigations, indictments and prosecutions involving the City's Carpenters Union, and still the International has failed to act.

- *Carpenters Local 17.* A recent indictment arising out of a Construction Industry Strike Force (CISF) investigation detailed Local 17's involvement in racketeering throughout the drywall industry. In the first prosecution of construction industry racketeering under the State's new Organized Crime Control Act (OCCA), Local 17 business agent Benedetto ("Benny") Schepis was charged with participating with officials from two other unions in a massive bribery and extortion scheme focused on the drywall industry. The indictment alleges that the criminal scheme was advanced by one individual who is an associate of the Genovese Crime Family.[10] Local 17's newly elected president, Nicholas Cirillo, is the nephew of Dominick ("Quiet Dom") Cirillo, who, according to another pending Organized Crime Task Force indictment, is a captain in the Genovese Family.

- *Carpenters Local 135.* The Moscatiello indictment also charges that, from March 1986 through December 1988, Schepis and Louis Moscatiello, an associate of Genovese capo Vincent DiNapoli and president of Plasterers Local 530, funneled sixteen bribes, totaling $38,000, from several contractors to a Local 135 official. According to the indictment, the bribes were paid so that the union would tolerate violations of the Carpenters Union collective bargaining agreement. The grand jury charged that the affairs of Local 135 were run through a pattern of criminal activity that arose out of and was supported by the Genovese Crime Family. Israel (Izzy) Hubelbank, business agent of Carpenters Local 135, pleaded guilty in August 1989 to criminal violations of the state labor laws for accepting cash payments from contractors who did business with Local 135.

- *Carpenters Local 257.* Business agents Attilio Bitondo and Gene Hanley were accused in 1987 in a seventy-nine count indictment of engaging in a pattern of labor racketeering from 1977 through 1986.[11] Demanding bribes of up to $25,000, they threatened to put contractors out of business by refusing to assign skilled labor to the jobs and by otherwise creating labor unrest on the job site.

- *Carpenters Local 531.* In November 1988, business agent Henry Walaski was convicted of extortion, Taft-Hartley violations, and RICO Act conspiracy for extracting bribes from contractors in exchange for labor peace.[12] Walaski has since been indicted for perjury and criminal contempt for his refusal to testify before a state grand jury in the Moscatiello case.[13] Robert Waller, Jr., Local 531 president, pleaded guilty in 1989 to extortion following his indictment on charges that in 1985 he, along with a Teamsters Local 282 working teamster foreman, extorted money from a nonunion contractor doing scaffolding work during construction of the International Design Center of New York in Long Island City, Queens.[14]
- *Carpenters Local 902.* Business agent Arthur Giangrande (who was also first vice-president of the District Council) was convicted in 1986 of conspiracy, mail fraud and violation of the Taft-Hartley Act. The indictment charged that, through his position in the District Council, he assisted the contracting firm of Standard Drywall to defraud the Carpenters Union Benefit Funds.[15]
- *Carpenters Local 608.* Vice-president and business agent John O'Connor was charged in 1987 in a 127 count indictment with soliciting bribes, extortion and taking unlawful gifts from seventeen contractors between 1980 and 1986.[16] Chief shop steward William Holden was accused of perjury and contempt for lying to the grand jury in its investigation of construction site sabotage by the Carpenters Union. Holden was convicted and sentenced in January 1990 to one year in prison.[17] Business agent Martin Forde has also been charged with extortion and related offenses.[18]

The international unions have chosen not to take action despite the revelation and documentation of extensive racketeering. The rank-and-file has produced "dissident" movements, but it has proved extremely difficult to mount an effective challenge.[19] Reformers may be laid off, blacklisted, intimidated, beaten, or even killed, and the agencies whose mandate is to protect their rights, offer such victims little support. The National Labor Relations Board, for example, has jurisdiction over disputes concerning hiring halls, but resort by rank-and-file reformers to the Board often requires years of persistence and victories there are inevitably followed by further delays occasioned by appeals.

- John Kuebler, a member of Teamsters Local 282, was fired in October 1977 after joining a Local 282 dissident group called FORE (Fear of Reprisal Ends). Because of this, and because he received no new assignments from the hiring hall, he took his case to the National Labor Relations Board, where, after twenty-five days of trial, an Administrative Law Judge (ALJ) ruled that the union was liable to

Kuebler for backpay. Local 282 unsuccessfully fought the decision to the U.S. Supreme Court. When the Supreme Court refused to hear the case, it was remanded to the National Labor Relations Board for computation of damages. After a twenty-two day hearing, an ALJ determined the amount due to Kuebler. The union appealed this decision to the full Board, which, in July 1988, affirmed the ALJ's decision. However, the Board remanded the matter to the ALJ for determination on a further, relatively minor point. At the time of his death, in June 1989, eleven and a half years after seeking help from the National Labor Relations Board, the case was still in litigation and Kuebler had yet to receive any money.[20]

Once racketeers infiltrate and gain control of a union, it is very difficult to wrest control from them. Corrupt union officials use several means to stay in office and to prevent opponents or dissidents within the union from instituting reform measures. These include control over union elections, appointments and grievance processes; the union hiring hall or hiring referral service; union communications; and the power, through the union constitution, to expel from the union a member whose conduct is determined not to be in the best interests of the union. In particular, control over work assignments gives the union a very powerful weapon to use against those who might be inclined to challenge the leadership. As one commentator has noted:

The union hiring hall has been one of the major developments in twentieth-century labor relations. It has provided many industries with a means for efficiently matching unemployed workers with job vacancies and has replaced a system of haphazard, unjust, and corrupt employment practices. Yet it has also developed substantial problems of its own. A hiring hall is fraught with potential for abuse, and indeed, that potential is all too frequently realized. The largely unreviewable discretion of business agents and inadequate protection for workers can combine to make hiring halls a mixture of whim, nepotism, prejudice, and irrationality.[21]

Many construction workers lack formal education and are unskilled or semiskilled laborers. They are well aware that few jobs are open to them that pay as well as construction. Ultimately, the power to ensure that a "nonconformist" or "troublemaker" never again works in the construction industry is a powerful and effective deterrent to reform. When this power is in the hands of the mob, resistance to racketeer domination is difficult, if not impossible, to sustain.

Finally, when racketeers control a union, they also can and do threaten physical violence against union "dissidents."

- FBI affidavits describe Ralph Scopo, president of the Cement and Concrete Workers District Council, and Carl DiSilvio of Laborers Local 2 in Chicago, as responsible for the brutal assault on Dennis Ryan. As Ryan stood on the floor of the 1981 Laborers International Union of North America convention in Hollywood, Florida, to nominate himself as a candidate to run against Angelo Fosco for president of the union, a dozen thugs surrounded and beat him. Agents said the violence against Ryan was a carefully orchestrated attack to ensure Fosco's leadership.[22]

Characteristics of the Collective Bargaining Process Contributing to Racketeering Susceptibility

Several special characteristics of construction labor relations contribute to the industry's racketeering susceptibility, including the balkanization of bargaining units and the weakness of the employer associations.[23]

By describing the jurisdictional bargaining units in the industry as balkanized, we mean that collective bargaining in the construction industry is marked by numerous specialty unions, each with exclusive jurisdiction over discrete tasks or functions. Thus, there are separate unions for electricians, carpenters, plumbers, boilermakers, ironworkers, and so on. The large number of specialty unions, each fiercely protecting its exclusive jurisdiction, creates the potential for constant disputes between contractors and unions, as contractors seek to reduce the number of different unions whose workers must be used to perform a specific task.

As one example, the installation of metal modular furniture, which could be efficiently performed by members of either the Iron Workers Local 580 (Ornamental and Window Installation) or the Carpenters Union, must often be undertaken by composite crews comprised of members of both unions. This inevitably leads to superfluous labor costs.[24] There are numerous other examples throughout the industry. A simple electrical job may require that a member of one union pull a cord through a pipe and that a member of another union plug the cord into a socket. Putting up a sign at the Javits Convention Center required two carpenters to nail several blocks of wood, a pipe fitter to hold the metal pipe that goes between the blocks, and two electricians to attach the wires. Carpentry and electrical work are not the only problem areas; because the Elevator Constructors Union and the Operating Engineers Union each have partial jurisdiction over hoists or elevators, two hoist operators, one to haul workers and the other to haul materials, must be assigned to each hoist.

A contractor who attempts to avoid the consequences of balkanization by hiring from only one union, where two or three might be required, inevitably faces job actions or strikes. As a result, the construction industry is filled with inefficiencies and featherbedding, which provide incentives either to pay union officials not to press their jurisdictional claims or to reach out to racketeers who can dictate accommodations with the unions.

A second important feature of the construction industry's collective bargaining structure is the imbalance between strong unions and weak employer associations. Employer associations are associations of contractors in the same trade who voluntarily band together for purposes of collective bargaining. All members of the association are represented by the same negotiator(s) at the bargaining table and agree to be bound by the agreement which the negotiations produce.

Despite what would appear to be a unity of interest shared by all construction employers during the negotiation process, the associations representing them at the bargaining table are often divided by conflicting interests. For example, the Building Contractors Association is comprised of both high-rise building contractors and a large number of smaller contractors specializing in alteration work; each group has different concerns when negotiating with their common union counterparts. Featherbedding positions such as the working teamster foreman or the master mechanic affect only the high-rise builders and impose no costs on the alteration contractors. Accordingly, this latter group has no reason to resist union demands for the inclusion of these particular featherbedding positions in collective bargaining agreements. Union negotiators can thus take advantage of these conflicting interests. Court decisions permitting members of employer associations to withdraw from their associations during stalled negotiations and to sign their own interim agreements further facilitate whipsawing by union negotiators and the breakdown of association solidarity.[25]

Furthermore, some employer associations have difficulty obtaining meaningful participation and financial contributions from their members. Contractors are generally reluctant to volunteer time and effort to serve on association committees that undertake studies of work practices, new technology, legislation, and collective bargaining provisions. Moreover, it is a common practice in New York City's construction industry for some employer associations to rely on unions—their nominal adversaries—to collect employer association dues. Some employer associations in New York City actually rent office space from the unions with whom they negotiate.

Employer associations have less economic leverage at the bargaining table than unions, which can impose significant economic harm on contractors through work slowdowns or stoppages. The dire consequences of delay to contractors, coupled with their ability to pass along costs, explain their accession to the perpetuation of inefficient and functionally indefensible work practices in collective bargaining agreements. While a strike completely shuts off contractors' flow of cash, construction workers usually collect strike benefits and even unemployment insurance. During construction booms, they can find employment in other geographical areas. Because unions monopolize the supply of labor in New York City construction, contractors lack the bargaining leverage that builders in other parts of the country derive from being able to hire competitive nonunion workers.

As a result of this imbalance of power, many onerous and inefficient contract provisions characterize collective bargaining agreements in New York City construction. For example, contractors have agreed to mandatory minimum crew sizes for defined tasks, whether the number of workers is needed or not; ratios of foremen and nonworking stewards to journeymen, whether or not the foremen are actually needed; working teamster foremen and shop stewards who perform only union work and carry out no tasks for the employer who pays their salaries;[26] and master mechanics who are paid whenever a certain number of operating engineers are working,[27] even though the master mechanic is not at the site and has no actual supervisory responsibility.[28] Other examples abound:

- Operating Engineers Locals 14 and 15 have been accused by the General Contractors Association of imposing the following work practices:

  1. A two-member crew from each local union must operate cherry pickers (hydraulic cranes) that need only one operator.

  2. A compressor operator's sole responsibilities are to start the compressor in the morning and turn it off at night.

  3. Several operating engineers must be assigned to pumps easily staffed by a single person

- IBEW Local 3 requires similar practices:

  1. Superintendents who have no actual duties, supervisory or otherwise, are required to be on the job.

  2. Standby electricians must be present whenever any trade has four workers working overtime under temporary lights

- Mason Tenders Local 59 of the Laborers Union requires that gatemen be hired on large projects in order to open the entrance gate in the morning. Security guards working for the general contractor could easily open a gate, as could the working teamster foreman.

We recognize that labeling work practices inefficient and unreasonable necessarily involves subjective judgments. One person's "featherbedding" is another person's "safe working condition" or "job preservation." Nevertheless, as others have previously observed, we cannot escape the conclusion that certain work practices in New York City construction are wasteful and dysfunctional for consumers and the public. More importantly for our analysis, these practices give contractors and builders incentives to bribe union officials to obtain waivers of costly and unnecessary contract provisions. They also provide corrupt union officials with numerous opportunities to extort payments from contractors by threatening to enforce even the most trivial and inefficient contract provision.

Another feature of construction labor relations that enhances racketeering susceptibility is the inclusion of frontline supervisors in unions. In most industries, frontline supervisors are key members of the management team. In a typical manufacturing setting, before a round of collective bargaining negotiations, frontline supervisors work with top management on desired contract changes needed to improve discipline and productivity. In the construction industry, by contrast, foremen are members of the same unions as the workers they supervise.[29] Contractors are unable to benefit from such advice and counsel, and may find it difficult to count on supervisors to represent the employer's interests rather than those of their fellow union members. This encourages the perpetuation of inefficient and wasteful work practices, and may make it more difficult to detect abuses and frauds. A supervisor whose allegiance runs to a union, rather than to his employer, will be less likely to blow the whistle on workers engaged in systematic theft or "mungo" rings, sabotage or slowdowns.

Competitive and Fragmented Economic Environment
The construction industry is characterized by a large number of general contractors, and an even larger number of subcontractors, engaged in intense competition, moving from one short-duration contract to another, chronically insecure about obtaining future work. Many subcontractors are small firms, with only a handful of full-time employees. In any given geographical region, including the New York City metropolitan area, large numbers of such firms continually appear and disappear. Because they are not publicly held corporations, they are often not subject to strenuous regulation or external audit.

Three decades ago, labor analyst Philip Taft noted the connection between intense competition and racketeering susceptibility:

> Systematic racketeering appears to depend upon the existence of a highly competitive industry. In industries where labor racketeering has been "institutionalized," in the sense that it has continued over long periods of time and in a number of local jurisdictions, the common characteristic has been keen competition in their product or service markets. In such industries, with many competing employers, the union occupies a position of strength with respect to the single hirer of labor. The building trades, the trucking industry, sections of the amusement industry, and the distributive and service trades where corruption is endemic, all have this common characteristic.[30]

The combination of intense competition among construction contractors and racketeer control of the critical components capable of providing competitive advantage produces a high level of racketeering susceptibility. Contractors are motivated to reach out to anyone with the ability to help them gain an economic advantage by reducing labor costs or eliminating competition. Labor racketeers, especially those with access to the use of violence, are in the best position to provide such services. Any contractor who might attempt to compete with favored firms or protected cartels would be faced with labor problems, cutoffs of critical supplies, or other costly delays. Conversely, labor racketeers can provide competitive advantages to favored firms through sweetheart contracts which permit costly collective bargaining provisions to be avoided, and through cartels which allocate contracts among a small number of firms.

Intense competition not only creates a voluntary market for the services of racketeers, it also makes legitimate businessmen vulnerable to extortion. Racketeers can extort payoffs from contractors by threatening the loss of labor or supplies. Given the highly competitive economic environment, the high cost of delay, and the fragility of the construction process, a businessman cannot easily risk standing up to such threats.

High Cost of Delay

The high cost of delay is a key contributor to racketeering susceptibility for two reasons: (1) it creates incentives for builders to pay bribes to insure that construction proceeds expeditiously and without disruption; and (2) it increases the racketeers' leverage for extorting money by threatening disruption of the construction process. In his account of New York City construction racketeering in the 1890s, labor historian Harold Seidman cited the high cost of delay as the most important explanation of the industry's susceptibility to racketeers:

> Construction has always involved an element of speculation. The promoter and the investor do not receive any return until the building has been completed and during the process of construction a considerable sum of money has been tied up. The interest on the million to the three or more million dollars invested in a building is considerable even for a few weeks, so that to the investors, time is costly. Delay can be disastrous if it prevents the completion of a building in time for the fall renting season. Sometimes the builder is forced to pay a substantial penalty if his work is not finished by a certain date. Unscrupulous walking delegates [business agents] were well acquainted with these peculiar factors in the building industry and did not hesitate to take advantage of them. Employers soon found that it was cheaper to pay off the delegates than to try to fight them. And since in the long run the added cost could be passed on to the owner or to the public, the builders seldom made any trouble.[31]

Delay inflates costs of every critical component in the process, including capital, labor and supplies. For example, calculating on the basis of a 200 working-day year, one day's delay on a $100 million construction loan at a fifteen percent interest rate would cost a builder $75,000!

Delay also means paying contractual penalties, paying workers who sit idle as they wait for their skills to be used, and ultimately paying large overtime payrolls to make up for lost time. Delay means acceding to change orders to cover the cost of contractors' inactivity or accepting the disruption that occurs when contractors withdraw from the project. Delay means escalating costs of supplies. Storage costs mount up for materials that cannot be immediately utilized. Suppliers and subcontractors, whose scheduled involvement has been determined months earlier, will withdraw or pass along the costs they incur by having to readjust their plans.

The costs of delay are particularly high in New York City because of the number and magnitude of up-front costs—those requiring builders to expend or borrow large amounts of money before commencing construction. Assembling land in New York City, particularly in Manhattan, is an enormously expensive process. Moreover, parcels are typically encumbered by occupied buildings. New York City's ordinances are highly favorable to tenants facing eviction for development purposes.[32] Thus, tenants (and their lawyers) are able to obtain generous settlements from developers, further increasing up-front costs.[33] Demolition in congested Manhattan is complicated by permit requirements and the need to attend to the safety of pedestrians, motorists, and occupants of adjacent buildings.

Fragility of the Construction Process
The power of so many people in the construction process to impose delay costs on a construction project is what we mean by "fragility." Construction differs from a typical industrial assembly line process. The "product" is not standard, and it cannot be broken down into small mechanical steps. Moreover, and more importantly, construction requires the coordination and integration of dozens of subcontractors, specialized craftspeople and groups of laborers. Site clearance, demolition and excavation

must be undertaken, concrete poured, superstructures raised, plumbing installed, and carpentry and electrical work carried out—all in a predetermined and often unalterable sequence.[34] For example, drywall installation cannot begin until the electrical wiring is finished and ready to be covered. Because subcontractors, specialized workers and suppliers have to be coordinated within a production schedule, any one of these parties, and the unions on which they depend, have the power to delay or even shut down an entire project. This is one important form of fragility.

During the construction process, builders face more complex logistical and transportation problems on high-rise projects in Manhattan than in other large cities. These problems further contribute to the fragility of the process. Manhattan's narrow and congested streets, and the absence of vacant lots, make the cost of debris removal and hauling extremely high. Crowded roads and limited parking require that some materials be delivered at night, and that workers prepare sites at costly night-shift rates. Heavy supplies and materials can only be transported over certain roadways. Because of traffic congestion, there is always uncertainty about when a particular shipment will arrive.

The fact that Manhattan is an island exacerbates the fragility of the process. Goods must be brought into Manhattan over a bridge or through a tunnel. When the bridges and tunnels are jammed by commuters, transporting materials and supplies becomes practically impossible. Because certain large transport vehicles could disrupt traffic at these pressure points, they are permitted to cross the rivers only at particular times. The use of ready-mix concrete presents a special problem. Unless delivered and poured within approximately ninety minutes of being loaded at a batching plant, wet batches of concrete can harden in the truck's mixing drum, causing loss of the concrete and extensive damage to the truck. Given the congestion on, and difficulty of transporting to, the island of Manhattan, it is necessary to locate batching plants at strategic points on the island or within a radius of only a few miles.

Compared to New York City, other metropolitan areas usually have more space adjacent to a building site for trucks to park and materials to be stored.[35] In Manhattan, every square foot of space is at a premium. Supplies from distant markets cannot be delivered at the same time, but only as needed. This further escalates costs.

Given all of these logistical complexities, when a union problem arises or a critical supply arrives late at the site, even a brief delay can be compounded. For example, if a truck does not arrive before the morning rush hour, its supplies may not be available until afternoon. Thus, the entire day is lost. Because of such geophysical factors, fragility increases the power of those with control over essential supplies and services.

The myriad laws and regulations governing the building process in New York City also contribute to fragility.[36] New York City's byzantine building code makes the required permit processes lengthy and frustrating.[37] Permits for building plans, demolition, construction, hoisting, and so on, require inspections and approvals from a large number of agencies, including the City Planning Commission, the Department of Environmental Protection, the Buildings Department, the Fire Department, the Department of Transportation, the Landmarks Commission and the Bureau of Highways.[38]

Because the construction process is fragile, it is highly susceptible to racketeering. A racketeer with influence or control over suppliers, union officials or inspectors can exacerbate or reduce this fragility; he thus has many opportunities to extract money from the construction process. In this context, high susceptibility exists because the structure of the industry presents extensive opportunities for extortion.

Conversely, builders and contractors may reach out to racketeers who, through influence, expertise, position, threat of violence and control of unions, can assure that construction costs due to industry fragility are minimized. In this second context, high susceptibility exists because there are substantial incentives for contractors and builders to enlist the illicit aid of someone capable of insuring stability and predictability in the construction process.

Racketeering Potential in the Industry
Susceptibility explains the vulnerability of the construction industry to corruption and racketeering, but does not com-

pletely explain why racketeers enter the industry. They would not do so unless they found it profitable. This is what we mean by the construction industry's high "racketeering potential."

There are five major reasons why New York City's construction industry has an extremely high potential for racketeering: 1) enormous amounts of money are involved; 2) large quantities of cash for illegal payments can be easily acquired and concealed; 3) valuable nonmonetary rewards exist; 4) illegal payments can be passed on to consumers; and 5) there are unique features of public construction that provide special opportunities for profitable racketeering.

Opportunity for Illicit Profits

The New York City construction industry annually undertakes projects worth billions of dollars. At any given time, there may be several billion dollar projects and dozens of $100 million projects in progress. Thus, huge sums of money are at stake. A skim of just one percent represents tens of millions of dollars annually. For this reason alone, the construction industry is highly attractive to racketeers. Union employee benefit funds worth hundreds of millions of dollars are another attractive target contributing to high racketeering potential.

Ease of Generating and Concealing Cash Payments

The construction process involves a large number of monetary transactions. These provide numerous opportunities for contractors to generate money for illegal payments and for racketeers to introduce schemes to conceal those payoffs. On a large project, general contractors must make payments to subcontractors, materials and building supply vendors, employee payrolls and union benefit funds. Subcontractors make similar payments. All these monetary transactions provide opportunities for such illicit schemes as no-show and fictitious employees, false invoicing for supplies and materials that were never delivered, and overcharging for those that were.

For a number of reasons, it is exceedingly difficult to provide careful monitoring or to demand strict accountability in order to prevent illegal payoffs. The sheer number of parties and the many independent contractual relationships account for part of the problem. Unlike other industries, there is no overall "top management" with responsibility for the many companies, workers and suppliers on a construction site. Developers contract with construction managers, who contract with general contractors, who contract with subcontractors, who may engage in further subcontracting. Each company also contracts with many vendors of supplies and materials. No one party has contractual relationships with, or responsibility for, all companies on a construction site. General contractors and construction managers responsible for general supervision of large construction projects sometimes acknowledge their awareness of racketeering, but claim to be ignorant of specific illegal activities.

Another serious problem results from the difficulty in monitoring much activity during the construction process, and the impossibility of uncovering it after the project is completed. Subcontractors may have workers spread over many acres of a large construction site or on different floors of several buildings. It is virtually impossible to determine the exact number of workers or the precise number of overtime hours worked on any given day. After a project is completed, who can say how much dirt was removed, how many tons of concrete poured, how much scaffolding used, or how many miles of wire or conduit installed? The inability to make such determinations precisely invites false invoicing and overcharging.

Nonmonetary Rewards
Another measure of the construction industry's racketeering potential is the opportunity it offers racketeers to extract valuable nonmonetary rewards. Many racketeers lack legitimate sources of income. No-show "jobs" provide a legitimate cover for income tax purposes. Control of legitimate companies also provides racketeers with a valuable means of laundering money obtained in illicit activities. In addition, legitimate jobs allow racketeers to conceal their underworld positions and offer convenient explanations for questionable associations.

Racketeers can also convert their positions in the construction industry into status, prestige and political power. Some industry racketeers have enjoyed "Man of the Year" accolades from charities and civic groups. Labor racketeers can obtain political power through their control of political action committees, their ability to provide campaign workers and phone banks, and their perceived ability to deliver votes. This provides a link to and potential influence with politicians at every level.[39]

The construction industry, with its vast array of jobs, provides racketeers with enormous patronage. They can reward friends, crime syndicate members and associates with jobs, often demanding kickbacks in one form or another. Patronage creates a debt owed by the recipient to the racketeer.

Another nonmonetary reward which the construction industry provides to racketeers is a market for illicit goods and services. A large construction site creates a voracious market for gambling, loansharking, narcotics trafficking and stolen property. Finally, racketeers can exploit their leverage over contractors to compel them to purchase ancillary goods and services, such as security, debris hauling, food wagon franchises and window washing, from companies controlled by or which kick back to those racketeers.

Special Features of Public Construction
Public construction is an easier and more lucrative target for racketeers than private construction. Because of its special vulnerabilities to corruption and racketeering, this subject is treated in detail in Chapter 5. It is necessary to note here, however, that at almost every stage of the construction process it is easier to extract money from public builders. Many public projects fail to provide adequately for experienced site project managers, engineers and supervisors who, in any event, are expensive and hard to recruit.[40] This means that there are inadequate checks on whether contractors have performed the amount and quality of work they claim to have done. When confronted with requests for contract change orders, government agencies frequently lack the capacity to make an informed determination.[41]

Furthermore, public works contractors who submit fraudulent bills for supplies and labor often run only a minimal risk of being caught. Government entities generally lack the resources to audit billings adequately. Even if they did, without effective site supervision, they are not in a position to dispute bills involving "unknowables" such as the amount of concrete and other materials used, the number of workers actually employed, or the amount of overtime actually worked.

The Criminal Syndicate's Role as a Rationalizing Body in New York City's Construction Industry

> Whether by violence or by effective mutual understanding, the stabilization of the market is highly desired in established business. . . . The gangster undertakes to effect by illegitimate means what is a normal tendency in legitimate business. [42]

The large concentration of racketeers in New York City capable of exploiting the construction industry's racketeering susceptibility and potential, along with the instabilities and uncertainties created by the industry's fragility and fragmentation, create a need for a "rationalizing body." This body must be able to regulate the predatory activities of the racketeers and must have the influence necessary to bring coordination and predictability to the construction process. Organized crime syndicates can, and do, play both these roles. [43]

By controlling the activities of disparate groups of racketeers preying on the industry, syndicates can assure contractors that they will only have to pay off once for a specified result, that the amount to be paid will be "reasonable," and that "services" paid for will be delivered.

- In 1981, Matthews Industrial Piping Co. won a $10 million contract to replace the piping in a deep-water oil storage and pipeline facility at Port Mobil in Staten Island. When $10,000 in bribes to George Daly, Steam Fitters Local 638 business-agent-at-large, were insufficient to prevent union picketing, Matthews called on more influential figures. He paid $100,000 to Jules Miron, a lumber contractor with organized crime connections. Miron gave part of the money to Daly to pay off other union officials and part of it to Gambino Crime Family boss Paul Castellano. Gambino in turn gave a portion of it to Louis Giardina, a member of the Genovese Crime Family, who served as a business agent in Mason Tenders Local 23. In the end, Matthews was forced to sign a collective bargaining agreement anyway, and when he threatened to go to the authorities, $50,000 of the bribe money was returned to him. According to FBI wiretaps, Castellano blamed the entire problem on Daly's not clearing the original bribe through him. [44]

This rationalizing function is not provided for altruistic reasons; it serves Cosa Nostra's interest to have stable relationships within a profitable industry. Where, for example, a racketeer-dominated union threatens financial harm to a company controlled by, or paying off to, a criminal syndicate, the syndicate will restrain the union by whatever means are necessary.

Cosa Nostra's services as a "rationalizing body" go beyond making the demands of racketeers predictable. To the extent that the industry's structure creates fragmentation and fragility, an organized crime syndicate can use its network of relationships throughout the construction industry to reduce uncertainties and promote needed stability. For example, when more than one union has a jurisdictional claim over a particular construction task, an organized crime syndicate can, in return for a payoff, work out a reasonable arrangement between the contractor and the affected unions. In this role, the syndicate serves the same functions, albeit by criminal means, as a highly effective, legitimate labor consultant. Cosa Nostra's capacity for violence and its influence in both the legitimate world and the underworld makes its construction specialists more "effective" at conciliation, dispute resolution and expediting than most lawyers, mediators, labor relations or construction consultants. Similarly, where a crime syndicate can regulate the groups of racketeers who control components critical to the production, delivery and installation of a necessary supply (such as concrete), the syndicate has the power to bring predictability and stability to a process that could otherwise be easily and frequently disrupted.

Thus, the characteristics of the construction industry not only explain the presence of racketeers, but also generate a demand for a rationalizing body. The functions of that rationalizing body define its attributes. It must have influence or control in all segments of the industry. Its power may stem from an institutional or political position it actually holds, from one it is perceived to hold, or from its ability to prevent and cause economic loss, intimidation or injury.

FOOTNOTES

1. By components we mean all discrete inputs of an industry, be they tangible goods or definable services. By critical components we mean those goods or services which are essential to the industry's functioning, i.e., those which, if disrupted, cause the industry substantial costs and dislocation.

2. See Herbert R. Northrup, *Open Shop Construction Revisited* (Philadelphia: The Wharton School, Industrial Research Unit, University of Pennsylvania, 1984) 188.

3. See, generally, Northrup, "Training and Development," 409-65.

4. See Armand J. Thieblot, Jr., *Prevailing Wage Legislation: The Davis-Bacon Act, State "Little Davis-Bacon" Acts, the Walsh-Healey Act, and the Service Contract Act* (Philadelphia: The Wharton School, Industrial Research Unit, University of Pennsylvania, 1986).

5. National Labor Relations Act, 29 U.S.C. §§ 151-69 (1982).

6. Usually the prehire agreement is renewable every three years and is renewed indefinitely on a three-year basis. Under a decision by the National Labor Relations Board, *John Deklewa and Sons and International Association of Bridge, Structural and Ornamental Iron Workers, Local 3, AFL-CIO*, 282 NLRB No. 184 (1987) *order enforced* 843 F.2d 770 (3d Cir. 1988) *cert. denied*, 109 S.Ct. 222 (1988), construction unions will no longer have a presumption of majority status when the prehire contract expires. The contractor can refuse to bargain with that particular union until the union proves it represents a majority of the workers. In theory, this decision should strengthen the position of contractors who are willing to challenge weak unions. It is, however, expected to have little impact on union contractors in the New York City area, since few appear prepared to mount such a challenge.

7. The 1987-1990 High-rise Industry Agreement between the Contractors Association of Greater New York and Teamsters Local 282 provides in Section 14 (4) that:

> The Employer shall notify the Union of any job opening in a category covered by this Agreement and shall afford the Union an opportunity to refer applicants for the position.

> The Employer shall retain the right to reject any job applicant referred by the Union. In the event of such rejection, the Employer shall notify the Union. The Union shall then have the opportunity to refer other applicants to the Employer until the required number of applicants are obtained.

The 1987-1990 Agreement between the Associated Brick Mason Contractors of Greater New York, Inc., and the Mason Tender's District Council provides in Article III, Section 1(C):

> The Union, on ten (10) days' written notice to the Employer shall have the right to institute a hiring hall system in lieu of, or in addition to the hiring system contained in this Section 1(b). . . . Further, the Employer retains the right to reject any job applicant referred by the Union, but in the event of such rejection, the Employer shall reapply to the Union for further referrals until a referral is accepted. . . .

> If a hiring hall is instituted, the Union's right to refer Mason Tenders from
> such hall shall be limited to fifty percent (50%) of the Mason Tenders
> employed on any job. Further, the Employer reserves the right to employ
> directly all foremen and assistant foremen.

The 1987-1990 Agreement between an Independent Employer of Cement and
Concrete Workers and the District Council of Cement and Concrete Workers provides in Article V, Section 3:

> The Employer agrees that the Union shall have the right, in its sole and
> absolute discretion to establish a Union hiring hall system, provided,
> however, that if a hiring hall is instituted, the Union's right to refer
> Employees from such shall be limited to fifty percent (50%) of the Employ-
> ees employed on any job, and provided further that the Employer reserves
> the right to employ directly all Working Foremen.

8. There are legal limitations on the power of unions to run hiring halls, but they
provide little real protection to workers. Under the Taft-Hartley Act of 1947, 29
U.S.C. § 144 *et seq.* (1973), Congress outlawed "closed-shop" agreements, i.e.
management labor agreements restricting employment to union members.
However, § 8 (a)(3) of the National Labor Relations Act does permit "union
shop" provisions, i.e., collective bargaining agreements requiring a nonunion
employee to join the union within thirty days of his or her being hired. Because
of the temporary nature of the employment in the construction industry, special
treatment was given to union shop agreements in the construction trades by
shortening the grace period for joining the union to seven days. In reality, little
difference exists between a closed shop and a union shop in New York City construction, since few employers, except those who pay off a union representative
to look the other way, would risk hiring nonunion workers, out of fear of union
retaliation.

9. Labor-Management Reporting and Disclosure Act of 1959, 29 U.S.C. § 401 *et seq.*
(1985), commonly known as the Landrum-Griffin Act.

10. *People v. Moscatiello*, Ind. 8081/89 (N.Y. County 1989).

11. *People v. Bitondo*, Ind. 7952/87 (N.Y. County 1987).

12. *United States v. Cervone*, 87 CR 579 (E.D.N.Y. 1987).

13. *People v. Walaski*, Ind. No. 8079/89 (N.Y. County 1989) and Ind. No. 9494/89
(N.Y. County).

14. *United States v. Waller*, 88 CR 466 (E.D.N.Y. 1988).

15. *United States v. Standard Drywall*, 617 F.Supp. 1283 (E.D.N.Y. 1985).

16. *People v. O'Connor*, Ind. No. 7953/87 (N.Y. County 1987).

17. *People v. Holden*, Ind. No. 9352/87 (N.Y. County 1987).

18. *People v. Forde*, Ind. No. 7951/87 (N.Y. County 1987).

19. It is fair to say that the New York City groups and individuals who have strug-
gled to democratize corrupt unions (e.g., the Association for Union Democracy
and the Teamsters for a Democratic Union) have had only modest successes.

20. Kuebler's fight against corruption in Local 282 is documented in Kenneth C.
Crowe "John W. Kuebler, Teamsters' Reformer," *Newsday*, 15 June 1989, N.Y. ed.:
49.

21. Robert M. Bastress, "Application of a Constitutionally-Based Duty of Fair
Representation to Union Hiring Halls," *West Virginia Law Review* 82 (Fall 1987):
31, 31. See also Barbara J. Fick, "Political Abuse of Hiring Halls: Comparative

Treatment under the NLRA and the LMRA," *Industrial Relations Law Journal* 9 (1987): 339.

22. See "The Mob on Trial: A Union Dissident is Beaten as Ordered," *Newsday*, 10 September 1986, New York ed.: 26-27. Scopo, a soldier in the Colombo Crime Family, was subsequently convicted of labor racketeering in the Commission case, *United States v. Salerno*, 85 CR 139 (S.D.N.Y. 1985).

23. For a thorough analysis of construction labor relations, see Arthur Smith, *Construction Labor Relations* (Chicago: Commerce Clearing House, 1984).

24. "In a market like New York's that has such a potentially high demand for housing, restrictive labor practices and onerous labor costs actually limit employment in the construction trades, thereby working against the interests of laborers." Commission on the Year 2000, *New York Ascendant* (June 1987) 148.

"New York's labor costs, which are pushed up by restrictive labor rules and practices, are higher than in all cities except Los Angeles and San Francisco, and exceed the national average by 21 percent" (149).

25. Smith, 16.

26. "Working teamster foreman" (WTF) is a contradiction in terms. A WTF does not perform any construction work, drive a truck, or supervise any workers. The general contractor pays the WTF an average of $75,000 per year in wages and fringes, including overtime for hours when the WTF is not even present at the construction site. The WTF is assigned by the Teamsters to check that all drivers making deliveries are dues paying members of the local and to prevent nonunion drivers from coming onto the site unless a penalty claim payment is made.

27. A Local 14 master mechanic, who is required to be hired whenever four or more operating engineers are on a job site, rarely performs or supervises any construction work. One master mechanic known in the industry, George Morrison, cost his employer, Olympia & York, almost $500,000 in 1984, including pay for more than twenty-four hours per day on 221 days at Battery Park City. Once a master mechanic is on the payroll, Local 15 requires that a "working foreman maintenance engineer" also be added to the crew. One working foreman maintenance engineer cost the Port Authority almost $300,000 in 1984, including pay for hundreds of overtime hours when he was nowhere near the Port Authority's World Trade Center.

28. New York State, Commission of Investigation, *Investigation of the Building and Construction Industry: Report of Conclusions and Recommendations* (December 1985) 30-31.

29. A related situation that also contributes to racketeering susceptibility arises when inspectors belong to the same union as the craftsmen whose work they are required to inspect. For example, New York City Buildings Department electrical inspectors and independent electricians both belong to Local 3 of the IBEW.

30. Philip Taft, *Corruption and Racketeering in the Labor Movement* (Ithaca, N.Y.: N.Y.S. School of Industrial and Labor Relations, Cornell University, 1958) 34.

31. Harold Seidman, *Labor Czars: A History of Labor Racketeering* (New York: Liveright, 1938) 8.

32. Under New York's rent control and rent stabilization laws, tenants cannot be evicted without cause. See Michael Hinds, "Holdouts Battle Developers in Site Wars," *New York Times*, 29 September 1985, late ed.: Sec. 8, 1.

33. In one midtown development, the last remaining tenant in the building turned down $650,000 to leave her $165 a month rent controlled apartment. The

developers had previously paid a total of $2.4 million to other holdouts to leave their rent controlled apartments so that the development project could be started. Esther Fein, "A Rent Control Holdout Showing Her Gumption," *New York Times*, 13 February 1986, late ed.: B1.

34. Before commencing the actual construction of a project, builders prepare projections called "milestone events schedules" that set forth the projected time frame in which each trade will commence and complete operations. On very large projects, a milestone events schedule projects three and four years into the future.

35. See "An Avenging Convoy Stalks Contractors," *New York Times*, 27 October 1989, late ed.: B1.

36. These laws and regulations are found in a maze of statutes and regulations, including the Administrative Code, the City Charter, the Zoning Resolution, the Uniform Land Use Review Procedure (ULURP), the City Environmental Quality Review (CEQR), the Landmarks Preservation Law, and the Department of Transportation Rules.

37. Manhattan's construction costs of $200 per square foot are higher than in any city in the nation except San Francisco. Some costs are pushed up by regulations. New York has a stringent building code which, while having mostly suitable provisions, has some archaic restrictions that drive up costs. One effect of the outmoded building code is the effective exclusion of most manufactured housing. Similarly, the enormously detailed zoning code is often far behind the natural development of the city.

Commission on the Year 2000, 148.

38. In November 1984, Mayor Koch appointed a panel, chaired by Richard Shinn, to review City policies and procedures covering approval of building plans and issuance of construction permits. The Shinn panel concluded that: a) there was little communication among the agencies involved; b) the agencies lacked regularly scheduled training sessions, written guidelines and objective standards to measure employee performance; c) agency staffing levels were critically low; d) there were marked differences in filing procedures and requirements among borough offices; e) little had been done in the last fifty years to improve the methods used to catalog and preserve files; and f) the 1961 Zoning Resolution was outdated, inconsistent and procedurally awkward. City Environmental Quality Review was cited as the most significant source of delay. The panel made recommendations to address each of these problems. It also recommended that some oversight organization, perhaps the Mayor's Office, coordinate the regulatory functions of all the agencies involved in the plans approval and permit process. City of New York, *Report of the Mayor's Blue Ribbon Panel on Building Plan Examination and Review* (August 1986).

39. Legislators and executive officials from mayors to presidents have treated notorious Cosa Nostra figures with deference and respect because of their union positions. One such figure was Anthony Scotto who, before his 1979 conviction on racketeering charges, enjoyed prominence in New York City government. Scotto was listed in the *Official Directory of the City of New York* as a member of Mayor Lindsay's Council on Port Development and Promotion and as head of the Marine Port Council. Scotto was also listed in state directories as a member of Governor Hugh Carey's executive search committee and Economic Development Board. His political contacts were such that Carey and former mayors Robert Wagner and John Lindsay testified as character witnesses at his 1979 racketeering trial. Upon his release from prison, several political figures

attended his welcome home dinner. "The Mob on Trial: Organized Crime, Organized Labor and Organized Politics — No Strange Bedfellows Here," *Newsday*, 10 September 1986, New York ed.: 7.

President Richard Nixon entertained several labor officials associated with Cosa Nostra. In May 1970, Nixon entertained such corrupt officials as Sidney Glasser (a convicted extortionist who served as business manager of the Glazier's Union), Biagio Lanza (a convicted bookmaker who served as business agent of the Plasterer's Union), Charley Johnson (a construction racketeer who served as president of the Carpenters New York City District Council), and Thomas (Teddy) Gleason (a subject of the Waterfront Commission investigations). "Nixon and the Bums," editorial, *Scanlan's*, September 1970: 1.

40. Under the provision of the Wicks Law, the government is prohibited from delegating responsibility and financial accountability for supervision and coordination to a single contractor.

41. Seven years ago, the New York City Corporation Counsel's Office took a tough stand on change orders in an effort to reduce the millions of dollars paid annually to contractors who claimed that City changes and delays had increased costs. See "Schwartz Says Builders' Suits Are Costing the City Millions," *New York Times*, 2 February 1983, late ed.: B3. According to the *Mayor's Management Report* (September 18, 1985), "As a direct result of the City's past success in litigating cases vigorously rather than settling, the number of actions brought against the City by construction contractors has decreased markedly, from 233 in Fiscal 1984 to 182 in Fiscal 1985" (531-32).

42. John Landesco, *Organized Crime in Chicago* (Chicago: University of Chicago Press, 1929) 151.

43. By "organized crime syndicate" we mean a criminal business organization which allocates black markets, provides a ruling or governing body to the underworld and resolves disputes among its members or affiliates, who may pursue a variety of criminal enterprises and ventures. For discussion and definitions of "organized crime syndicates," see Thomas Schelling, "Appendix D — Economic Analysis and Organized Crime," *Task Force Report on Organized Crime*, President's Commission on Crime and the Administration of Justice (Washington, D.C.: GPO, 1967) 115; Paul H. Rubin, "The Economic Theory of the Criminal Firm," *The Economics of Crime and Punishment*, American Enterprise Institute for Public Policy Research (Washington, D.C.: American Enterprise Institute for Public Policy Research, 1973) 155; G. Robert Blakey, Ronald Goldstock, Charles Rogovin, *Rackets Bureaus: Investigation and Prosecution of Organized Crime*, Appendix A, National Institute of Law Enforcement and Criminal Justice (Washington, D.C.: GPO, 1978).

44. The scheme is described in detail in *United States v. Daly*, 842 F.2d 1380 (2d Cir. 1988) and *United States v. Gallo*, 671 F.Supp 124 (E.D.N.Y. 1987). In the latter opinion, the court observed "The pipe-welding contractor conspired with Daly, Miron, Giardina and Castellano in a classic payoff-sweetheart deal" (137).

CHAPTER 3

How racketeers have exploited and rationalized the construction industry

Introduction

History provides at least two examples of syndicated criminal groups playing a "rationalizing role" in the construction industry. In the early twentieth century, Robert Brindell and his cronies, known as the "Annex of Tammany Hall," preyed on the industry through a variety of racketeering schemes. Today, New York City's five Cosa Nostra Families play a similar, albeit more complex, role.

Racketeering by Robert Brindell

During the second decade of this century, the construction industry in New York City was largely controlled by Robert Brindell. Using the influence of the powerful United Brotherhood of Carpenters and Joiners of America, with which his own Independent Dock Union had recently affiliated, Brindell established connections with a network of trade union officials. In 1919, he organized a Building Trades Council, chartered by the American Federation of Labor. Brindell placed the business agents on his payroll, thus giving them an independent power base. In return, he was able to call upon their assistance in carrying out his racketeering activities.

Brindell used his control over labor to extort money from construction contractors, principally through the sale of "strike insurance." If a contractor failed to pay off to Brindell's satisfaction, some pretext would be fabricated on which to call a strike. In addition, Brindell leveraged his power over labor into control over the awarding of construction contracts; a contractor who obtained a contract without Brindell's approval would find himself without a workforce.

The implications of Brindell's power were not lost on the Building Trades Employers Associations. To solidify control over its members, drive out any remaining independent contractors, and enforce the rules of its cartels, it allied with Brindell's Council. Brindell's labor force was only available to Association members; they, in turn, used only Council labor.

As a result, Brindell became the power broker through whom all contracts were let, all materials furnished, and all labor assigned in New York City's construction industry.[1] He further exploited his power by organizing manufacturers and dealers of construction materials and supplies into specialized trade associations. Builders were not permitted to purchase supplies directly from manufacturers. They could buy only from supplier trade associations which fixed minimum prices three or four times above free-market levels. Some associations, such as the Marble Industry Employers Association, had bylaws that prohibited members from bidding on work outside their assigned geographic zones. The associations were also able to prevent technological advances from being introduced into the construction industry.[2]

The City paid heavily for Brindell's stranglehold on construction. Because of the pervasive pricefixing, graft and violence that characterized his reign, the cost of construction tripled and, in some instances, quadrupled; honest contractors were driven out; and competition was stifled. Rental costs rose sharply to compensate for the increased cost of building apartments and other housing. Eventually the cost of construction became so high that building came almost to a standstill. This, along with complaints about the intolerable conditions in the industry, caused the New York State Legislature, in April 1919, to appoint a Joint Legislative Committee on Housing to investigate housing conditions and the causes for lack of construction in New York City. This committee, chaired by Charles C. Lockwood, conducted a two-year investigation (1920-1922) and documented corrupt practices that are remarkably similar to those prevalent today.

The practices of the Brindell era sound painfully familiar. Brindell used his control over the supply of labor to extract huge sums from the industry through systemic extortion and solicitation of bribes. By controlling the exploitation of the construction industry's racketeering susceptibility and potential, Brindell "rationalized" the practices of the many racketeers active in the industry. While many participants in the industry resented his exploitations, some contractors and suppliers praised Brindell for the order and predictability he brought to the industry. An official of the employer's association reminded a complaining contractor, "Brindell is doing a wonderful work in the business . . . we must stand behind him."[3] Indeed, Brindell performed such a vital function, at least to those who prized stability, that both labor and management rallied to his defense when he was under attack by the Lockwood investigation. One officer of the Building Trades Employers' Association termed the legislative inquiry a "Russian-Polish-Turkish inquisition which should never have been permitted in the United States." The president of the New York Federation of Labor branded the charges against Brindell a "darned shame" and announced that he would "stick with him through thick and thin." An assemblyman criticized the entire investigation "as part of a deep seated propaganda to discredit organized labor." The Building Trades Council assessed every member ten dollars for Brindell's defense.[4] Despite this support, he was convicted and sent to prison.[5] This was in 1921, a time when a new breed of racketeers first arrived on the scene.

Racketeering by Cosa Nostra

The exploitive and rationalizing roles of Brindell and his organization are now filled by the heirs of the 1920s mobsters, New York's five Cosa Nostra Families—Gambino, Genovese, Lucchese, Colombo and Bonanno.[6] While not every act of corruption or racketeering in the construction industry is performed by or at the direction of a member of Cosa Nostra, Cosa Nostra's influence nonetheless pervades the industry.

The complexity and scale of the industry no longer allows any one person—or any one organization—to achieve Brindell's monolithic power. Nonetheless, because of its nature and structure, Cosa Nostra can and does act as a "rationalizing body." It provides many of the same kinds of services Brindell performed, and is even more capable than Brindell of exploiting its position within the industry.

Cosa Nostra's organizational structure and expertise is ideally suited to this rationalizing and exploitive role. As a syndicate, it engages in crime as a business. Its successes are in large part attributable to its tight structure, code of secrecy and ruthlessness. Membership in Cosa Nostra must be earned by years of demonstrated loyalty and service to the family, and by success in running criminal enterprises or by providing useful services, such as violence and intimidation, theft and fraud.

Cosa Nostra's strength and its ability to control networks of criminal enterprises and ventures is based upon its members' recognition that their criminal activities, whether in legitimate or illegitimate businesses, are conducted for their family's benefit. Violations of rules by members or challenges by outsiders are regarded as serious offenses, often punishable by death.

Although each family's influence and power in the construction industry is dispersed through its members and associates, some members are construction industry specialists to whom other family members or associates look or are directed when construction-related opportunities or problems arise. Intra- and interfamily structure and outside relationships provide the networks, power and connections that enable Cosa Nostra to be effective. Its hierarchical structure facilitates the resolution of conflicts that arise from overlapping ventures and makes possible joint ventures among families or crews within a family.

Each of New York City's five crime families is headed by a "boss," who oversees his family's criminal operations, maintains order and represents the family on the interfamily commission. Beneath the boss is an "underboss," who relays messages and information up and down the chain of command and acts in the boss's stead when the boss is absent. The *consigliere* (counselor) provides advice and counsel and serves as ombudsman and arbiter of intrafamily disputes. In some families, the *consigliere* play an operational as well as advisory role. Below the underboss are the *caporegime* (also known as the "capos" or "captains").

Caporegime constitute the middle-management layer and insulate the boss and underboss from contact with most lower-echelon family members. The lowest ranking family members are called "soldiers." They are assigned to the "crew" of a *caporegime*, although some high-earning "specialists" work directly for the boss or underboss. Soldiers are entrepreneurs, directing criminal enterprises and ventures, such as gambling, loansharking and truck hijacking. Below the soldiers are a large number of family "associates," who are not "made members" of any family, but who operate under the control of a soldier (or in the case of a "proposed member," under the control of a capo). Capos represent their soldiers in resolving disputes over criminal activities within their crime families and in disputes with members of other crime families.

New York City has by far the largest number of Cosa Nostra members and associates of any city in the country. In 1983, the New York City Police Department estimated 870 "made members" of the five families (Gambino 250, Genovese 200, Colombo 115, Bonanno 195 and Lucchese 110).[7] Estimates of criminal associates run into the thousands. Thus, New York City is the home base of a large corps of sophisticated and ruthless racketeers who not only engage in traditional organized criminal activity (including loansharking, gambling, narcotics and redistribution of stolen goods), but who also play a major role in numerous legitimate industries, including private sanitation, garment, cargo freight and construction.

Because of its extensive criminal activities in so many different industries, and because of the large number of businesses in which it has interests, Cosa Nostra has developed extensive networks in both the underworld and the legitimate world. Disputes often arise among families over control of certain ventures or the appropriate division of turf and proceeds. The Cosa Nostra Commission has, at least in the past, provided a mechanism for dispute resolution—a mechanism that also strengthened Cosa Nostra against internal and external threats. Formed more than fifty years ago, the Commission has been comprised of the bosses of all five of New York City's Cosa Nostra families. The 1985 RICO indictment of the Commission's members described the duties and roles of the Commission in the following terms:

1. regulating and facilitating relationships among the five families;

2. promoting and carrying out joint ventures between the families, including the domination and control of labor unions and construction companies;

3. resolving actual and potential disputes among the families, and regulating the operation and control of their respective criminal enterprises;

4. extending formal recognition to newly elected bosses of the families, and resolving leadership disputes within the families;

5. authorizing assassination of Cosa Nostra members; and

6. approving the initiation or "making" of new members or soldiers into the families.[8]

Cosa Nostra's effectiveness is grounded in its power to provide illegal services to its own members and, for a price, to other racketeers and legitimate businessmen. Among the more valuable services are mediation of disputes with other criminals; criminal enterprises and ventures; allocating turf to Cosa Nostra and other criminal groups; fending off incursions by others into those territories; providing financing, muscle, or a corrupt contact necessary to the success of a criminal venture; and providing other means, skills or manpower required to take advantage of constantly arising criminal opportunities.

Within the construction industry, Cosa Nostra has successfully exploited a variety of racketeering opportunities.[9] Because of its influence and control over construction unions, it organizes cartels around the threat of labor unrest, disruption of materials delivery and/or the promise of labor peace. It finances and regulates gambling and loansharking at construction sites. It uses its all too credible threat of violence to eliminate or control what other organized crime groups and individual racketeers can do, how much they can do, and where they can do it.[10] It uses money earned from other illegal activities to finance new ventures in the construction industry and uses its foothold in unions and companies to earn illicit profits or to conceal profits earned in other criminal ventures.

With respect to its "rationalizing role," Cosa Nostra serves two essential and related functions. First, where there is fragmentation, its presence and power provide simplification and coordination; it can solve labor problems and assure that supplies are delivered and competition reduced. Second, it can assure that extortion will not exceed predictable and "reasonable" levels and can be the guarantor of the *quid pro quo* for illegal payments.

Cosa Nostra's Influence in Construction Unions

Cosa Nostra's primary power base in the construction industry is found in many of the construction trade unions.[11] Paul Castellano, boss of the Gambino Crime Family until his murder in 1985, put it bluntly: "Our job is to run the unions."[12] The 1986 Report of the President's Commission on Organized Crime found that more than a dozen New York City construction union locals "have a documented relationship with one or more of the New York City families, often through the holding of union office."[13] Our investigations have revealed an even more extensive Cosa Nostra involvement. Cosa Nostra's infiltration of or control over the district councils is particularly significant, because it provides the means for manipulating and sometimes dominating the locals under that district council's jurisdiction. Cosa Nostra family members or their close associates also often hold key offices in these union locals and district councils. Likewise, they exercise control over employee benefit funds.

Criminal investigations, including those conducted by OCTF, have revealed examples of Cosa Nostra's control over or influence in New York City construction unions:

- Local 282 of the International Brotherhood of Teamsters is one of the most powerful construction unions in New York City and Long Island. Its officials have been closely associated with or controlled by members of Cosa Nostra for decades. As early as 1954, New York County District Attorney Frank Hogan reported that gangsters were threatening concrete suppliers with labor problems. John O'Rourke, president of Local 282 from 1931 to 1965, was closely associated with Lucchese Family members John "Johnny Dio" Dioguardi and Antonio "Tony Ducks" Corallo. From 1976 to 1984, Local 282's president was John Cody, a close associate of the Gambino Crime Family. An investigation revealed that Cody paid $200,000 per year to Carlo Gambino, the Family's boss. In 1982, Cody was convicted of operating Local 282 as a racketeering enterprise through extortion, kickbacks and bribery.[14]

- Cosa Nostra has long dominated Cement and Concrete Workers Local 6A of the Laborers Union. Until recently, Cosa Nostra controlled this local, as well as the District Council of which it is a member, through Ralph Scopo, a soldier in the Colombo Crime Family. Scopo resigned as president of the District Council in 1985 after being indicted on federal racketeering charges of which he was later convicted. Scopo's sons, Joseph and Ralph, continued to be affiliated with both the District Council and Local 6A, with Joseph serving as president of Local 6A, until their resignations in 1987.[15]

- Cement and Concrete Workers Local 20 of the Laborers Union, also a member of the Concrete Workers District Council, was until recently controlled by Luigi "Louis Beans" Foceri and Frank Bellino, both of whom were former vice-presidents of Local 20 and members of the Lucchese Crime Family. In November 1988, business agent Joseph Frangipane, who controlled the union, was convicted on federal racketeering charges.[16] Frangipane's indictment alleged that he acted together with officials from other unions to force contractors to make payoffs in exchange for labor peace, and that he was under the control of Basil Cervone.

- Cement and Concrete Workers Local 18A of the Laborers Union, another District Council member, was controlled by Vincent DiNapoli, a Genovese Family capo. DiNapoli exercised control through the local's secretary-treasurer, Eugene McCarthy. DiNapoli, who was convicted in 1980 for labor racketeering in the drywall industry, was recently convicted, along with fourteen other members and associates of Cosa Nostra, on various charges of construction-related racketeering.

- The New York City and Vicinity District Council of the Carpenters Union has long been used by Cosa Nostra to control New York City's drywall industry. Genovese Family capo Vincent DiNapoli has been significantly involved in a variety of racketeering schemes orchestrated through the District Council. DiNapoli directly controlled Theodore Maritas, the former president of the District Council, who disappeared on the eve of trial and is believed to have been murdered. Our investigations and indictments have confirmed that racketeering in the industry continues at the District Council and local levels.

- Laborers Local 66 has been controlled by Peter Vario, formerly a vice-president of the local, and a member of the Lucchese Crime Family. He is the nephew of Lucchese Family capo Paul Vario. In December 1988, Peter Vario, along with Michael LaBarbara, Jr., the business manager, and James Abbatiello, an assistant business manager, were charged with operating Local 66 as a criminal enterprise and sharing the proceeds of their illegal activities with the boss and underboss of the Lucchese family.[17]

- Mason Tenders Local 23 of the Laborers Union was, until his 1986 conviction for labor racketeering, controlled by Louis Giardina, a former president of the local and soldier in the Gambino Family. Local 23 controls concrete masonry on many building jobs in the New York metropolitan area.

- Mason Tenders Local 59 of the Laborers Union has been controlled by the Pagano faction of the Genovese Family for many years. In June 1974, Patsy D. Pagano, secretary-treasurer, pleaded guilty to violations of the Hobbs Act and the Taft-Hartley Act. The union was later run by Daniel Pagano, a Genovese Family member and business manager for the local, until his conviction in one of the

LILREX prosecutions. It is currently controlled by his cousin, also named Daniel Pagano, a soldier in the Genovese Crime Family. In a telephone conversation intercepted through court-ordered electronic surveillance by OCTF, the late Joseph Pagano, also a Genovese Crime Family soldier, claimed that Local 59 had "belonged to [his] family for fifty years."[18]

- Steam Fitters Local 638 of the Plumbers Union was represented by George Daly in 1987. Daly was an associate of Gambino Family boss Paul Castellano and soldier Thomas Bilotti, both of whom were murdered in December 1985. Daly served as Local 638's business agent until his 1987 conviction for soliciting bribes to insure labor peace.

- Blasters and Drill Runners Local 29 of the Laborers Union has long been controlled or influenced by a number of Lucchese Family members. Secretary-treasurer Amadio Petito was indicted in 1981 and subsequently convicted of criminal contempt and perjury for his refusal to testify in a grand jury investigation seeking to determine whether president Louis Sanzo had received illegal payoffs and whether Lucchese Family soldier Samuel Cavalieri, who was not a union member, actually controlled Local 29 and shared payments with Sanzo.[19] The government produced evidence that Sanzo considered Cavalieri to be his "boss" and that Cavalieri's son was the administrator of Local 29's pension fund. Sanzo was convicted of tax evasion and conspiracy to defraud, based on payments he received as part of a money laundering scheme involving mob related construction companies.[20]

- Teamsters Joint Council 16, the largest of the International Brotherhood of Teamsters joint councils, with several construction locals as members, has several officers tied to the Genovese and Lucchese Crime Families. Joseph Trerotola is both president of Joint Council 16 and a vice-president of the Teamsters International Union. His appointment as International Vice-President required the approval of Cosa Nostra. Joint Council 16's vice-president is Patsy Crapanzano, a convicted labor extortionist tied to the Genovese Crime Family. Listed as a member of Joint Council 16's advisory board is Gerald Corallo, president of Teamster's Local 239 and son of former Lucchese Crime Family boss Antonio "Tony Ducks" Corallo.

- Housewreckers Union Local 95 of the Laborers Union is controlled by Vincent "Chin" Gigante, boss of the Genovese Crime Family. In June 1984, Local 95 union officials Joseph Sherman (president), Stephen McNair (business manager), and John "Pegleg" Roshetski, (secretary-treasurer) were convicted of labor racketeering in connection with an extortion from a contractor, Schiavone-Chase Corporation.

- Mason Tenders Locals 47 and 13 of the Laborers Union were identified as long ago as 1969 as racketeer-dominated unions. Local 13, based in Queens, was found to be controlled by "Trigger Mike" Copolla, a capo in the Genovese Family. Local 13 secretary-treasurer George Cervone was murdered in 1961 during a bitter struggle for control of the local. Shortly thereafter, his brother, Basil Cervone, assumed control, and eventually Basil's sons, Joseph and Basil, Jr., were installed as officers. Until his conviction in 1988 for labor bribery, fraud, extortion and racketeering, Basil controlled Local 13 as well as the District Council. Also convicted at that time were Joseph Cervone, two Local 13 shop stewards, officials from three other unions, and several contractors. Basil Cervone, Jr. testified at the trial that he regularly picked up payoffs and "ghost employee" checks for his father.[21]

• Peter A. Vario, business manager of Mason Tenders Local 46 of the Laborers Union, was convicted in 1988, along with Basil Cervone, of labor racketeering and accepting bribes from contractors in exchange for labor peace. Vario is linked to the Lucchese Crime Family, in which his late uncle, Paul Vario, was a capo.

• Genovese Family capo Vincent DiNapoli was directly responsible for the creation of Plasterers Local 530. Local 530 is run by business manager Louis Moscatiello, a Genovese Crime Family associate, currently under indictment for bribe receiving, enterprise corruption and other offenses.[22]

Cosa Nostra members' control of unions on behalf of their families is convincingly illustrated in the following OCTF intercepted conversation between two Lucchese Family soldiers. In the conversation, Salvatore Avellino explained how Peter Vario, the Lucchese soldier then serving as the vice-president of Laborers Local 66, once had to be reminded that he held his union position in stewardship for Lucchese Family boss Antonio "Tony Ducks" Corallo:

> AVELLINO: Before he [Vario] straightened out, he's telling me that the union is his, you know. So I'm saying, what, what do you mean, the union is yours? He believes the fuckin' union is his...[and so I tell him] nothing is yours. Everything is the boss. And he, we only ah got the privilege of working it, or running it....

Cosa Nostra's recognition of the critical value of controlling labor unions is illustrated by another electronically intercepted conversation, in which Avellino informed his business associates of the most effective means of controlling an industry. Although the Lucchese Crime Family already controlled an employers' association, Avellino explained that an industry can be controlled more effectively when "wise guys" (members of a crime family) "control the men" (employees):

> AVELLINO: But we gotta have the strength so that when a fucker comes along and bids [on a contract which is supposed to be limited to members of a Cosa Nostra family sponsored cartel] tomorrow he's got four Gold Tooths [Lucchese controlled Long Island union delegates] in front of him saying "now that [you've got the contract] where are all the workers?" That's the power.
>
> Now, as the Association, we control the [employers]. When we control the men we control the [employers] even better because they're even more fuckin' afraid.
>
> Do you understand me? When you got a [employer] who steps out of line, you got the whip. You got the fuckin' whip. This is what he [one of the crime bosses] tells me all the time. A strong union makes money for everybody, including the wise guys. The wise guys even make more money with a strong union.

Cosa Nostra's role in a union may sometimes be less direct. Organized crime can control a union (at least with respect to key issues and goals) without any organized crime members holding union office. Roy Williams, past General President of the International Brotherhood of Teamsters, testified that from his earliest days in the Teamsters he was controlled by Nick Civella, head of the Kansas City crime syndicate.[23]

As Genovese Crime Family member Vincent ("Fish") Cafaro recently explained:

> My family [Genovese] made a lot of money from gambling and the numbers rackets. We got our money from gambling, but our real power, our real strength, came from the unions.
>
> With the unions behind us, we could shut down the city, or the country for that matter, if we needed to get our way.
>
> Our brugad [family] controlled a number of different unions, some of which I personally dealt with, some of which I knew about from other amico nostra. In some cases, we got money from our dealings with the unions, in some cases we got favors such as jobs for friends and relatives—but, most importantly, in all cases, we got power over every businessman in New York. With the unions behind us, we could make or break the construction industry, the garment business, the docks, to name but a few.[24]

Cosa Nostra's Interest in Legitimate Businesses

Construction unions are not Cosa Nostra's only base of power and influence in the industry. Cosa Nostra "sponsors" or has direct interest in numerous construction companies, principally contractors and suppliers. It also operates as a "labor consultant" to contractors and subcontractors.

In most instances, Cosa Nostra members and associates hide their interests in construction-related companies by operating through nominees who "front" for them on public records.[25] Some examples are:

- Through nominees, Anthony "Fat Tony" Salerno, convicted as boss of the Genovese Crime Family, controlled S & A, a concrete contracting company, and Certified, one of the two major concrete suppliers in Manhattan
- Vincent DiNapoli, Genovese Crime Family capo, for many years controlled Cambridge Drywall Company and Inner City Drywall, two of the City's largest drywall contractors
- Paul Castellano, until his murder the boss of the Gambino Crime Family, controlled Scara-Mix Concrete Company. The company was created in 1980 by its present owner, Paul Castellano's son Phillip, and immediately won a huge subcontract for sewer construction on Staten Island, Castellano's home territory.

In some cases, Cosa Nostra members or their close associates are openly owners or principals of construction companies, and their involvement is accordingly disclosed on legal and financial forms. Some examples are:

- Salvatore "Sammy" Gravano, *consigliere* of the Gambino Crime Family, who reportedly handled street operations for Family boss John Gotti during Gotti's incarceration in the mid-1980s, is president of JJS Construction Company
- William Masselli, a Genovese Crime Family soldier, was the president of JOPEL Contracting and Trucking Company
- John Gotti, Jr., son of the Gambino Family boss, is president of Sampson Trucking Company
- Alphonse "Funzi" Mosca, a Gambino Crime Family capo, was the owner of Glenwood Concrete Flooring, Inc., a major concrete contractor in the New York metropolitan area
- Louis Di Bono, a Gambino Crime Family soldier, is the president of Mario & Di Bono Plastering Company.

In other cases, Cosa Nostra members or associates held salaried positions in construction firms. In these situations, the employment is "on the books" and in the person's true name because it provides a legitimate position in the community and a reportable source of income. Examples include:

- John Gotti, Gambino Crime Family boss, has held the position of salesman with ARC Plumbing Company
- Aniello "Neil" Migliore, Lucchese Crime Family capo, has held the position of salesman with Port Dock and Stone, one of the principal suppliers of trap rock to the two firms that monopolized the production of concrete in New York City
- Steven Crea, another member of Cosa Nostra, has drawn a salary from Inner City Drywall, one of the City's largest drywall contractors.

In still other cases, Cosa Nostra members and associates serve as "sponsors," "representatives" or "labor consultants" of and for certain construction companies, thereby receiving fees for services, contracts and business opportunities. Some recent examples include:[26]

- Vincent DiNapoli, Genovese Crime Family capo, represented the interests of Standard Drywall Company in its dealings with the New York City drywall contractors.
- Aniello Migliore, Lucchese Crime Family capo, represented the interests of Northberry Concrete, a Brooklyn based contractor and member of the concrete club.

Cosa Nostra's Exploitation of the Industry

Cosa Nostra is a business. One of its objectives is to extract as much money as possible from the multibillion dollar construction industry. The greater its power and influence within the industry, the greater its success. Cosa Nostra families have ingeniously developed and ruthlessly implemented numerous schemes, including the racketeering activities cataloged in Chapter 1, for converting position and power into wealth.

As a result of its role in establishing and policing cartels or "clubs," Cosa Nostra dictates who can participate in certain subindustries, who can obtain which contracts, and at what price. Cosa Nostra profits from these cartels in two ways. First, it extracts payments from cartel members for the benefits that club membership provides: protection from competitors, inflated profit margins, noncompliance with collective bargaining agreements, quality labor force, guaranteed market share, availability and timely delivery of supplies, and protection from other criminal groups. Second, it extracts money by operating its own companies as favored members of the protected cartel.

Cosa Nostra enforces the cartel's rules by threats of labor unrest, withholding essential supplies, violence and sabotage. Prosecutions have shed light on the operations of three clubs, one in the drywall industry and two in the concrete industry.

In the case of the drywall club, the policing function was played by the New York City District Council of Carpenters, which the Genovese Crime Family dominated for many years. In a conversation intercepted by an eavesdropping device in his office, Theodore Maritas, president of the District Council and a Genovese Crime Family associate, explained to a drywall contractor that the contractor was in "hot water" because he had underbid a drywall club company owned by Genovese Crime Family capo Vincent DiNapoli:

MARITAS:	Close the door, Friend, we got a problem... you got to understand something, all right? This guy [Vincent DiNapoli] was being set up, okay, by very, very heavy people, okay, including myself, okay? The prices were all inflated okay? If you weren't in there, I want to tell you what kind of ball game you're in, okay? The lowest price he [Vincent DiNapoli] had was a million dollars more than what you were asking for... I don't know if you understand what you're into, you know, when I tell you okay?
CONTRACTOR:	You're laughing because you're in a lot of hot water.
MARITAS:	I'm laughing because you're in a lot of hot water.
CONTRACTOR:	Who is?
MARITAS:	You.
CONTRACTOR:	Why... I don't understand.
MARITAS:	You have to understand something, okay? Everybody [got] together, okay, specifically to see a certain guy [got] the job, okay, and people had it set up that way, okay? Now you come along a million dollars less than we do, okay?... I mean, you're a friend of mine... I'm not trying to hurt you, okay, swear to God. I want you to understand... take my word for it because everybody

that submitted a bid was set up... this thing had been set up for eight or nine months. I mean, like, everybody [had] been in on it and you come along, innocently, okay—and come in a million less than the low bidder—a million dollars, a million dollars I'm saying... Yeah.

The concrete club demonstrates the sophistication and complexity of Cosa Nostra's role in the construction industry. According to evidence presented at the "Genovese Family" and "Commission" trial,[27] Cosa Nostra was able to regulate the concrete subindustries through its domination of the Laborers Union District Council of Cement and Concrete Workers and of Teamsters Local 282, and through its control of Certified Concrete Company and Transit Mix Concrete Corp., the two main suppliers of ready-mix concrete in Manhattan. On all concrete pouring contracts up to $2 million, the Colombo Family extorted a one percent kickback. Contracts from $2 to $15 million were reserved for a club of contractors selected by Cosa Nostra's Commission. These contractors were required to kick back two percent of the contract price to the Commission. Contracts valued at more than $15 million were the exclusive province of S & A Concrete Co., in which Anthony "Fat Tony" Salerno (convicted boss of the Genovese Crime Family) and Vincent DiNapoli (Genovese Crime Family capo) had alleged hidden interests.

- Engineers estimated the concrete contract for the Jacob K. Javits Convention Center at $18 million. The Center twice rejected bids from S & A Concrete and Dic Underhill Company because they were too high. Nevertheless, S & A Concrete eventually won the contract with a bid of $30.3 million.

In the following intercepted conversation, Colombo Crime Family soldier Ralph Scopo (who, as president of the Cement and Concrete Workers District Council, served as Cosa Nostra's "enforcer" throughout the concrete industry) described to a nonclub contractor that the Commission itself had to approve membership in the concrete club.

SCOPO: ... The concrete's gotta be twelve million?

CONTRACTOR: Yeah. Why can't I do the concrete?

SCOPO: You can't do it. Over two million you can't do it. It's under two million, hey, me, I tell you go ahead and do it.

CONTRACTOR:	Who do I gotta go see? Tell me who I gotta go see?
SCOPO:	You gotta see every Family. And they're gonna tell you, "no." So don't even bother.
CONTRACTOR:	If Tommy goes and talks to them?
SCOPO:	They'll tell you no. No matter who talks. I know they'll tell you no. I went through this not once, a hundred times. I can't get it for myself. How could I get it for somebody else?

In addition to enforcing cartels, Cosa Nostra exploits its power to extract money from the construction industry in several other ways. It extorts payoffs from individual contractors or suppliers by threatening labor unrest or violence, and solicits bribes, either explicitly or implicitly, by promises of sweetheart contracts and waivers of collective bargaining provisions. For example, Ralph Scopo's control of the supply of concrete provided him leverage to obtain payoffs from contractors throughout the City. In one recorded conversation, Scopo described how easily he could deal with a contractor's refusal to make a Christmas payoff:

SCOPO:	I called up, "no concrete." He called back. I told the office, "Don't order no concrete for tomorrow cause you're not getting any." That was the end of that. He seen I had the fuckin' stranglehold on him, the next move...
D'AMBROSI:	Yeah.
SCOPO:	... he calls... I forget what the fuck I got from him. It was 15 thousand and it was a promise that Christmas...
D'AMBROSI:	Yeah.
SCOPO:	... he would give me somethin', you know, for Christmas.
D'AMBROSI:	Yeah, yeah.
SCOPO:	He paid the fifteen thousand.

OCTF has identified a second concrete conspiracy made possible by the Lucchese Family's control of Laborers Local 66 on Long Island. An investigation by the Construction Industry Strike Force, which was prosecuted jointly by OCTF and the United States Attorney's Office for the Eastern District of New York, established that a Long Island concrete contractors club paid bribes to union officials to permit the contractors to operate a double-breasted shop; avoid employment of union shop stewards on the job; pay union workers below scale; and withhold employer contributions to the union benefit and welfare funds.[28] The club, organized by the Lucchese Family through Local 66 vice president Peter Vario, met regularly to discuss bids and allocate jobs. In return for the benefits of club membership, the contractors paid one percent of the price of certain contracts to Vario. A large portion of these payoffs were then allegedly transferred to the Lucchese Crime Family.[29]

In a 1983 conversation that was secretly recorded by OCTF pursuant to court authorized electronic surveillance, Salvatore Avellino described to Salvatore Santoro, underboss of the Lucchese Family, the various racketeering methods used by Vario to control and profit from the Long Island concrete industry:

AVELLINO: Well, ya see... there's three things involved over here. See, Peter's [Vario] got something to do with a ... concrete plant.

SANTORO: Yeah.

AVELLINO: That's number one.

SANTORO: Oh yeah, I know that.

AVELLINO: OK. Then Pete has got a guy that lays the stuff [concrete], Sal Spilabotte.

SANTORO: Yeah, he's got something to do with him.

AVELLINO: He's got something to do with him, he gets a pay, a payroll there... He [Vario] wants this guy [Spilabotte] to get all the [concrete-pouring] work. Now, this is the highest [priced] guy that there is...

SANTORO: Yeah...

AVELLINO: Right, then he's [Vario] got the, a Club. Follow. Some other Club [believed to be concrete suppliers] yeah, that they all pay fifty-cents a yard [of concrete].

SANTORO: Right, right.

AVELLINO: ... That's the Club. But ya see... Peter [Vario] would like Racanelli to, number one, use Spilabotte,[30] and then, Spilabotte, in turn, buys from Keyway.

SANTORO: Right.

AVELLINO: And also pays the fifty cents a yard, so he [Vario] gets a triple header here.

Because of its network of control and domination of a variety of construction unions, Cosa Nostra can use its leverage in one union to support the legitimate or illegitimate goals of other unions. In the following intercepted conversation, for example, Ralph Scopo describes how he used his control of the Cement and Concrete Workers union to resolve problems faced by others:

SCOPO: That's why, see with me, if, a lot of times, there's a grievance on the job, they call a grievance on the teamsters, carpenters, the masons, the lathers, you know. . . . They don't even know what to do. I call up the yard. Say you're gettin' concrete from uh, F. and M. I call 'em up, "Giulio, don't send no fuckin' concrete over because we got a problem." He stops it. He don't listen to me, I stop his whole plant.

FERRARA: Stop the plant.

SCOPO: The whole plant! Now he can't make no deliveries. So there's no problem.

Another example involves Louis D. Moscatiello, president of Plasterers Local 530 and an associate of Genovese Family capo Vincent DiNapoli, and Benedetto (Benny) Schepis, a business agent and business manager of Carpenters Local 17. In 1989, Moscatiello and Schepis were charged with serving as middlemen, or "bribe brokers," in the payment of bribes from construction companies to a Carpenters Local 135 official. As brokers, they both received bribe money on behalf of the Local 135 official and told him which companies were safe to accept bribe payments from and how other companies were to be treated.[31] In exchange for the bribes, the union official was to permit the companies to violate the Carpenters Union collective bargaining agreement and assign to those companies' projects stewards who would overlook such violations. Six contractors were also indicted, charged with Bribery of a Labor Official, Conspiracy and other crimes.[32]

Cosa Nostra also extracts money from the construction industry by forcing contractors to place nonworking Cosa Nostra members, associates, or fictitious workers on their payrolls. These are convenient and lucrative sinecures for family members and associates or, alternatively, a tax cover for others who merely serve as conduits for the payments.

- Collective bargaining agreements require the presence of a "working teamster foreman"[33] at every construction site in order to verify that drivers delivering building materials are members of the union. These are the most lucrative assignments in the Teamsters Union, often paying $75,000 or more in wages and fringe benefits. The SIC has documented that many Cosa Nostra members hold no-show positions as working teamster foremen and that twenty-four percent of the working teamster foremen assigned to contractors' payrolls in 1984 by Local 282 had been convicted of some criminal offense.[34]

- In a suit brought by dissident union members against Teamsters Local 282 challenging the union's refusal to appoint the plaintiffs as working teamster foremen, Local 282 president Robert Sasso "conceded that relatives of union officials who were not even union members were appointed working teamster foremen."[35]

- Frank DiCicco, the underboss of the Gambino Crime Family, who was murdered by a car bomb in April 1986, used his Teamsters Local 282 job placements as a cover. Testimony before the SIC disclosed that DiCicco was on the payroll of Leon DeMatteis Construction Corp., a major New York State builder. Although paid overtime, DiCicco was rarely present at any construction sites.[36]

- Tishman Construction carried on its payroll Harry Gross, a Teamsters racketeer, and Phillip Doran, a Teamsters business agent convicted of bribe receiving and extortion.

- A 1986 indictment alleged that Anthony Vitta, a soldier in the Joseph Armone crew of the Gambino Crime Family, extorted three years of salary at $500 per week by threatening to put the victim, E.M. Mechanical, a small Bronx construction firm, out of business.[37]

- Henry Hill, a Lucchese Family associate, recounted how Lucchese Family capo Paul Vario presented him with a Bricklayers union card and a no-show construction job on his 14th birthday to mark the Family's recognition of Hill's growing accomplishments as a gangster.[38]

Through its influence in the construction unions, Cosa Nostra placed its members and associates as trustees in various union employee benefit funds and has exploited these funds through embezzlement and fraud. Cosa Nostra also takes kickbacks from those to whom it steers fund business and investments.

- John Cody, a Gambino Family associate, served as president of Teamsters Local 282 and as both a trustee and administrator of the local's pension and welfare funds. In 1978, he tried to lend $20 million (one-third of Local 282's entire pension fund) to purchase land and construct a hotel and gambling casino in Las Vegas. The proposed transaction was terminated by the U.S. Department of Labor.[39]

Five months later, Cody was approached by Anthony Angelos,

president and chairman of the board of Des Plaines Bancorpora-
tion, which was seeking a loan for its wholly owned (and sole) subsidiary, the Des Plaines bank. One month later, Cody pushed
through a $2 million loan from the union's pension fund. The bank,
which was little more than a shell corporation, subsequently
closed, returning little of the money borrowed from the union. In
an action brought initially by union members, and later joined by
the Department of Labor, the court held the pension fund trustees
directly and severally liable for losses incurred and removed the
defendants as trustees in favor of a court-appointed manager.[40]
Cody was convicted in 1982 of, among other charges, conducting
the affairs of both the union and its benefit plans through a pattern
of racketeering that spanned a fourteen year period.[41]

The employee benefit funds provide many services for union
members, including medical, dental, and legal services, and life
insurance. The power to direct this business provides enormous
kickback opportunities for Cosa Nostra.

- A Securities and Exchange Commission investigation of investor
  John Giura exposed a scheme in which he steered more than a billion dollars of Teamster employee benefit funds to favored brokers,
  including the son of Teamsters Local 282 President John Cody. The
  brokers kicked back a portion of their large commissions to trustees, their families and friends.[42]

- Some of organized crime's abuse of pension and welfare funds
  were disclosed by Senator John McClellan's committee's investigations (1957-61) of improper practices in labor-management relations. In one case, almost immediately after receiving a license as
  an insurance broker, the son of a major organized crime figure in
  New York City was chosen as the broker for a number of such
  funds. The youthful broker's only explanation for his success was
  that he had advertised in the classified pages of the telephone
  directory.[43]

- LILREX indictments alleged that companies belonging to the "drywall club" operated double-breasted shops which paid no withholding tax, social security or unemployment insurance, and made
  no contributions to the employee benefit funds.[44]

Through its control of unions, Cosa Nostra compels contractors to purchase ancillary goods and services (window washing,
security, carpeting, and so on) from favored firms either controlled by or kicking back to Cosa Nostra.

- Corky Vastola, a member of the DeCavalcante New Jersey crime
  family, coerced building material suppliers to buy carpet material
  from a single carpet supplier from whom he received kickbacks.

Cosa Nostra also uses its connections in the construction industry to organize and dominate the rackets which supply illicit goods and services at construction sites. These goods and services include gambling, loansharking, narcotics and stolen goods. Control over several of these rackets was discussed in the following intercepted conversation between Ralph Scopo and three other Cosa Nostra family members:

> SCOPO: There's a super [site superintendent hired by general contractor] on that job, and Rudy went out after it to find out when they're gonna start. So the super says to him, "Let me, let me, explain everything to you now, so there's no problems later. I got the coffee shanty, I got the numbers, I got bookmaking, I got shylocking, I got the five dollar bags." So Rudy says, "I don't know what you got, but whatever you got, keep it." And he walked away and he comes to me.

A 1989 OCTF indictment charged that Joseph Pagano and his son Daniel, both soldiers in the Genovese Crime family, attempted to control a waterfront construction project in Yonkers, so that they could control gambling, loansharking and other illegal activities at the construction site. According to the indictment, when a dispute over that control arose with another faction of the Genovese family, Daniel Pagano sought the intervention of Genovese family boss, Vincent "the Chin" Gigante. Gigante allegedly resolved the dispute with an agreement that, among other things, the Paganos would receive $400,000 and control of the on-site gambling and loansharking. [45]

During the hearings conducted by the President's Commission on Organized Crime, an undercover informant from the New York City construction industry testified:

> WITNESS: There were occasions when I was approached by organized crime seeking certain favors, such as union membership cards, which would give access to their people to get on construction sites and allow them —
>
> QUESTION: Why was organized crime interested in getting union books [cards] so as to get access to construction sites?
>
> WITNESS: Construction sites tend to be sealed off and guarded. In order to gain access to a site, you would have to show some sort of union membership and show that you were working on that site.

QUESTION: And why did organized crime want to get onto a con-
                struction site, to engage in what kinds of activity?

WITNESS: On a typical construction of a large scale project you
                may have many, many workers who are literally on
                the site all day. There are dice games, card games,
                bookmaking going on, loansharking. By gaining
                access to the site, the organized crime members can
                engage in those activities and control it.[46]

Implications of Organized Crime Racketeering

Racketeers enter an industry because its structure, organization
and other characteristics make it susceptible to infiltration and
domination, and because of its high level of racketeering potential. If a racketeering syndicate is able to control or influence such
critical components as unions, suppliers or contractors, and has
sufficient power to control all or most of the racketeers preying
on the industry, it has the power to play a rationalizing role in the
industry.[47] Such a role is valued by those who appreciate the need
for certainty and predictability in an industry marked by high
fragmentation, competition, fragility, bribery and extortion.
Once capable of playing a rationalizing role, the racketeering
syndicate can create cartels in which the companies it controls
play dominant roles. The syndicate will thus benefit in two ways:
directly, by payments for its interests in the rationalizing services, and indirectly, through profits made by the firms making
up the cartels.

Cosa Nostra's domination of the construction industry has
profound implications. During the past five decades, Cosa Nostra has become an entrenched part of the industry. Its presence is,
to a large extent, accepted by developers, contractors and suppliers—in some instances as a necessary evil to promote stability
and predictability; in other instances, as a provider of valuable
illicit services. Even those who resent Cosa Nostra's presence in
the industry perceive it as a parasite that society is powerless to
remove. As in the Brindell era, the industry has learned to live
with its exploitive activities and, to some extent, has become
dependent on its rationalizing role.

This accommodation between legitimate businessmen and
syndicate racketeers is inherently unstable. A criminal syndicate
by its nature seeks to exploit its power to the limit. Ultimately, its

demands become greater and greater. We have seen that Cosa Nostra has achieved power and prominence in many of the construction industry's labor unions, as well as in supply and contracting companies. If left unchecked, the balance between the legitimate and illegitimate elements in the construction industry will tip overwhelmingly toward the illegitimate. One economist has described this phenomenon:

> To the extent that large criminal business firms provide governmental structure to the underworld, helping to maintain peace, setting rules, arbitrating disputes, and enforcing discipline, they are in a position to set up their own businesses and exclude competition. Constituting a kind of "corporate state," they can give themselves the franchise for various "state-sponsored monopolies." They can do this either by denying the benefits of the underworld government to their competitors or by using the equivalent of their "police power" to prevent competition. . . . Where the line between business and government is indistinct, as it appears to be in the underworld, dominant business firms become regulators of their own industries, and developers of state monopolies.[48]

It is therefore probable that more and more legitimate companies will be squeezed out of the industry, and more and more honest unionists will be forced into silence or a different career. Such a dismal vision must not be allowed to materialize.

FOOTNOTES

1. Brindell was able to maintain his influence within the industry in part because of political backing from Tammany Hall—this explains why his Buildings Trades Council was known as "the Annex of Tammany Hall." The power of Tammany resulted in quashed prosecutions and fixed cases, and ensured that Brindell was perceived in the industry as an "untouchable."

2. State of New York, *Intermediate Report of the Joint Legislative Committee on Housing* (Albany, N.Y.: J. B. Lyon Company, 1922).

3. Harold Seidman, *Labor Czars: A History of Labor Racketeering* (New York: Liveright, 1938) 74.

4. *Id.*, 82-83.

5. This pattern of support for indicted and convicted racketeers continued in the 1940s, when Joe Fay, vice-president of the International Operating Engineers Union, was incarcerated for his part in a conspiracy to extort more than $700,000 from contractors. He was visited in prison by politicians and labor leaders, including Arthur H. Wicks, Lieutenant Governor, State Senate Majority Leader and author of the "Wicks Law." Harold Danforth and James Horan, *The D.A.'s Man* (New York: Crown, 1957) 271.

6. The literature on the origins of Cosa Nostra in the United States is voluminous. Some of the most important works are: John Landesco, *Organized Crime in Chicago* (1929; Chicago: University of Chicago, 1968); Donald Cressey, *Theft Of A Nation* (New York: Harper, 1969); Humbert Nelli, *The Business of Crime* (New York: Oxford University Press, 1976); Virgil Peterson, *The Mob: 200 Years of Organized Crime in New York* (Ottowa, Ill.: Green Hill Publishers, 1983); Stephen R. Fox, *Blood and Power: Organized Crime and Twentieth Century America* (New York: William Morrow, 1989).

7. New York City Police Department, *Report on Organized Crime in New York City to the United States Senate, Committee on the Judiciary* (New York: NYPD, July 1983).

8. *United States v. Salerno*, 85 CR 139 (S.D.N.Y. 1985), known as the "Commission Case."

9. Cosa Nostra's infiltration of the construction industry is not limited to New York. The New Jersey Commission of Investigation reported that the Bruno Organized Crime Family of Philadelphia, headed by Nicodemo "Little Nicky" Scarfo, controlled construction of many of the casinos, as well as numerous public works in Atlantic City, New Jersey, during the 1980s. This was done through control of key labor unions—specifically, Cement and Concrete Workers Local 33 and Ironworkers Local 350—and through ownership of companies that supplied concrete and steel. See State of New Jersey, Commission of Investigation, *18th Annual Report and Report and Recommendations on Organized Crime-Affiliated Subcontractors at Casino and Public Construction Sites* (Trenton, N.J., 1987) and State of New Jersey, Commission of Investigation, *Organized Crime Roster-Profiles of Bruno/Scarfo Group Members, Associates, Affiliated Businesses and Influenced Labor Unions* (Trenton, N.J., May 1988).

10. Cosa Nostra is not the only organized crime group to have preyed on the construction industry. Among the others are the Westies, an Irish-American gang, which operated independently in the construction industry but which has a working relationship with Cosa Nostra. See *People v. Kelly*, Ind. No. 5471/86 (N.Y. County 1986) and *People v. Gotti*, Ind. No. 358/89 (N.Y. County 1989).

11. For a comprehensive overview of labor racketeering see, G. Robert Blakey, Ronald Goldstock, and Gerard Bradley, *Labor Racketeering: Background Materials* (Ithaca, N.Y.: Cornell Institute on Organized Crime, 1979); John Hutchinson, *The Imperfect Union: A History of Corruption in American Trade Unions* (New York: Dutton, 1970); John Hutchinson, "The Anatomy of Corruption in Trade Unions," *Industrial Relations* 8 (1969): 135; Philip Taft, *Corruption and Racketeering in the Labor Movement*, 2d ed. (Ithaca, N.Y.: N.Y.S. School of Industrial and Labor Relations, Cornell University, 1970); Daniel Bell, *The End of Ideology* (Glencoe, Ill.: Free Press, 1960).

For Congressional investigations of labor racketeering, see United States, Senate, Select Committee on Improper Activities in the Labor or Management Field, *First Interim Report*, 85th Cong., 2d Sess. (Washington, D.C.: GPO, 1958); United States, Senate, Select Committee on Improper Activities in the Labor or Management Field, *Second Interim Report*, S. Report No. 621, 86th Cong., 1st sess. (Washington, D.C.: GPO, 1959); United States, Senate, Committee on Governmental Affairs, *Labor Management Racketeering: Hearings Before the Permanent Subcommittee on Investigations of the Committee on Governmental Affairs*, 95th Cong., 2d Sess. (Washington, D.C.: GPO, 1978).

12. Conversations of Paul Castellano intercepted on May 5, 1983, by the Federal Bureau of Investigation pursuant to court-authorized electronic surveillance.

13. President's Commission on Organized Crime, *The Edge: Organized Crime, Business, and Labor Unions* (Report to the President and the Attorney General) (Washington, D.C.: GPO, March 1986) 225-26.

14. *United States v. Cody*, 722 F.2d 1052 (2d Cir. 1983), *cert. denied*, 467 U.S. 1226 (1984). The Teamsters connection to Cosa Nostra has been the subject of much investigation and documentation. See Dan Moldea, *The Hoffa Wars: Teamsters, Rebels, Politicians and the Mob* (New York: Paddington, 1978); Lester Velie, *Desperate Bargain: Why Jimmy Hoffa Had to Die* (New York: Simon and Schuster, 1978); Steven Brill, *The Teamsters* (New York: Simon and Schuster, 1978); James Cook, "The Invisible Enterprise—Part 4: The Most Abused, Misused Pension Fund in America," *Forbes*, 10 November 1980: 69.

In June 1988, the U.S. Department of Justice filed a civil RICO action against the International Brotherhood of Teamsters; their General Executive Board, including the president, secretary-treasurer, sixteen vice-presidents, and one former vice-president; and the Commission of La Cosa Nostra. *United States v. International Brotherhood of Teamsters*, 708 F.Supp. 1388 (S.D.N.Y. 1989). The action alleged that the union's board had deprived its 1.7 million members of their rights by allowing the union to be dominated by organized crime. In March 1989, the Justice Department and the union leadership reached a settlement which provided for the appointment of three administrators to supervise specific areas of the union's operations and to oversee a free election.

15. In March 1987, pursuant to a civil RICO suit by the United States Attorney for the Southern District of New York, Local 6A and the District Council of Cement and Concrete Workers agreed to replace many of their leaders and accept supervision by a court-appointed trustee. *United States v. Local 6A, Cement and Concrete Workers*, 86 Civ 4819 (S.D.N.Y. 1986).

16. See *United States v. Cervone*, 87 CR 579 (E.D.N.Y. 1987).

17. See *United States v. Vario*, 88 CR 719 (E.D.N.Y. 1988). In September 1989, LaBarbara and Abbatiello pleaded guilty to multiple counts of accepting payoffs totaling $18,000 from seven Long Island contractors. Abbatiello also pleaded guilty to obstructing justice by instructing a witness to lie to the grand jury. In December 1989 they were each sentenced to fourteen months imprisonment, and each

ordered to pay approximately $37,000, including fines and the cost of imprisonment.

Vario, indicted in December 1988 as a result of a CISF investigation, resigned as vice-president of the union and as a welfare fund administrator. Vario was convicted in March 1990 on thirty-eight counts, including Taft-Hartley Act violations and participating in a RICO conspiracy that included receiving twenty-five illegal payments between 1979 and 1986.

18. *People v. Pagano*, Ind. No. 120/89 (Rockland County 1989). In this case, Daniel Pagano, Joseph Pagano's son, was charged with heading—along with his father—the Pagano faction of the Genovese Family. He pleaded guilty in the case to Criminal Usury in the First Degree and Promoting Gambling in the First Degree.

19. See *United States v. Petito*, 671 F.2d 68 (2d Cir.), *cert. denied*, 459 U.S. 824 (1982).

20. See *United States v. Sanzo*, 673 F.2d 64 (2d Cir.), *cert. denied*, 459 U.S. 858 (1982).

21. See *United States v. Cervone*, 87 CR 579 (E.D.N.Y. 1987).

22. *People v. Moscatiello*, Ind. No. 8081/89 (N.Y. County 1989).

23. Affidavit of Roy Williams in *United States v. International Brotherhood of Teamsters*, 708 F.Supp. 1388 (S.D.N.Y. 1989) (civil RICO action seeking to place Teamsters Union in trusteeship).

24. "Affidavit of Vincent Cafaro" filed with the United States, Senate, Permanent Subcommittee on Investigations of the Committee on Government Affairs, April 1988, 16-17.

25. A Certificate of Incorporation, which must be filed with the Secretary of State, need list only the corporations' "incorporators"; there is no requirement that shareholders or officers be listed. N.Y. Bus. Corp. Law § 402 (McKinney 1986). While city and state agencies can require additional information from companies who seek contracts from them, the common practice of listing relatives or other "fronts" as nominal owners defeats most efforts to determine true ownership.

26. For a not so recent example, consider Jack McCarthy, a reputed associate of the Gambino Crime Family. As far back as 1966, McCarthy was the subject of hearings before the Senate Permanent Subcommittee of the Committee on Government Operations. See United States, Senate, Permanent Subcommittee on Government Operations of the Committee on Government Operations, *Hearings on Labor Racketeering Activities of Jack McCarthy and National Consultants Associated, Ltd.*, 89th Cong., 2nd sess., Sept. 27, 28, and Oct. 4, 1966 (Washington, D.C.: GPO, 1967.) It is also interesting that a number of mob figures who attended the 1957 Appalachian Conference, including Carlo Gambino, described themselves to law enforcement as "labor consultants."

27. *United States v. Salerno*, 86 CR 245 (S.D.N.Y. 1986); *United States v. Salerno*, 85 CR 139 (S.D.N.Y. 1985).

28. See *United States v. Vario*, 88 CR 719 (E.D.N.Y. 1988).

29. For a further description of this conspiracy, see: Robert W. Greene, "The LI Concrete Trial," *Newsday*, 11 March 1990, Long Island ed.: 3; Tom Morris, "LI Prices Among Highest," *Newsday*, 11 March 1990, Long Island ed.: 3; Steve Wick, "How A Small Firm Became the Island's Largest Supplier," *Newsday*, 11 March 1990, Long Island ed.: 27.

30. In June 1989, concrete contractor Silvestro Spilabotte pleaded guilty to paying a bribe to Laborers Local 66's business manager, Michael LaBarbara, and was sentenced to six months imprisonment.

31. *People v. Moscatiello*, Ind. No. 8081/89 (N.Y. County 1989).

32. Henry ("Hank") Walaski, a business representative of Carpenters Local 531 until his federal racketeering conviction in December 1988, was indicted for criminal contempt and perjury in the same case. Walaski testified before the grand jury that while he had accepted unlawful payments from "everybody," he could not recall the name of a single contractor from whom he had taken a bribe. See *People v. Walaski* Ind. No. 8079/89 (N.Y. County 1989) and *People v. Walaski*, Ind. No. 9494/89 (N.Y. County 1989).

33. The official title of this position has been changed to "on site steward," but it is still commonly referred to as "working teamster foreman."

34. State of New York, Commission of Investigation, *Investigation of the Building and Construction Industry: Report of Conclusions and Recommendations* (December 1985) 28.

35. See *Kudla v. Local 282 International Brotherhood of Teamsters*, 821 F.2d 95, 101 (2d Cir. 1987).

36. See testimony of SIC Investigator Louis Montello at public hearings held in June 1985 before the New York State Commission of Investigation.

37. *United States v. Gallo*, 86 CR 4525 (E.D.N.Y. 1986).

38. Nicholas Pileggi, *Wise Guy* (New York: Pocket Books, 1985) 24.

39. *Marshall v. Teamsters Local 282 Pension Trust Fund*, 458 F.Supp. 986 (E.D.N.Y. 1978).

40. *Katsaras v. Cody*, 744 F.2d 270 (2d Cir.), *cert. denied*, 469 U.S. 1072, (1984). In 1984, almost five years after the above loan closed, the fund trustees brought an action against Angelos and nine others, asserting two counts of securities fraud under federal law and one count each of fraud and negligent representation under Illinois law. The action, which was barred by the statute of limitations, was dismissed.

41. *United States v. Cody*, 722 F.2d 1052 (2d Cir. 1983), *cert. denied*, 467 U.S. 1226 (1984).

42. Jonathan R. Laing, "The Rogue of Stein Roe," *Barrons'*, 24 November 1986: 6; Gerard Bray and Jon LaFayette, "Top Lawyer Quits as Insider Probe Widens," *New York Post*, 15 July 1986, Wall Street extra: 2; Gary Langer, "SEC Charges Kickback Schemes by Investment Advisor," *Associated Press*, 15 July 1986; James Sterngold, "3 Face SEC Charges," *New York Times*, 15 July 1986, late ed.: D16.

43. Interview with James P. Kelly, former investigator for the Senate Select Committee on Improper Activities in the Labor or Management Field, November 23, 1966, in President's Commission on Law Enforcement and Administration of Justice, *Task Force Report: Organized Crime* (Washington, D.C.: GPO, 1967) 5.

44. *United States v. Maritas*, 81 CR 122 (E.D.N.Y. 1981).

45. *People v. Pagano*, Ind. No. 120/89 (Rockland County 1989).

46. President's Commission on Organized Crime, *Organized Crime and Labor-Management Racketeering in the United States, Record of Hearing VI, Chicago, Illinois* (Washington, D.C.: GPO, April 1985).

47. See Bell, *The End of Ideology*.

48. Thomas Schelling, "Appendix D—Economic Analysis and Organized Crime," *Task Force Report: Organized Crime*, President's Commission on Crime and the Administration of Justice (Washington, D.C.: GPO, 1967) 118.

CHAPTER 4

Official corruption

Introduction

Official corruption in the New York City construction industry, like labor racketeering, has persisted throughout the twentieth century.[1] Official corruption occurs when a public official (1) solicits or receives a bribe in exchange for favorable exercise of official authority; (2) extorts a benefit by threatening unfavorable exercise of official authority;[2] (3) takes official action to further the official's self-interest; or (4) enriches himself or herself through the wrongful use of inside information or connections.[3] While official corruption arises in the context of practically all government functions and activities, it is an especially difficult problem in the construction industry. The reason is obvious: construction involves large amounts of money, and government officials are inevitably and critically a part of virtually every stage of the construction process.[4]

Corruption susceptibility is high among those public officials with discretionary authority over the construction process. Like labor union officials, public officials can escalate costs, cause delays or even shut down a project. By leveraging and manipulating their regulatory powers (and, in public construction projects, their power over the contracting process itself), corrupt public officials can substantially help or hinder developers and contractors.[5] Like labor racketeers, they typically do not have to extort or even solicit payoffs; many contractors voluntarily make payoffs simply to ensure smooth relationships.

Corruption potential is high because profits on New York City's multimillion and multibillion dollar projects are substantial, and opportunities for payoffs plentiful. Payoffs to lower level officials generally take the form of cash bribes. Higher level officials and politicians can be paid off in favors, deals and business opportunities. Moreover, given the extent to which developers and builders are dependent upon political and legal "inputs" to get their projects approved, started and completed, it is hardly surprising to find that developers and contractors are large contributors to political campaigns.[6]

This chapter describes New York City's long history of official corruption in both public works administration and in regulation of public and private construction projects. It will also present evidence that this official corruption is part of an environment in which developers and contractors cultivate and seek favors from public officials at all levels.

History of Official Corruption in the New York City Construction Process

New York City's construction industry has long been afflicted with official corruption.[7] Perhaps the most notorious public scandal of the nineteenth century involved the construction of the New York County Courthouse. In 1858, the County Board of Supervisors allocated $250,000 for its construction. Four years later, boss William Marcy Tweed and his supporters gained control of the Board. By the time the Courthouse was completed, over a decade later, its cost had escalated to more than $13 million, from which Tweed and his friends had siphoned off $9 million.[8]

> The [Courthouse] scheme was launched when Tweed and [District Attorney Peter] Sweeney made arrangements with businessmen of easy conscience, the contractors of the courthouse. The operation then swung into the bailiwick of Richard Connolly, the City Comptroller, and his right-hand man, the ex-convict James Watson, the County Auditor. It was Connolly's job as the Ring's bookkeeper and financial expert to supervise the assault on the soft underbelly of the city treasury. The contractor submitted a bill for this work, so ill-disguised that the most untutored could recognize it as being padded to its final decimal point. Connolly made sure the Ring received 65 per cent as its commission, with 35 per cent going to the contractor.[9]

Tweed and his associates also profited from the construction of numerous other public works, including the Brooklyn Bridge. In addition to the usual percentage kickback on public contracts, Ring members bought or simply took stock in the company constructing the bridge. Corruption also existed within the construction companies building the bridge. Several assistant engineers with the Roebling Company took large bribes from various steel companies to accept inferior wire for the suspension cables. Another major fraud involved massive overcharges for the storage of cable wire.[10]

William Riordon, a chronicler of turn-of-the-century machine politics, described how one Tammany Hall ward heeler, George Washington Plunkitt, became a millionaire by awarding contracts for the building of many City docks to his own construction company. In addition, as a member of several City and State boards which funded public works, Plunkitt was able to inflate payments on his own construction contracts. He also converted public trust to private wealth by inside trading on projects. In Plunkitt's colorful words:

> [S]upposin' it's a new bridge they're goin' to build. I get tipped off and I buy as much property as I can that has to be taken for approaches. I sell at my own price later on and drop some more money in the bank. Wouldn't you? It's just like lookin' ahead in Wall Street or in the coffee or cotton market. It's honest graft, and I'm looking for it every day in the year.[11]

This kind of graft has continued to be a New York City tradition. Developers and contractors have retained New York City political party officials to handle negotiations with public construction regulators and administrators whose appointments (and often entire careers) the party officials have orchestrated. Elected public officials have often received significant campaign contributions from developers and contractors whose businesses depend on public contracts.[12]

Of course, contributions are not often accompanied by explicit requests for favors. Developers and contractors are constantly seeking good will, favorable dispositions and access to decision makers. They can realistically assume, without explicit and specific agreements, that public officials who are economically dependent on or indebted to them will act favorably on matters in which they have an interest. Such implicit agreements are, perhaps, more appropriately considered "honest graft" than is the kind of conduct for which Plunkitt coined the term.

Official corruption has afflicted the City's regulatory process as well as its bid letting and project implementation. Lincoln Steffins, writing in 1902, observed pervasive corruption in the

operation of the New York City Department of Buildings, the
agency responsible for enforcing the City's Building Code.

> Some of the richest graft in the city is in the Department of Buildings:
> $100,000,000 a year goes into building operations [construction] in
> New York. All of this, from outhouses to skyscrapers, is subject to
> very precise laws and regulations, most of them wise, some impos-
> sible. The Buildings Department has the enforcement of these; it
> passes upon all construction, private and public, at all stages, from
> plan-making to actual completion; and [it] can cause not only
> "unavoidable delay," but can wink at most profitable violations.
> Architects and builders had to stand in with the department. They
> called on the right man and they settled on a scale which was not
> fixed, but which generally was on the basis of the department's esti-
> mate of a fair half of the value of the savings in time or bad material.
> This brought in at least a banker's percentage on one hundred mil-
> lions a year. [13]

The 1931 Seabury Commission uncovered corruption in building regulation similar to that described by Steffins a generation
earlier:

> William E. Walsh ... resigned as chairman of the Board of Standards
> and Appeals after he was indicted for accepting a gratuity from an
> applicant before the board. . . . Fred F. French, who heads a large
> building corporation . . .,followed Walsh to the stand. He had nego-
> tiated with Donnelly [a Tammany Hall lawyer] several times, he
> admitted under examination by Judge Seabury, to have [had] modifi-
> cations of the building code granted for projects in which his com-
> panies were the builders. On a graduated scale he paid $75,000 in
> "legal fees" for permission to make alterations in the plans of "Tudor
> City" at East River and Forty-second Street. He paid $35,000 in simi-
> lar fees on a Madison Avenue office building. [14]

In 1940, Mayor Fiorello LaGuardia expressed a desire to eradi-
cate inspectional corruption in the wake of a scandal in the
Department of Housing and Buildings. He personally suspended twenty-six elevator inspectors who had extorted payments from contractors, a "well-known" practice he had been
trying to expose since 1919, when he was president of the City
Board of Aldermen. LaGuardia's Commissioner of Investigation, William B. Herlands, later reported that extortionate inspections in the elevator division had been going on for thirty years. [15]

Since the 1940s, scandals in the inspectional services corps
have surfaced with almost predictable regularity. Municipal officials have inevitably expressed outrage and pledged stern mea-

sures. Commissions have been formed, investigations launched, reports issued, and in the weak light of waning public interest, some organizational changes have been implemented.

- *March 1942*: Thirty-two plumbing inspectors were suspended for extorting five dollar payments in return for prompt inspection of new construction.[16]

- *June 1947*: As a result of an investigation of the Department of Housing and Buildings, clerks were indicted for removing and destroying records showing that certificates of occupancy had been issued to at least twelve buildings without inspections.[17]

- *October 1950-January 1951*: Several building inspectors were convicted of perjury relating to statements about the source of large sums of money. Bribes amounted to several multiples of an inspector's salary.[18]

- *November 1957*: Manhattan District Attorney Frank Hogan announced an investigation into the sale of building condemnations by inspectors to realtors. Buildings inspectors were bribed to list scores of building violations or to condemn properties which realtors wished to acquire. The latter could then buy the buildings for development at greatly reduced prices. The State Assembly Committee on Government Operations then commenced an inquiry into construction inspection and regulation.[19]

- *March 1958*: A Special Mayoral Commission on Inspectional Service recommended daily, nonsequenced rotation of inspectors to prevent the development of close relationships between inspectors and contractors and realtors. Investigators disclosed that realtors maintained hidden bank accounts for officials of the Department of Buildings in exchange for the officials' favorable actions on their buildings.[20]

- *January 1959*: The acting chief inspector for Manhattan in the Department of Buildings was arrested for taking bribes to ignore building violations. The Department undertook its third reorganization in five years; lines of authority were to be strengthened and supervision reinforced.[21]

- *February 1959*: Kings County Judge Hyman Barshay ordered a grand jury investigation of the Brooklyn Department of Buildings (DOB) after the indictment of an inspector for "mutilating and destroying official records." The Manhattan DOB office was under a separate investigation by a New York County Grand Jury, and the Department of Investigation was conducting a citywide inquiry.[22]

- *March 1959*: A New York County grand jury criticized the Department of Buildings as being run so poorly that "essential services were administered in a completely disorganized, if not chaotic manner." The grand jury's presentment said that maladministration had led to "improper and corrupt practices."[23]

- *July 1960*: The State Commission on Governmental Operations reported that a Department of Buildings inspector had backdated a building permit for a contractor seeking favor with Staten Island Borough President Albert V. Maniscalco. The permit was for a garage at the borough president's home.[24]
- *January 1961*: Buildings Commissioner Peter Reidy reported on his department's anticorruption efforts. Among the changes were higher pay for inspectors, an increased engineering staff, better liaison with the building industry, and reduced time for application processing. Subsequently, the State Commission of Investigation released a report charging that corruption existed "at every stage of operations in the plan-examining division of the City Buildings Department."[25]
- *February 1962*: Mayor Robert Wagner suspended construction at residential developments in Canarsie and Mill Basin because of revelations resulting from an investigation by a Brooklyn grand jury. Charges of fraudulent inspections and police shakedowns were corroborated by complaints of residents of completed units. A week later, the Board of Estimate funded the position of Special Assistant to the Commissioner to "strengthen the control of the inspectional activities of the Buildings Department."[26]
- *May 1966*: Buildings Commissioner Charles Moerdler transferred eighteen Staten Island construction inspectors who were extorting payments to approve residential construction begun since the start of the Verrazano-Narrows Bridge.[27]
- *January 1968*: The Department of Investigation, in a study of low-level employees dismissed for graft, found inspectors to be the group "most often...in trouble" and that the Buildings Department had "been hit most often by scandal in recent years." Other agencies were cited, including the Fire Department. Twelve of the thirteen electrical inspectors in the Fire Department had previously been suspended for allegedly taking bribes to ignore alarm, sprinkler and wiring violations.[28]
- *June 1972*: David Shipler's two-part report in the *New York Times* described the extent of corruption in the construction industry, including payoffs totaling $25 million per year. The report provided details of graft at every level, especially in the inspectional services. In reaction to the report, major investigations were launched by the Department of Investigation and several State agencies.[29]

The extraordinary and lengthy history of official corruption relating to the New York City construction industry can be explained by the same kinds of corruption susceptibility and potential that accounts for other types of racketeering endemic to the industry. An analysis designed to illuminate those features that promote such corrupt behavior is therefore in order.

Accounting for Official Corruption in the Contemporary Construction Process

Introduction
An analysis of official corruption in the building process should first note that public officials play three different roles in construction. The first is letting and monitoring public construction projects. The second is enforcement of City codes regulating the manner in which construction must be carried out. The third is powerbrokering by those whose political stature and/or connections give them the ability to control or influence decisions on all construction matters. Each of these roles generates its own corruption susceptibility.

Corruption in the Award and Administration of Public Construction Projects
Manipulation and fraud can infect contract letting, even in the face of apparent conformity with lowest-responsible bidding procedures. Corrupt officials can "sell" inside information about in-house estimates or about other bidders and their bids. Design specifications can be drawn in such a way as to favor certain contractors. Without proper safeguards, corruption can be even easier to effectuate when noncompetitive bidding procedures are used, as in the awarding of emergency contracts.[30]

- In 1966, James L. Marcus, commissioner designate of the Department of Water Supply, Gas and Electricity borrowed $10,000 from Antonio "Tony Ducks" Corallo, a capo in the Lucchese Crime Family. Under the terms of the loan agreement, Marcus was to repay Corallo $40,000 and to award emergency cleaning contracts at the Jerome Park Reservoir to S.T. Grand & Company, a company to which Corallo was connected. On his first day in office, Marcus awarded an $835,000 "emergency contract" — without competitive bidding — to S.T. Grand. The company president, Henry Fried, then kicked back a total of $40,000 to Marcus, Corallo, Herbert Itkin, a labor lawyer, and Daniel Motto, president of Local 350, Bakery and Confectionery Workers. (Marcus' share, $16,000, was used to pay off a portion of his loan from Corallo).[31] Marcus, who pleaded guilty, was sentenced to fifteen months in federal prison. Corallo, Fried and Motto were tried, found guilty and also sentenced to prison.

A public works project must pass through a gauntlet of reviews by public officials; their favorable actions are necessary if the project is to proceed. Private projects also require many approvals from zoning, landmarking, environmental protection, and other agencies. Once these "go-aheads" are obtained, construction projects require other favorable actions from officials who issue design approvals and building permits. For example, approvals for diverse types of construction need to be obtained from the following agencies: for highways, from the Department of Transportation; for sewers and water, from the Department of Environmental Protection; for electrical and building work, from the Department of Buildings; for fire prevention purposes, from the New York City Fire Department; for asbestos removal, from the Department of Environmental Protection. (Table 3 illustrates the number and complexity of approvals required prior to construction of a new building).

After public works projects are approved and funded, planners, administrators and site supervisors determine when and how billions of dollars are spent. These public officials and employees can delay or expedite progress payments, approve or deny change orders, and accept or reject the final product. Therefore, those who are corrupt are in a position to solicit payoffs, explicitly or implicitly, throughout this process.

- In 1983, the U.S. Court of Appeals for the Second Circuit described the corrupt activity of a Long Island construction engineer:

  Over a 12-year period ending in 1979 appellants engaged in an audacious pattern of corrupt and illegal activities in New York, New Jersey, and Connecticut. As consulting engineers on a number of major sewer construction projects in the tri-state area, and with the connivance of others, appellants extorted money from the project contractors under their control and fraudulently overstated payment claims. Equally outrageous, appellants then used the proceeds of these illegal actions to bribe public officials in order to obtain additional contracts and other forms of preferential treatment from the municipalities they were ostensibly serving.[32]

- In 1986, twenty-six employees of the Board of Education's Buildings Division were indicted for taking bribes and kickbacks from maintenance contractors over a nine-year period. The contractors were required to pay two percent of the original contract amount, ten percent on any additional work, and ten percent on any emergency work let outside the normal bidding procedures. Bribes were paid to expedite payments, inflate materials charges, and to release funds for work never done. Inspectors permitted the contractors to add the price of the kickbacks to the payments they requested. Contractors who did not pay were denied contracts.[33] According to then Kings County District Attorney Elizabeth Holtzman, the scheme had been going on for nearly a decade and involved "tens of millions of dollars" in bribes. Some of these employees were said to have received $60,000 in bribes per year. Blame for the scandal was placed by the Inspector General on poor or nonexistent construction management. Cited as one example was the practice of having the same officials write specifications for a particular job, inspect it, and then review and authorize change orders.[34]

- In 1980 an investigation disclosed widespread fraud and corruption in the City's "in-rem" residential building program. Under the program, the Department of Housing and Preservation (HPD) managed residential properties taken over by the City, through "in-rem" forfeiture proceedings, from owners who had failed to pay taxes. The investigation resulted in the conviction of twelve HPD employees and four construction contractors for the payment of hundreds of thousands of dollars in bribes to influence the award of repair and maintenance contracts, and to expedite the processing of payments under those contracts.[35]

- Eight years later, identical corruption was exposed in the same HPD "in-rem" program. Five employees and two contractors were convicted for receiving kickbacks of up to ten percent of the contract price on bids ranging from $500 to $10,000. In exchange, they funneled work to the contractors and overlooked City regulations pertaining to contract bidding and performance.[36]

- In 1989, two officials of the New York City Bureau of Water Supply each solicited $10,000 in bribes from officials of the Town of New Windsor, which was seeking to obtain increased access to the New York City water supply system. The two officials — Bruno Nagler, a project manager, and John Perykase, who directed management information and computer operations — also accepted bribes from both the owner and the general superintendent of a company seeking construction contracts for repair of the water supply system. In addition, Nagler accepted a bribe from a water meter company in return for steering repair and test work to the company. In March 1990, Nagler and Perykase pleaded guilty to violation of the federal anti-extortion statute. The three contractors pleaded guilty to interstate travel in aid of racketeering.[37]

Corruption among Building Inspectors

By far the greatest number of documented cases of official corruption in the New York City construction industry involves building inspectors. In part, this is because inspectors outnumber any other category of public officials with responsibility for construction regulation and administration. Furthermore, inspectors' corruption is easier to detect and expose because it involves soliciting and/or receiving bribes from a large number of people, many of whom are unknown to the bribe receiver. Even though some bribe givers may willingly accede to bribe solicitations, inevitably some will balk and complain to the authorities. It is also relatively easy for law enforcement to catch corrupt inspectors through sting operations in which under-cover agents pose as contractors or builders.

In 1974, the New York City Department of Investigation (DOI) released a study that was highly critical of the Department of Buildings (DOB).[38] In a two-year investigation, DOI undercover agents and informants uncovered an inspectional system rife with corruption. Ninety-five DOB employees were indicted, including nine managers, fifteen supervisors, forty-three inspectors, and twenty-three plan examiners and clerical support staff. In some cases, the corrupt officials collected weekly payments of several hundred dollars from a contractor. In other cases, payoffs up to $5,000 were made on individual jobs. DOI found that "aggressive corrupt inspectors are believed to make in excess of $20,000 to $30,000 a year from graft."[39] However, it was not necessary to be aggressive. One DOI undercover agent, posing as an inspector, was offered seventy-six bribes in a one-year period without any solicitations on his part. According to DOI, payoffs were offered in exchange for: 1) ignoring Building Code violations; 2) signing off on construction that did not meet code standards; and 3) expediting paperwork, approvals and certificates of occupancy.

In 1977, DOI released the results of another elaborate sting, this time focusing on demolition inspectors in the Department of Housing Preservation and Development. Again, rampant corruption was revealed.

> [B]ribes were expected and the amount was calculated on the con-tract price of each particular job arrived at by the inspectors, appar-ently throughout the industry. The formula given to us was a straight 2% of the contract price for those situations where a job proceeded in a routine manner. For that payment, inspectors did not enforce cer-tain minor provisions of the Code. . . . In return for the standard 2% of the contract price payment, inspectors provided a variety of ser-vices.[40]

In 1983, the Inspector General of the Department of Environmental Protection launched "Operation Norton," an investigation of corruption among the seven sewer connection inspectors in the Residential Office of the Bureau of Sewers. It revealed that four of the seven residential sewer connection inspectors routinely accepted bribes to allow improper connections with the City's sewer mains.[41] Depending on the size of the job, the corrupt inspectors expected between ten and fifty dollars for approving an illegal break-in connection or a connection without an inspection. During Operation Norton twenty-four of the approximately thirty plumbing contractors who specialized in City sewer connections had dealings with undercover investigators. Of those twenty-four contractors, twenty-one paid bribes totaling $1,250 over a six-week period.

In 1983, DOI began "Operation Ampscam," directed at inspectors in the Bureau of Electrical Control in the Department of General Services. DOI created two undercover electrical contracting companies and had them apply for permission to turn on power at twenty-five derelict buildings supposedly under construction. All twenty-five buildings chosen by DOI had serious code deficiencies; none met electrical code standards. Municipal law and departmental regulations required a code inspection of the premises before issuance of a turn-on permit. Nevertheless, and in spite of the danger involved, City electrical inspectors approved turn-on permits for all these buildings. Of the fifteen electrical inspectors involved, thirteen accepted bribes ranging from a mere ten to twenty dollars.

The investigation also revealed a "pad" in the inspectional division: each inspector was expected to turn over half of the bribe money to his supervisor. In addition, supervisors often received their own payoffs directly from contractors. Twelve inspectors and two borough supervisors were indicted on federal charges. All but one of the defendants ultimately pleaded guilty. The eighteen defendant contractors were acquitted on the strength of their defense that they had been victims of the inspectors' and supervisors' extortion. As a result of the sting, the Bureau of Electrical Control was transferred from the Department of General Services to the Department of Buildings.

In August 1986, two building inspectors were indicted for extorting more than $40,000 in bribes and kickbacks from contractors engaged in a $2 million masonry work job at Co-op City in the Bronx.[42] Both defendants pleaded guilty. One was sentenced to five years in prison and a $100,000 fine; the other received a three-year term and a $10,000 fine.

On June 13, 1989, the Construction Industry Strike Force obtained an indictment charging a New York City Buildings Department supervising inspector with extortion and bribe receiving for his solicitation and acceptance of $4,000 from a Manhattan contractor to expedite the issuance of two temporary and four final certificates of occupancy.[43] In March 1990, the defendant pleaded guilty to Bribe Receiving in the Third Degree and was sentenced to five years probation, a $3,000 fine, 180 hours of community service in the area of housing, and $1,000 restitution to cover the amount he received from the OCTF undercover investigator.

Building inspectors are in an almost ideal position to attract payoffs.[44] On the one hand, they can impose costly delays on developers or contractors; on the other, they can provide money-saving benefits by expediting the inspection process or overlooking noncompliance with rules and regulations.

The Building Code
Ambiguities in the regulations affecting construction substantially contribute to corruption susceptibility among construction inspectors. Regulations in the City's Administrative Code (e.g., the New York City Building Code, the Electrical Code, the Fire Safety Code, the Housing Maintenance Code) and zoning regulations are in many instances outdated, ambiguous, contradictory and irrelevant. In some instances, they need not and probably cannot be adhered to. As was pointed out by the Commission on the Year 2000:

> At least 20 separate city and state agencies have a role in some aspect of housing development. Many of the agencies are bound by statutory processes that complicate and delay development, including outdated portions of the building and zoning codes that drive up costs. When developers are delayed, they incur additional carrying costs that are eventually passed on to the buyers or renters of the units. Overall construction costs are higher here than in any other major American city, and 40 percent higher than the national average.[45]

Whoever has the discretionary power to interpret these regulations can impose heavy costs on builders and contractors, and thus is in a position to attract or demand payoffs.

In one OCTF-sponsored workshop, a group of architects expressed their frustration with the code. In sum, they described their position as follows:

> You are faced with Manhattan telephone book size volumes of regulations. You look up a specific requirement which is set forth in imprecise terminology which in turn refers to other sections in other volumes for definitions and examples. If you set out to find in another volume a definition of a particular term used in the first, the definitional language in this other volume refers you to certain sections set forth in still other volumes and then itself lists certain exemptions and exceptions which are set forth in still different sections. As frustrating and incomprehensible as this search may be, your real frustration lies in the recognition that ultimate resolution of all building code questions will rest in the discretion of plan examiners and inspectors who have far less training than you do.

A 1979 review of the Building Code by Joseph McGough and Thomas Roche of the New York City Department of Investigation pointed to a number of "corruption-encouraging" features:

> For example, the Code requires the installation of "Z bars" on a party wall of a building adjoining construction. Since the Code does not define what a "Z Bar" is, this may often lead to disputes between the contractor and an inspector as to whether or not a conforming "Z bar" has been installed. Another example... is the requirement to build catch platforms along the full length of the building when only part of the building is being worked upon.... Because the platform is put together from used lumber by workers, the primary cost is the cost of labor. Frequently, particularly in larger buildings, the requirement... is simply not needed since work is not being performed in many areas. Therefore, a contractor, rather than expend money to construct a full catch platform, may wish to build a mobile catch platform which he can place wherever he is working; in the event that an inspector raises the issue, it costs the contractor less to offer a "gratuity" to the inspector for overlooking the requirement than to comply.[46]

In 1986, a report by the Mayor's Panel on Affordable Housing stated: "One of the key issues raised by the development community is the system of often burdensome, and in some cases outdated, requirements contained in the City's Codes."[47] Examples included requirements that brass pipe (rather than thin copper tubing) be used for water supply and that BX electrical cable (with a metal covering) be used in all buildings rather than Romex cable (with a heavy plastic covering). Four years later, these outdated requirements are still in force.

Underfunding of Inspectional Services

Ironically, although construction has boomed in New York City during the past decade, the funding of inspectional services has fallen further and further behind. This means fewer inspectors, fewer double checks, less training and underinvestment in informational systems.

The number of construction inspectors and plans examiners in the Department of Buildings was cut by approximately eleven percent (from 419 positions in Fiscal Year 1973 to 371 positions in Fiscal Year 1989). At the same time, the number of construction permits granted annually in New York City has increased seventy-nine percent (from 25,261 permit applications in Fiscal Year 1973 to 45,228 permit applications in Fiscal Year 1989).[48] Clearly, fewer personnel are expected to inspect a larger number of construction projects.

Currently eighty-six Buildings Department construction inspectors are assigned to the boroughs: eleven in the Bronx; twenty in Brooklyn; twenty-seven in Manhattan; fifteen in Queens; and thirteen in Staten Island. In addition, twelve are assigned to the emergency unit (night shift), twenty to site safety and eight to place of assembly inspections. These numbers are clearly insufficient to cover the amount of construction which is in progress in the City.

When the number of field inspectors is inadequate, on-site inspections are delayed. Thus, building contractors have a strong incentive to make unsolicited payoffs to move to the head of the list. Likewise, inspectors can solicit bribes simply by claiming to be too busy to get to the site.

Productivity Measures and Performance Standards

New York City's fiscal crisis during the late 1970s affected all of its agencies. As personnel resigned or retired, many positions were not filled. The inspectional agencies responded to the widening gap between resources and responsibility by pressuring their personnel to produce more.

Each year New York City's productivity program has assessed the number of inspections made by construction (and other) inspectors, and set goals for the coming year; next year's goal is virtually always higher than the current year's performance. In Fiscal Year (FY) 1984, there were 8.9 Buildings Department construction inspections per person per day; the goal for FY 1985 was 9.2 inspections.[49] When this goal was exceeded (10.2 inspections per person per day in FY 1985), the goal for FY 1986 was higher still (10.5 inspections).[50] By FY 1988, the number of actual inspections was 13.0, with the goal for FY 1989 at 13.3.[51]

To the extent that quantity has been stressed over quality, morale has suffered, and the whole purpose of inspecting has been undermined. By making inspections a numbers game, the link between inspections and health and safety is attenuated. Although productivity standards must be established, unrealistic requirements lead to superficial inspections and deceit. Even realistic "productivity measures" should not be the sole criterion of acceptable performance. Accuracy and thoroughness in inspections must be given top priority.

Organizational and Management Problems
In July and October 1988, the Office of the State Controller for the City of New York released audits of inspectional productivity and practices in the Department of Buildings. The audits detailed a number of deficiencies that created serious corruption hazards:[52]

- None of the three inspectors observed put in a full day's work
- There were serious falsifications of route sheets; assigned inspections were left undone
- The frequency of inspection at several construction sites did not meet DOB's own standards
- Only two of the sixteen violations of a hazardous nature which were subsequently monitored were reinspected within ten working days as required by DOB regulations
- Only three percent of supervisors' time in Manhattan and Brooklyn was spent in field supervision
- Supervisors made no unannounced visits to inspection sites
- Brooklyn inspectors made required "call-ins" to supervisors only fifty-two percent of the time
- No inspection checklist was required for the Building Enforcement Special Team (BEST Squad) or for their supervisors.

Ineffective supervision and monitoring mean that corruption is easy to engage in and unlikely to be discovered.

Poor Supervision and Morale

Poor supervision and low morale increase corruption suscepti-bility among plan approvers and building inspectors. Poor morale is explained in large part by low pay, low status and lack of a sense of mission. Low pay is not only a major obstacle to recruitment and retention, it also provides psychological justifi-cation for accepting payoffs. For example, salaries for Depart-ment of Buildings' plumbing and electrical inspectors, who must have five years trade experience before their City employment, are between $28,000 and $35,000. In the City's private sector, annual income based on fifty compensable weeks for journey-men electricians and plumbers is between $50,000 and $60,000. The City of San Francisco pays construction inspectors in compa-rable positions between $47,000 and $59,000 per year.

In addition, New York City's inspectors do not appear to have a sense of the importance of their work in protecting the City's infrastructure and the public's health, safety and welfare. The result of poor morale and low self-esteem is cynicism about reform efforts. Consider the following 1980 report:

> Mayor Koch issued a sharply worded warning yesterday to 3,000 city inspectors, vowing to prosecute corrupt employees. But some mem-bers of the audience responded with more jeers than applause.

> At a raucous meeting at Brooklyn Technical High School that erupted several times in catcalls and boos for the Mayor, Mr. Koch said he was putting the inspectors on notice and vowed to "go after every single miscreant."[53]

Corruption among Powerbrokers and High-Level Political Leaders

Powerbrokers include public officials, political party bosses, and influence peddlers who have the ability to trade one benefit for another and to do political favors.[54] Officials throughout the com-plex construction process who perceive that they owe their jobs to powerbrokers will be susceptible to requests or demands for favors from those powerbrokers.

Political powerbrokers can assist developers and contractors through turbulent political and legal waters. A powerbroker exerts influence in many government agencies, assuring the issuance of public approvals and protecting the developer or contractor against shakedowns. In this sense, powerbrokers play a "rationalizing role" in political matters that is similar to Cosa Nostra's rationalizing role in labor relations.[55]

A powerbroker or influence peddler can exploit the public construction process for his own enrichment in many ways. The Donald Manes and Stanley Friedman scandals, for example, illustrated how effectively power and influence can be wielded over City agencies and operations. By controlling or influencing the appointment of commissioners, deputy commissioners and agency supervisors, and by virtue of their own positions in City government, political leaders can trade on the loyalty of those whose appointments they have secured. A contractor having difficulty with a building agency need only pay a large "consultant fee" to the county political leader; his "consultant" need only call the agency supervisors whose appointments he had secured, and the difficulty evaporates.

Under cross-examination during his 1986 trial on racketeering charges, Stanley Friedman provided a particularly vivid example of the influence peddler's power. The prosecutor asked Friedman about his role in obtaining approval of a City lease for a large building in lower Manhattan on behalf of the building owner, Jeff Gurrell. In the following exchange, Friedman, who was then Chairman of the Bronx Democratic Party but held no City office, boasted about his power:

Question: Now, you got paid for the services that you performed for Mr. Gurrell, isn't that correct?

Witness: Yes, I did.

Question: You got paid $10,000?

Witness: I believe that's absolutely correct.

Question: And you got paid $10,000 for making one phone call to Mr. Lieberman and one phone call to Donald Manes?

Witness: I think it was just for calling—one phone call...

Question: So it's your testimony that you got paid the $10,000 for that one phone call to Donald Manes...

Witness: I got paid $10,000 for 10 or 20 years of experience in government that made me aware of how the Board of Estimate works and made me aware who, you know, pulls the strings, so to speak...[56]

Conclusion

All official corruption undermines trust in and support for government, cheats the taxpayers and defrauds the citizenry. Construction, public and private, offers especially rich opportunities
for corrupt public officials, just as it does for corrupt labor officials and businesspeople.

Since the mid-nineteenth century, there has been a steady
stream of corruption scandals in contract letting and administration, as well as in the regulation of the construction process. The
extent and persistence of this official corruption can be understood in terms of the high levels of corruption susceptibility and
potential inherent in the roles of those public officials who regulate and implement public construction. The building inspectors
present particularly difficult problems; they can easily attract or
demand payoffs by expediting the approval process or by turn-
ing a blind eye to code violations. Such conduct is not only mor-
ally abhorrent, but can also pose especially grave risks to the
public. Corruption susceptibility among building inspectors is
reinforced by the byzantine building codes, underfunding of
inspectional services, low pay and poor morale, unrealistic performance measures, and inadequate management.

Perhaps no less disturbing than the amount of prosecutable
corruption that has been exposed in New York City in recent
years is the amount of unethical and corrupt conduct which is
not illegal. While payoffs to low-level building inspectors in
exchange for favorable action is unambiguously defined as bribery or extortion, much larger payments to high-level officials can
often best be characterized as "honest graft." A political culture
that accepts and promotes this kind of behavior provides a rich
breeding ground for all types of corruption.

FOOTNOTES

1. For general discussions of political corruption, see John G. Peters and Susan Welch, "Political Corruption in America: Search for Definitions and a Theory, or If Political Corruption Is in the Mainstream of American Politics Why Is It Not in the Mainstream of American Politics Research?," *American Political Science Review* 72 (1978): 974; Edward C. Banfield, "Corruption as a Feature of Governmental Organization," *Journal of Law and Economics* 18 (1975): 587; Michael Johnston, *Political Corruption and Public Policy in America* (Monterey, Calif.: Brooks/Cole, 1982).

2. See James Lindgren, "The Elusive Distinction Between Bribery and Extortion: From the Common Law to the Hobbs Act," *UCLA Law Review* 35 (1988): 815.

3. A corrupt act by a public official may violate one or more criminal statutes. For example, threatening official action in order to extract a benefit constitutes Grand Larceny by Extortion, N.Y. Penal Law Article 155; the offer and acceptance of a benefit by a public official upon an agreement that his or her official action will thereby be influenced constitutes Bribery and Bribe Receiving, N.Y. Penal Law §§ 200.00-200.15 (McKinney 1988); see also, the crimes of Rewarding and Receiving Reward for Official Misconduct, N.Y. Penal Law §§ 200.20-200.27 (McKinney 1988); Official Misconduct, N.Y. Penal Law § 195.00 (McKinney 1988); Scheme to Defraud, N.Y. Penal Law §§ 190.60 and 190.65 (McKinney 1988); Defrauding the Government, N.Y. Penal Law § 195.20 (McKinney 1988). Federal crimes which may be implicated by acts of official corruption include the Hobbs Act (extortion "under color of official right"), 18 U.S.C.A. § 1951 (West, 1984), and theft or bribery relating to programs receiving federal funds, 18 U.S.C.A. § 666 (West Supp. 1988).

Until recently, federal prosecutors had been using the federal mail fraud statute, 18 U.S.C.A. § 1341 (West 1984), to convict public officials of defrauding the citizenry of certain "intangible rights," including the right to have government affairs conducted honestly. See, e.g., *United States v. Mandel*, 591 F.2d 1347 (4th Cir. 1979), *cert. denied*, 445 U.S. 961 (1980) (defendant was governor of the State of Maryland), and *United States v. Margiotta*, 688 F.2d 108 (2d Cir. 1982), *cert. denied*, 461 U.S. 913 (1983), (defendant was chairman of the Nassau County Republican Committee). In 1987, the U.S. Supreme Court rejected this use of mail fraud in *McNally v. United States*, 483 U.S. 350 (1987), holding that the statute covered only frauds depriving victims of money or property rights. Congress responded by amending the mail fraud statute to cover those acts of public officials that "deprive another of the intangible right of honest service."

4. See generally, John A. Gardiner and Theodore R. Lyman, *Decisions for Sale, Corruption Reform in Land-Use and Building Regulation* (Westport, Conn.: Praeger, 1978).

5. "Operation Double Steal," a "sting" operation conducted by the F.B.I. in counties and municipalities across New York State from 1985 to 1987, revealed that corruption in procurement and contract letting is pervasive. Forty-four officials, including highways superintendents, parks managers and public works commissioners from forty towns outside New York City, were approached by undercover agents posing as vendors of snowplow blades, street signs and other products. Of 106 offers of bribes and kickbacks, 105 were accepted. Ralph Blumenthal, "F.B.I. Says Public Officials Accepted 105 of 106 Bribes Offered in 2-Year Operation", *New York Times*, 12 August 1987, late ed.: A1.

See also U.S. Department of Justice, Law Enforcement Assistance Administration, National Institute of Law Enforcement and Criminal Justice, *Corruption in Land Use and Building Regulation: An Integrated Report of Conclusions*, vol. 1 (Washington, D.C.: GPO, 1979), and *The Final Report to the General Court of the Special Commission Concerning State and County Buildings* (Boston: The Commonwealth of Massachusetts, December 31, 1980).

6. In hearings before the New York State Commission on Government Integrity, New York City real estate developers revealed how they were able to skirt the statutory proscription on corporate campaign contributions in excess of $5,000 per year. N. Y. Elec. Law § 14-116(2) (McKinney Supp. 1990). Real estate developer Donald Trump stated that his contributions to local campaigns in 1985 exceeded $150,000. Trump circumvented the State's $50,000 individual and $5,000 corporate contribution limits by spreading his payments among eighteen subsidiary companies. He said, "My attorneys basically said that this was a proper way of doing it." Transcript of "Hearing on Campaign Finance Practices of Citywide and Statewide Officials," State of New York Commission on Government Integrity (March 14, 1988), 251-56.

Developer Gerard Guterman contributed $100,000 to New York City Comptroller Harrison Goldin's campaign committee between December 27, 1984, and January 4, 1985, through the use of twenty-one corporations he controlled; on April 28, 1985, Robert Pressman and his family contributed $15,000 to Mayor Edward Koch's 1985 campaign through three corporations. See New York State Commission on Government Integrity, *Unfinished Business: Campaign Finance Reform in New York City* (September 1988) 9, n. 16. Such contributors' profits were directly affected by discretionary actions by these and other members of the New York City Board of Estimate, who in turn relied on such large contributions to fund their election campaigns.

7. The literature on official corruption is enormous. See, e.g., James Bryce, *The American Commonwealth* (New York: Commonwealth Publications, 1908); Robert C. Brooks, *Corruption in American Politics and Life* (New York: Dodd, Mead, 1910); Lincoln Steffins, *The Shame of the Cities* (New York: Hill & Wang, 1904); William L. Riordon, *Plunkitt of Tammany Hall* (New York: Dutton, 1963); Larry L. Berg, Harlan Hahn and John R. Schmidhauser, *Corruption in the American Political System* (Morristown, N.J.: General Learning Press, 1976).

A good deal of scholarship specifically focuses on official corruption in New York City: Seymour Mandelbaum, *Boss Tweed's New York* (Westport, Conn.: Greenwood Press, 1981); Alexander Callow, *The Tweed Ring* (New York: Oxford University Press, 1966);Edward K. Spann, *The New Metropolis: New York City, 1840-1857* (New York: Columbia University Press, 1981); Warren Moscow, *What Have You Done for Me Lately? The Ins and Outs of New York City Politics* (Englewood Cliffs, N.J.: Prentice-Hall, 1967); Jack Newfield and Wayne Barrett, *City for Sale: Ed Koch and the Betrayal of New York* (New York: Harper, 1988).

8. Callow, 198-206.

9. *Id.*, 201.

10. See David McCullough, *The Great Bridge* (New York: Simon and Schuster, 1972).

11. Riordan, 4.

12. See John T. Noonan, Jr., "The Donations of Democracy," *Bribes* (Berkeley, Calif.: University of California Press, 1984) 621-51.

13. Steffins, 208.

14. Walter Chambers, *Samuel Seabury: A Challenge* (New York: Century, 1932) 348-49.

15. "26 City Inspectors Face Graft Trials," *New York Times*, 9 November 1940, late city ed.: 19; "19 Lift Inspectors Dismissed by City," *New York Times*, 18 January 1941, late city ed.: 1.

16. "City Drops 32 Men on Graft Charges," *New York Times*, 9 March 1942, late city ed.: 21.

17. "Clerk Is Accused of Stealing Data on Housing; Graft Inquiry Seen," *New York Times*, 11 June 1947, late city ed.: 1.

18. "City Housing Official Indicted for Perjury," *New York Times*, 27 October 1950, late city ed.: 18; "Extortion Is Laid to Ex-Housing Aide," *New York Times*, 15 December 1950, late city ed.: 49; "$10,000 in 4 Banks, City Employee Out," *New York Times*, 5 January 1951, late city ed.: 42.

19. "Buildings Inquiry Pursued by State," *New York Times*, 6 November 1957, late city ed.: 37.

20. "City Maps Reforms in Realty Agencies," *New York Times*, 17 March 1958, late city ed.: 1; "'Hidden Accounts' Linked to City Aides," *New York Times*, 20 March 1958, late city ed.: 19.

21. "City Reorganizes Building Office," *New York Times*, 8 January 1959, late city ed.: 1.

22. "Building Graft Hunted in Kings," *New York Times*, 3 February 1959, late city ed.: 26.

23. "Jury Sees Wide Disorder in City's Building Agency," *New York Times*, 10 March 1959, late city ed.: 1.

24. "Maniscalco Case Brings New Trial," *New York Times*, 6 July 1960, late city ed.: 1.

25. "Building Chief Reports on Graft," *New York Times*, 1 January 1961, late city ed.: 52; "Building Chief Asks for More Aides," *New York Times*, 3 January 1961, late city ed.: 46; "Graft Is Charged in Building Unit," *New York Times*, 11 January 1961, late city ed.: 1.

26. "Police Shifted in Building Case," *New York Times*, 3 February 1962, late city ed.: 22; "Watch to Be Kept on Building Aides," *New York Times*, 9 February 1962, late city ed.: 16.

27. "Moerdler Transferring 18 on S.I. after Inquiry into Housing Graft," *New York Times*, 7 May 1966, late city ed.: 1.

28. "A Guide to Petty Graft Found on Scrap of Paper," *New York Times*, 10 January 1968, late city ed.: 1.

29. David K. Shipler, "Study Finds $25-M Yearly in Bribes Is Paid by City's Construction Industry," *New York Times*, 26 June 1972, late city ed.: 1; "City Construction Grafters Face Few Legal Penalties," *New York Times*, 27 June 1972, late city ed.: 1.

30. Emergency procurement—utilized in case of an unforseen danger to life, safety, or property—is exempted from competitive sealed bidding requirements.

31. *United States v. Corallo*, 413 F.2d 1306 (2d Cir.), *cert. denied*, 396 U.S. 958 (1969). See also Virgil W. Peterson, *The Mob: 200 Years of Organized Crime in New York* (Ottawa, Ill.: Glen Hill Publishers, 1983) 349-54.

32. *United States v. Walsh*, 700 F.2d 846, 849-50 (2d Cir.), *cert. denied*, 464 U.S. 825 (1983).

33. *People v. Andros*, Ind. No. 4114/86 (Kings County 1986). Two of these defendants were found guilty, one receiving two to six years imprisonment and a $5,800 fine, the other receiving one to three years imprisonment and a $5,000 fine. Fifteen others who pleaded guilty were fined $15,000 and/or placed on probation.

34. New York City Board of Education, Office of the Inspector General, "Division of School Buildings—A Review of Management Controls: Conclusions and Recommendations" (May 1987).

35. See, e.g., *People v. Badalamenti*, Ind. No. 4356/80 (N.Y. County 1980); *People v. Jackson*, Ind. No. 4353/80 (N.Y. County 1980); *People v. Lucks*, Ind. No. 4359/80 (N.Y. County 1980); *People v. Ambrosio*, Ind. No. 4351/80 (N.Y. County 1980).

36. *People v. Donfrio*, Ind. No. 3293/88 (N.Y. County 1988).

37. See *United States v. Nagler*, 90 CR 139 (S.D.N.Y. 1990); *United States v. Epstein*, 90 CR 78 (S.D.N.Y. 1990); and *United States v. Conrad*, 90 CR 129 (S.D.N.Y. 1990).

38. New York City Department of Investigation, *A Preliminary Report on Corruption in the Department of Buildings and in the Construction Industry* (1974).

39. *Id.*, 3.

40. New York City Department of Investigation, *Report on Corrupt Practices in the Demolition Industry and in the Demolition Unit of the Department of Housing Preservation and Development* (1977) 8-9.

41. Sewer mains on residential streets have interface junctions at several places. Rather than bringing a residential hook-up to a junction, many plumbing contractors prefer to hook into the main at the point closest to the house on which they are working, whether or not there is a junction at this point. The resulting "break-in" fractures and weakens the sewer main.

   Operation Norton resulted in both criminal and civil cases: In *United States v. O'Mara*, 85 CR 547 (S.D.N.Y. 1985), the government successfully prosecuted an inspector who, after initially cooperating in the investigation, returned to his corrupt ways. In *New York v. Joseph Balkan, Inc.* 86 Civ 1428 (E.D.N.Y. 1986), the City filed a civil suit to recover damages for the harm caused to the water mains by the illegal break-ins. The City claimed that the corrupt inspectors and their collaborators caused substantial structural problems to the City's sewer system.

   The City, which has settled with eight contractor groups, will receive several hundred thousand dollars in damages, the completion of all work needed to correct the problems, and a guarantee that the work will be satisfactorily completed. Video inspections of the sewer lines will confirm that all repairs have been properly made. The City has not yet settled with three contractor groups, two excavators, and four former sewer inspectors.

42. See *United States v. DeMeo*, 86 CR 703 (S.D.N.Y. 1986).

43. *People v. Emmolo*, Ind. No. 6037/89 (N.Y. County 1989).

44. For a scholarly treatment of the problem of corruption by low-level municipal inspectors, see Brian Jones, *Governing Buildings and Building Governments* (University, Ala.: University of Alabama Press, 1985).

45. Commission on the Year 2000, *New York Ascendant* (June 1987) 146-47.

46. Joseph McGough and Thomas Roche, "Corruption in New York City's Construction Industry," *Corruption in Land Use and Building Regulation*, U.S. Department of Justice, Law Enforcement Assistance Administration, National Institute of Law Enforcement and Criminal Justice (Washington, D.C.: National Institute of Justice, September 1979) 10.

47. City of New York, Office of the Mayor, *Report by the Mayor's Panel on Affordable Housing* (April 1986) 12.

48. For reference on Fiscal Year 1989 permit applications, see City of New York, *Mayor's Management Report* (New York: City of New York, September 17, 1989) 303. Other data was obtained from Office of the Assistant Commissioner, New York City Department of Buildings.

49. City of New York, *Mayor's Management Report* (New York: City of New York, September 18, 1985) 296.

50. *Id.*

51. City of New York, *Mayor's Management Report* (New York: City of New York, February 15, 1989) 243.

52. The Department of Buildings' official response to the State Audit disputed each of these findings. DOB asserted that adequate safeguards and supervision were already in place and that the problems noted were either misconstrued by the observer (e.g., faulting an inspector for making an inspection from his car, when that is all that is required in some cases) or isolated instances of bad conduct (e.g., cheating on route reports).

53. "Koch Jeered During Speech on Corruption," *New York Times*, 17 September 1988, late ed.: 29.

54. Former Queens Borough President Donald Manes, Brooklyn Democratic Party leader Meade Esposito and Bronx Democratic Party leader Stanley Friedman clearly qualify as powerbrokers. The investigations and prosecutions which led to their respective convictions illuminated their enormous influence throughout City government and their ability to act as "fixers" for their friends and private clients.

55. Corrupt powerbrokers and mob racketeers can and do have influence on each other by entering into corrupt deals and relationships. See the earlier description of the bribery-kickback schemes involving James L. Marcus, New York City Commissioner of the Department of Water Supply, Gas and Electricity, and Antonio (Tony Ducks) Corallo, then a capo in the Lucchese Crime Family, Fn. 31, *supra*.

56. Record at 4909-10, *United States v. Friedman*, 86 CR 259 (S.D.N.Y. Nov. 12, 1986).

CHAPTER 5

Fraud in public construction

Introduction

New York City public construction projects are multibillion dollar spending programs that hemorrhage money through fraud, waste and abuse. A number of recent studies have documented or described these serious problems.[1] For example, the New York State Commission on Government Integrity (Feerick Commission) concluded its investigation of public contracting by noting:

> The problems facing New York City's contracting system have reached a state of crisis, no less real and no less serious than the more conspicuous problems facing the City. A 12-month review has convinced this Commission that the City's labyrinthine contracting system wastes millions of taxpayer dollars—dollars which otherwise could be spent fighting crime, drug abuse and homelessness. It is mired in red tape, scares away vendors and remains vulnerable to corruption.[2]

This chapter describes the complex conglomeration of agencies, rules, regulations and personnel that characterize "public construction" in New York City; it defines and describes fraud, waste and abuse in the City's public construction programs and explains why the City's public works programs are so susceptible to fraud, waste and abuse.

Description of Public Construction in New York City

Public construction includes a vast array of public works programs that build or renovate roads, bridges, tunnels, pollution control plants, schools, courts, jails, hospitals, housing, and public buildings of all kinds. In New York City, all levels of government and numerous specialized public authorities carry out such projects. To speak of "the public works program" of any level of government is an oversimplification. In reality, each level of government—federal, state and local—has a multiplicity of programs, often governed by different laws and administered by different agencies and individuals.

New York City's municipal government is the City's largest builder—private or public. In Fiscal Year 1989, the City's capital expenditures were $6.35 billion.[3] In its Ten-Year Capital Plan for 1989-98, the City projected more than $57 billion of capital construction. (See Table 4.) A number of agencies are responsible for carrying out these public works. The largest two are the Department of Environmental Protection, which is building the multibillion dollar Third Water Tunnel and various pollution control plants that also cost billions of dollars, and the Department of General Services, which carries out the capital construction program for many City agencies. The Department of Transportation and the Department of Housing Preservation and Development also carry out large construction programs.[4] Not surprisingly, because of differences in resources, types and amounts of construction, and general administrative capabilities, these agencies are not equally competent as public works planners and administrators.

Some centralization of public works administration exists through the operations of such agencies as the Mayor's Office of Management and Budget, the City Planning Commission, the City Comptroller and (until September 1990) the Board of Estimate. The Office of Construction has some specific oversight responsibility with respect to construction affairs, but it does not provide centralized planning or administrative expertise and exerts no line authority over operating agencies.[5] Instead, it tries to persuade the City agencies involved in construction to cooperate and accommodate the needs of builders.[6] Thus, each of the major City agencies that carry out public works essentially acts as an independent developer, establishing its own practices, procedures and regulations governing contract letting, execution and supervision.

The public works picture is further complicated by a significant number of public authorities with large capital construction programs, such as the Port Authority of New York and New Jersey, the New York City School Construction Authority, the Triborough Bridge and Tunnel Authority, the Battery Park City Authority, the Metropolitan Transit Authority, the New York City

Health and Hospitals Corporation, the New York City Housing Authority, the Urban Development Corporation, and the Dormitory Authority of the State of New York. Each public authority has its own enabling legislation or charter, its own rules, and its own mandate. Although subject to some City and State oversight, the authorities are essentially independent.[7]

Public construction is governed by a large and diverse set of federal, state and local laws and regulations whose values often compete with the goals of controlling cost and increasing efficiency. These competing, and sometimes conflicting, values include "fairness" in contracting, the fiduciary or stewardship responsibilities of public officials, creation of opportunities for businesses owned by women and disadvantaged groups, and the promotion of organized labor. In addition, efficiency and quality are sacrificed in the selection of contractors to the extent that public agencies must award contracts to the lowest bidder.[8] The Wicks Law further constrains public agencies by requiring public construction projects to be let to at least four prime contractors rather than to a single general contractor, which is the usual practice in the private sector.[9] In addition, a certain percentage of the work on public construction contracts must be let or sublet to minority or locally-based business enterprises. Furthermore, detailed and complex procedures govern change orders and the release of progress payments. Although these procedures are intended to prevent fraud, they too often cause needless delay and escalate costs. As a result of these laws and regulations, letting and implementing public construction is more complicated, difficult and costly than private construction.[10]

Fraud, Waste and Abuse in Public Construction

The line between criminal fraud and noncriminal waste and abuse is difficult to draw, especially in a business environment rich in puffery, corner cutting, contract violations and disputes. Clear cases of fraud are also difficult to identify because unscrupulous contractors can often give at least a colorably plausible explanation for dubious costs and poor job performance. Often these explanations take the form of counterclaims against the City for alleged design errors, delays, and/or explicit or tacit City approvals. Therefore, it is useful to think in terms of fraud, waste and abuse, rather than in terms of fraud alone.

> The basic concept that ties the words together (and makes the phrase politically potent) is that some productive value, potentially available to the government, is being lost: that somehow the public is not getting what it intended to buy, or as much of what it intended to buy. What distinguishes the separate ideas of fraud, waste, and abuse are distinctions that originate in the culpability of those who inflict the loss on the government and the objectivity with which a certain loss can be established.

> Fraud is the clearest concept. It defines situations in which some potential claimant against the government (for example, a contractor or client) willfully misrepresents some fact that entitles him to something of value from the government (for example, a payment for services to the contractor or the delivery of a benefit to clients), and the government provides the payment or service even though it is undeserved (for example, the contractors have done no work for the government or the client is ineligible for the government benefit). . . .

> The concepts of waste and abuse are inherently more ambiguous. Like fraud, they suggest that something of potential value to the government is being lost—that funds are being paid out and services provided but without any benefit to the government or the public. One difference is that the culpability of the person responsible for the loss seems less. In the case of abuse, the culprit may be badly motivated, but not clearly in violation of any laws. The official may have taken advantage of some loophole in the structure of rules guiding expenditures within a program to benefit himself or others in a way that differs from the common understanding of what the rules intend. . . .

> In the case of waste, the culpability seems even less; it suggests negligence or incompetence rather than sharp-dealing within the rules. Officials aren't perceived to be advancing their own interests or those of friends. They are just being less careful than they should be with the government's money.[11]

Fraud, waste and abuse have a variety of manifestations. Contractors and subcontractors may make claims for work not performed, for labor and materials not used, or for materials not meeting specifications. Such frauds are frequently facilitated by bribes to inspectors, resident engineers or other public employees.[12] Contractors may fail to meet contract specifications with respect to materials, labor and workmanship. They may unjustifiably front-load charges, intentionally cause delays, fail to perform or falsely claim to have complied with mandated affirmative action programs in order to qualify for special preference on public contracts. They may engage in collusive bidding, bribe construction managers, make unauthorized use of insider information on in-house cost estimates, make false statements and misrepresentations in prebid and bid documents, or engage in spurious litigation.[13] Contractors are able to make claims against the City that are difficult and often not cost-efficient to refute, confident that the City will settle.[14] We cannot emphasize too strongly that agency officials are under enormous pressure to keep their projects moving and, therefore, are greatly disinclined to charge their contractors with criminal fraud.

The Extent of Fraud, Waste and Abuse
Inspectors general have told us that they believe that there is significant fraud on every major public construction project. Nevertheless, the City has no way to quantify the extent (either in terms of frequency or magnitude) to which it has been defrauded. A DOI report states that the potential for corruption in the New York City Department of Environmental Protection is enormous, and that "[t]here is reason to believe that collusive bidding, bribery, extortion, fraud, embezzlement, labor racketeering and conflicts of interest are commonplace occurrences in the agency's capital construction program." The report found that:

> The City employs an elaborate network of resident engineers, inspectors, and auditors to safeguard its interests in capital construction. ...At the North River Water Pollution Project in Manhattan, for example, DEP has a force of more than forty full-time engineers on the site. [Nevertheless], the Inspector General has learned that Federal Chandros Incorporated [an electrical contractor] paid bribes to almost sixty City engineers or inspectors. The bribes ranged from a few hundred to several thousand dollars in each instance. Some of the bribes were paid for approval of substandard work, in other cases for expediting payments.

> Unfortunately, all too often the corruption of a resident engineer or inspector was not necessary in order to defraud the City. FCI project managers and other witnesses have indicated that often the City employees were not present or were not paying attention at critical phases of the construction.

While extensive documentation is not available, indications of widespread fraud throughout New York City's public works are not hard to find.

The Federal Chandros Investigation:
Case Study of a Corrupt Contractor

In 1986 a conscientious New York City Department of Environmental Protection (DEP) Engineering Audit Officer received an anonymous complaint alleging that Federal Chandros Inc. (FCI), an electrical contracting company which held 135 City contracts between 1980 and 1986, had submitted an inflated invoice defrauding the City of $10,000. Investigation showed that the Gelb Brothers, the company's owners, had spent $18,950 on an electrical transformer for the City's Owls Head Pollution Control Plant. On the photocopy submitted to DEP for reimbursement, the transformer's purchase price had been changed to $29,000.

After verifying this fraud, the City reviewed all change order invoices submitted by FCI for the Owls Head Project. It soon became apparent that the Gelbs had routinely altered invoices, both large and small, before submitting them to the City for reimbursement. Execution of a search warrant at FCI's offices revealed that the Gelbs had perpetrated their frauds by "whiting out" and recopying invoices and by using blank invoices and letterheads obtained from a number of suppliers. These frauds were not limited to altering the amount paid for an item; in some cases, FCI would take an invoice from one project, "white out" the delivery information and make it appear that the material had been shipped to a completely different job. In this way, the company was paid two or three times on the same invoice. After reviewing the documents obtained from the search, the scope of the investigation was expanded to include all FCI contracts with the City.

A review of Department of General Services' invoices uncovered three other frauds against the City. On a Metropolitan Museum of Art project, FCI submitted a fictitious invoice and was paid $55,000, via a change order, for a piece of equipment that, in fact, was never received or installed. The vendor listed on the invoice did not even carry such equipment.

FCI's fraudulent activities extended to New York City Transit Authority projects as well. In these schemes, FCI used a corporate shell called Overseas Electric. In one case, Overseas purchased electrical wire and then "resold" it to FCI. FCI then submitted an invoice inflated by $177,955. According to one cooperating witness, the ease with which FCI repeatedly defrauded the Transit Authority became an office joke.

FCI also defrauded the City by claiming that Overseas was a minority business enterprise (MBE). The Gelbs submitted claims of $2.4 million for work done by Overseas as an MBE. In fact, Overseas provided no genuine services for the project and was a fictitious MBE completely controlled by the Gelbs.

Other City agencies employing FCI as an electrical contractor did not have even the rudimentary sort of document control maintained by DEP. While DEP required copies of invoices as proof of contractors' purchases, the other City agencies either had no such requirement or did not enforce whatever requirements they had. For example, on the Coney Island Subway Car Wash project, FCI doubled or tripled the cost of certain materials. No one from the Transit Authority had asked for supporting invoices. The payment files for the Housing Authority and Health and Hospitals projects also lacked invoices, and the Department of General Services had invoices only for payments made pursuant to change orders. Consequently, the full extent to which FCI defrauded the City will never be known.

The Co-op City Repair Program:
Case Study of a Corrupt Public Works Project
While in the past no law enforcement agency has routinely focused criminal investigations on major public works projects, there is reason to believe that fraud is extensive and systemic in public construction. For example, in 1981 the State Commission of Investigation received allegations of fraud and corruption on the multimillion dollar repair program in Co-op City, a state-financed 15,000-unit cooperative housing complex in the Bronx. The Commission's hearings, held between 1981 and 1983, revealed substantial corruption. The Commission found that "prior to October 1981, there was widespread abuse characterized by mismanagement, waste and corruption and that subsequent to October 1981, progress in accomplishing repairs... virtually ceased."[15] Emergency contracts (not competitively bid) had been let at a cost greatly exceeding prevailing competitive rates. Inspections were inadequate, and contractors' disbursements were not audited.

As a result of the SIC's final report, which was forwarded to the U.S. Attorney's Office, twenty people, including Co-op City employees, contractors, vendors and state building officials, were ultimately indicted. Sixteen of those charged were found guilty.

- George Steiner, the general manager of the Co-op City construction repair program, was convicted of extortion and evasion of taxes on more than $1.2 million in kickbacks and bribes received from contractors. [16]
- Fernando Bragaglia, an inspector on the Co-op City construction repair program, accepted bribes from contractors not to report various frauds, such as padded payrolls. Bragaglia said during the allocution on his guilty plea that Rey Caulking Co., Inc. had fictitious employees on its payroll. These fictitious employees were added to the time and material contract costs charged to Co-op City and ultimately paid by the State. [17]
- A Citibank branch manager was convicted of money laundering in connection with his assistance to a corrupt contractor on the Co-op City project. He allowed the contractor to cash checks made out to fictitious employees in order to generate cash for the bribes paid to employees supervising the government project. [18]
- Two officials were convicted of extorting $45,000 from a masonry contractor on the Co-op City construction repair project. The defendants threatened that if the money was not paid, the contractor would be excluded from future contracts. [19]
- Five contractors were charged with paying off State officials at Co-op City to obtain lucrative caulking contracts. [20] Upon conviction, the principal defendant was ordered to pay $770,000 in back taxes.

Even this list of criminal cases does not provide the complete picture of the fraud, waste and abuse at Co-op City. The following letter, filed in connection with Steiner's sentencing, offers a telling commentary on the susceptibility of public works projects to corruption and fraud.

George Steiner took advantage of an environment at Co-op City which was an incubator for corruption. The State did not provide adequate resources to protect the expenditure of its money. [The Co-op City] Board of Directors, management and professional advisors were more interested in spending State funds first and later determining whether the expenditure was appropriate. The total lack of effective controls over State funds which were used to pay for construction defects permitted contractors to make a fortune even after having made payoffs to Steiner and others.

MBE Fraud: A Public Works Scam

Federal, state and local affirmative action programs are commonly referred to as MBE (minority business enterprise), DBE (disadvantaged business enterprise), WBE (women's business enterprise) and LBE (locally based enterprise). These programs require that a certain percentage of the aggregate contract price on designated federal, state or local construction projects be performed by minority or "disadvantaged" business enterprises. [21]

While MBE or LBE programs have laudable goals, they have been plagued by fraud. For example:

> 1. A prime contractor sets up a phony MBE, to which he purports to subcontract work. In reality, the prime contractor does all the work and supplies all the labor. Frequently, the phony MBE lists as its president one of the prime contractor's minority employees.

> 2. A member of a qualifying minority group sets up an MBE, allowing his "firm" to be hired as a subcontractor. In fact, he performs no work, and may be no more than a shell company through which billings are processed.

In 1984, the State Commission of Investigation concluded that illegitimate MBE contractors outnumbered legitimate ones. [22] Several criminal prosecutions have alleged fraudulent compliance with MBE programs:

- In 1987, the principals of Federal Chandros, Thomas and Michael Gelb, were indicted for fraud in subcontracting work to a sham MBE that was employed only to meet federal and state MBE requirements. The indictment charged the Gelbs with falsely certifying that the MBE was providing goods and services as a subcontractor, thereby enabling the Gelbs to receive a credit for $5.3 million under the MBE program. [23]
- Nanco Contracting Corporation and two of its officers were indicted for filing false documents in order to evade requirements set forth by the MBE program. Nanco and its officers allegedly established two dummy MBE companies to which they purported to subcontract highway construction work. [24]

The Susceptibility of Public Construction Projects to Fraud, Waste and Abuse

All factors contributing to high levels of corruption susceptibility and potential in the private sector operate even more potently in the public sector. To the extent that the administration of public works is underfunded, bureaucratically muscle bound and inefficient, it will be especially susceptible to fraud, waste and abuse.

A widely shared perception exists, born of a century of experience, that public construction always costs more than private construction. In part, this perception is based on reality. Contractors pass along the increased cost of preparing public bids to the awarding authority and, ultimately, to the public.[25] Contractors often believe they must raise their contract bid prices to accommodate higher costs occasioned by requirements peculiar to public contracting rules, including those flowing from politically generated executive or legislative decisions or from social policy goals. Additional costs also result from poor designs and slow payments by the City. General inefficiency in government results partly from relatively low pay, and the consequent inability to recruit and retain the most qualified staff. Because of a culture of cost overruns, contractors expect to increase the contract price as the project progresses.

Community pressures can also increase the cost of public construction. In exchange for community acceptance of the North River Water Pollution Control Plant, for example, the City agreed to build a large park, including a number of recreational facilities, on top of the waste disposal plant. This added millions to the cost of construction, since it required major changes in design and engineering.

The Politics of Public Construction
It is unfortunately understandable that agency heads typically do not assign high priority to the investigation and prevention of fraud, waste and abuse. Because politicians are under constant pressure to achieve results, their appointed commissioners correctly believe that they are judged more on their ability to begin and complete funded capital projects than on their ability to reduce fraud, waste and abuse. Criticism is far more likely to be leveled at the cautious commissioner who does not commit or spend budgeted construction funds, than at the commissioner who builds, albeit with large cost overruns. The constraining influence of the profit motive simply has no role in public construction. Ironically, the tension between completing the job and protecting the public from fraud, waste and abuse only increases

as problems arise and delays occur during the course of a project.

Even when fraud, waste and abuse are brought to light, administrators frequently do not take advantage of the available legal options for obtaining recoupments and restitution and sanctioning wrongdoers. Because the issuance of a grand jury subpoena or the overt use of any other criminal investigative technique is likely to slow down a construction project, agency managers may strain to define their problems as civil rather than criminal.

In addition, law enforcement agencies have not placed a high priority on the identification and prosecution of construction frauds. Prosecutors with few resources are reluctant to mount investigations and prosecutions which will not be fully supported by the "victim" agency. Their reluctance is also a product of experiences like that in the Durante Construction Corporation case, in which the dedication of scarce resources produced a conviction but no significant sanction. This paving contractor and its principal were indicted in August 1987 for defrauding three City agencies by a scheme involving phony invoices and load-trip tickets. In exchange for their guilty pleas to eighty-two counts of fraud, Louis Durante, Jr., was sentenced to probation and a $25,000 fine, and the corporation was fined $50,000. No provision was made for restitution.[26] In this instance, crime paid.

The Lowest Responsible Bidder System
One of the pillars of public construction law is the "competitive bidding" system.[27] Generally, all state, county and city agencies must award construction (as well as many other) contracts to the lowest responsible bidder.[28] This system was implemented as a reformist antidote to favoritism in the award of public contracts.[29]

Although it may have succeeded in reducing favoritism and bribery in the contract award process, the competitive bidding system has facilitated fraud, waste and abuse by undermining government efficiency. A contractor on a private construction project has a strong incentive to please his client, whose satisfaction determines whether the contractor will be hired again and/ or be recommended to other developers. Overcharging, waste and litigation will not endear the contractor to his private sector employer. A contractor working in the public sector, however, does not share the same incentives or disincentives. Neither the quality of performance nor the ability to work within budgets influence that contractor's chance of obtaining future contracts. Only submitting the lowest bid will be determinative. Public builders can neither reward good performers nor, except in extreme situations, penalize poor ones.

The singular importance of tendering the lowest bid encourages contractors to underbid, while counting on change orders and other "add ons" during construction to boost their compensation. In addition, the competitive bidding system provides incentives and rationalizations for contractors to cut costs and maximize profits not possible at the bid price by cheating on specifications or bribing labor officials to ignore key terms of labor agreements.

Arguably, a builder or developer's most important decision is the choice of contractors. A builder who has the freedom to choose proven and reliable contractors with whom he has a good relationship can confidently move ahead on projects. The lowest responsible bidder system denies public agencies this control and security. According to a 1987 report by the Institute of Public Administration:

> The fallacies of low bid restrictions in complex projects have been proven nationwide time and time again. Managers involved in contractor selection must develop the skills and be encouraged to exercise the discretion to weigh low bids against realistically estimated costs, against the quality and past performance of a potential contractor, against the needs for innovation and flexibility in implementation. New York's ratio of change orders to original bids is high. In the case studies, the IPA did not find much awareness of how final project costs related to original bids. Nor was anyone reviewing the relationship between various contract selection methods and project results.[30]

The weakness of the competitive bidding system is exposed when unscrupulous contractors submit low bids and subsequently boost costs through unjustified change orders and law suits. Speculative lawsuits have been encouraged by lawyers' contingency fees in construction suits and by the willingness of judges to read exceptions into a law which explicitly disallows claims by contractors for damages due to delay occasioned by the City.[31] A conscientious contractor who is not interested in playing this game is not likely to bid on public contracts; if he does, he is not likely to submit a bid lower than the contractor who is an experienced and willing player in the game.

The disadvantages of the lowest responsible bidder system are exacerbated by the absence of a viable prequalification and responsibility review process. A prequalification review requires contractors to submit their credentials to the agency, which then decides whether that contractor should even be allowed to bid on an agency contract. If properly administered, this system could eliminate the least competent and most dishonest contractors from the process.

A responsibility review process, which comes into play after a low bid has been selected, serves the same ends by requiring the winning bidder to meet the threshold of "responsibility." Although the New York courts have held that prior criminality would support an administrative finding of lack of responsibility, the City has rarely sought to deny a contract to the low bidder on a finding that the bidder was not "responsible."

The Wicks Law

The Wicks Law is another legal requirement that facilitates corruption in the public construction process. The Wicks Law requires public agencies on construction projects valued at more than $50,000 to divide such projects into at least four separate prime contracts. This law, like the lowest bidder requirements, had honorable intentions. Although its goal was to protect the State and its municipalities from perceived abuses by general contractors and to decrease the cost of public construction, it too has backfired and accomplishes the opposite result. Indeed, the State and City of New York are today's most vociferous proponents of repeal.[32]

The Wicks Law can create an administrative nightmare. It mandates that government agencies use a "multiple contract system," under which separate designs and specifications must be prepared, bids solicited and contracts awarded in each of four categories: heating, ventilation and air conditioning; electrical; plumbing; and general contracting. The judiciary has made the Wicks Law even more onerous by interpreting its provisions as prohibiting state and local governments from contracting out the responsibility and financial accountability for supervising and coordinating the four multiple prime contractors.[33] Thus, the

Wicks Law requires the work of the four prime contractors to be supervised by the government agency itself.

> The New York law poses special problems. First, it elevates a few categories of specialty subcontractors to equality with the general contractors while ignoring the practice of bid shopping with respect to other categories of specialty contractor. Second, since the general contractor is a coequal with the three principal specialty contractors, part of responsibility for project coordination (especially involving control of the flow of funds) falls to state contracting officials. This organizational arrangement makes the general contractor's management task more difficult and increases the likelihood of litigation arising from conflicts among contractors. The rigid enforcement of the separate contract procedure for all contracts, regardless of the relative amounts of work being performed by the general and the three principal specialty contractors, seems unlikely to promote efficient management of the work and may well result in the elimination of any apparent cost savings over single contract procurement. [34]

The Wicks Law, in effect, prohibits the "single contract system" used not only by virtually all private developers, but also by the federal government and the majority of states. [35] Under that system, a private or government builder contracts with one general contractor, who is then responsible for subcontracting specialty work and coordinating the project. In weighing the merits of the multiple and single contract systems, a Court of Claims judge familiar with the constant barrage of construction claims filed against the State commented:

> The Court would like to observe that [the Wicks Law] . . . should be studied with the express purpose of either eliminating or amending the law to permit the state to let such contracts as this one to one bidder, instead of five, six or more bidders, with none having authority over the others but all having the same privilege of screaming for help from the State engineer on the job, whose own efficiency is often diluted because too often he has to mother the disputing contractors, rather than performing his primary duty of progressing the job. Experience would indicate that under the prevailing system the State squanders huge sums of money in trying to keep the jigsaw puzzle together, whereas under the one [contract] system, the responsibility of efficiency and coordination would not only be on the one contractor, but it would be to said contractor's financial advantage to move with coordination, for the basic reason that the contractor could not place upon the shoulders of others, but only on himself, any blame for a slowdown or uncoordinated work. [36]

More relevant to our concerns is the Wicks Law's substantial contribution to racketeering susceptibility and potential. By multiplying the number of prime contractors, it not only facilitates collusive bidding and the formation of cartels, it also increases opportunities for fraud, bribery and extortion. Because competitive, low-bid procedures preclude negotiated contract letting, agencies are deprived of a powerful means to detect and frustrate collusive bidding among contractors. In effect, superimposing the Wicks Law on the competitive low-bid procedures multiplies fourfold the opportunities for collusive agreements.

The Wicks Law also encourages bid rigging. Specialty contractors bidding on prime contracts form cartels more easily than general contractors bidding on whole projects. Collusive arrangements are facilitated because specialty contractors are generally members of the same association(s), meet regularly and are familiar with each other's bidding patterns. General contractors, on the other hand, are less able to establish and enforce barriers to entry. Any contractor, specialty or other, can choose to bid as a general contractor, perform the work appropriate to its specialization and subcontract whatever work is outside its scope of expertise.

The Wicks Law further enhances racketeering susceptibility and potential by increasing opportunities for fraud. As noted in a 1984 Mayor's Office report:

> The City's inability to coordinate its construction contractors under the Wicks Law compounds its difficulties with project funding, design and specifications, with security, with community relations and with other aspects of its construction program. Because construction is a somewhat disorganized, disruptive, labor intensive and unpredictable process in the best circumstances, it requires thorough coordination from project inception to completion. In short, the central problem of public construction is coordination and the Wicks Law makes coordination four times as difficult as it has to be in most instances.[37]

Public agencies do not have sufficient numbers of experienced, competent personnel to supervise directly the on-site operations of their large public construction projects. Given inadequate supervision and the resulting disputes between prime contractors over design specifications, integration of construction timetables, and responsibilities for work which arguably falls within (or between) two or more contracts, opportunities are inevitably created for substantial fraud, waste and abuse.

Inadequate and Inefficient Administration of Public Works
In New York City, inadequate administration of public works fosters fraud, waste and abuse. Lack of resources, incompetence, inefficiency and dysfunctional bureaucratization frequently mean inaccurate and inappropriate designs and specifications, poor site supervision, needless delays on processing change orders and ineffective auditing.[38]

The funds allotted to planning and supervising public works are almost always insufficient, and the salaries for City engineers and consulting engineers are too low to attract enough people with the requisite ability and experience. Even major construction projects are undersupervised. A number of builders have stated to us that the City devotes far less resources to the management of *multibillion* dollar construction projects than private builders devote to the management of *multimillion* dollar projects.

Another cause of inadequate project supervision is insufficient clerical support. This forces project engineers to spend time on clerical tasks rather than on the technical and supervisory matters that are their primary responsibility. One study conducted by the Mayor's Office of Operations found that "project engineers, who are the key personnel in moving the consultant's design projects, are spending over 18 percent of their time performing clerical tasks."[39]

The few City engineers who are available to serve as resident engineers are usually assigned to small construction and repair projects. Frequently, funds are not available to hire architects, engineers and construction supervisors. Thus agencies must often "contract-out" for project design and management.[40] "Contracting-out," in addition to being extremely costly, generates its own corruption susceptibility. For example, when the construction manager is the same engineer who designed the project, there is great temptation to treat design errors (chargeable to the architect/engineer) as design changes or improvements (chargeable to the City).

There is no City-wide system for tracking a project from inception to completion; no consistent tracking of construction schedules against targeted goals; and no individual accountability. Work is simply passed on from one group to another within the agency. Consequently, the City lacks the ability to estimate accurately or maintain ongoing cost control.

Because monitoring and auditing procedures are inadequate, corrupt contractors can easily defraud the City by padding their bills. Insufficient documentation prevents auditors from determining if money was properly spent or was lost due to fraud, waste and abuse.[41] Audits usually occur after a project has been completed; if proper records have not been maintained, some frauds are no longer discoverable.

Inefficiency and disarray breed fraud, waste and abuse. "Reforms" that minimize discretion, scatter decision making authority and mandate checks and counterchecks on routine decisions also create more bureaucracy, paperwork, defensive decision making, delay and, ultimately, paralysis.[42] This, in turn, spawns additional fraud, waste and abuse. This degenerative cyclical process feeding on itself threatens to grind public works construction to a halt.[43] In 1989, the Citizens Budget Commission reported that fewer than one-tenth of the City's construction projects are completed on schedule, and that more than one-half are not even under construction by the originally scheduled completion date.[44]

Among the "horror stories" about New York City public works projects are:

- *LaGuardia High School*. Intended to replace the famous High School for the Performing Arts, LaGuardia was designed in 1969, the estimated cost being $9 million. Bid in 1972, it was begun in 1973. Construction, which was halted in 1974, resumed in 1979. Completion was expected in 1982 at a cost of $39 million. By 1989, the project had cost $90 million, and major features of the school were still not completed, had failed, or had been abandoned. Several prosecutorial and investigative agencies are investigating this public construction debacle.[45]
- *The Wollman Skating Rink*. The inability, after five years and $12.9 million, to build an ice-skating rink in Central Park was perhaps this generation's most dramatic example of paralysis in the City's public works program. The City finally accepted private developer Donald Trump's offer to build the rink. Trump completed the job in less than five months (six weeks ahead of schedule) for under $3 million (almost $800,000 below budget).[46]

In February 1990, the influential non-profit Settlement Housing Fund, which promotes affordable housing, issued *Housing*

New York Revisited,[47] an update of its 1986 study of state and local
housing programs. Citing administrative inefficiencies, mismanagement and the Wicks Law, it estimated that the City's much
publicized $5.1 billion affordable housing program may end up
costing more than twice that amount. In one example, the report
contrasted the $90,000 per unit cost of large-scale developments
undertaken by the City's Construction Management Program
with the $50,000 average cost per unit on smaller projects (100
units or less) undertaken by the Vacant Building Program, utilizing small owner-developers.[48] In an analysis devoted to each of
nineteen housing programs, this study found:

- **Capital Budget Homeless Housing Program—**
  "There are too many levels of City inspectors, and it takes too long
  to pay contractors."[49]
- **Special Initiative Program—**
  "Wicks law slows construction."[50]
- **Partnership New Homes Program—**
  "Endless reviews around site approvals and building permits delay
  projects and increase space costs. New fees keep mounting."[51]
- **Division of Alternative Management Programs, Tenant Interim
  Lease (TIL) Program—**
  "HPD has problems as a construction manager; contractors make
  bad repairs that last only a short time. Repairs are made too slowly,
  sometimes as much as a year after projects enter TIL program."[52]
- **Division of Alternative Management Programs, Community Man-
  agement Program—**
  "There is too much paperwork; also payments from the city are
  delayed months after bills are submitted."[53]
- **Capital Improvement Program—**
  "Bidding and payments to contractors too cumbersome. Wicks law
  is further complication."[54]

As it becomes harder to start up, carry on, and complete construction projects (in part, because of intensified efforts to prevent corruption), the pressure mounts on commissioners and
their staffs to keep projects on track, and so does the temptation
to approve questionable charges and change orders in order to
keep projects moving.

Unwillingness or Inability to Sanction Wrongdoers
Although State and City laws do not require that a municipality
contract with other than a "responsible" bidder, New York City

has been unable to avoid contracting—sometimes directly, sometimes indirectly—with firms that have performed poorly on previous contracts, or even with firms that are alleged to have organized crime connections. There are three reasons for this.

First, the City has no single, reliable database collecting information necessary to investigate whether contractors are "responsible." We recognize, of course, that it is difficult—if not impossible—for any agency, or even any multi-agency system, to keep abreast of all the relevant information that enters into the public record. Reports suggesting that a contractor is not responsible may appear in any of hundreds of newspapers and magazines, in the files of dozens of different courts or governmental agencies, in the oral testimony of witnesses testifying in courtrooms inside or outside the State, or in any other of a wide variety of places. Even when allegations of organized crime ties are available, legal rules mandating the secrecy of grand jury and eavesdropping evidence, and strategic considerations requiring the non-disclosure of other investigative information, may preclude contracting agencies from obtaining pertinent evidence documenting or refuting the allegation.

Nonetheless, a comprehensive effort must be made by or on behalf of contracting agencies to gather relevant information. When the public record suggests a basis for a finding that a contractor is not responsible, an inquiry can be made—at a minimum by reviewing the available documents and questioning the principals under oath—even where other investigative information cannot be disclosed or used for that purpose. Taking such steps gives the contracting agency an appropriate mechanism for exploring whether or not to award the contract and gives the contractor a forum in which to establish his responsibility. If such steps are not taken, an agency awarding a contract despite the public record information is subject to criticism for ignoring it, and a contractor denied a contract based upon charges not documented in the public record is denied an opportunity to respond to them:

- Inner City Drywall Inc., a major carpentry contractor, was awarded nearly $32 million in contracts for low-income housing rehabilitation in the Bronx. OCTF's Interim Report and several newspaper articles had previously identified Inner City as mob dominated. It was subsequently discovered that Inner City had failed to file City tax returns. None of this information was in the City's Vendex system—the information base utilized by City agencies to determine responsibility

- A $2.1 million contract was awarded by the Department of Housing Preservation and Development to M & C Lazzinnaro Construction, owned by Mario Lazzinnaro. Lazzinnaro has been identified by an FBI agent in trial testimony as an associate of the Genovese and Gambino crime families.[55] Again, had this information been known to the City, appropriate investigative steps could have been taken prior to contract award in the course of a "responsibility" review.

Second, much of the work on large capital projects is subcontracted, and the City has little control over which companies are chosen as subcontractors. Thus, even if the City denies a contractor a contract on a finding of nonresponsibility, that contractor can reappear as a subcontractor on the same job.

Third, in some instances, only a few contractors furnish a particular service or material. Where these contractors are mob connected, tainted by a prior criminal record or have a history of poor performance, the City must either do business with them or accept that certain public needs will not be met.

A case in point is the City's purchase of asphalt. In early 1987, the City announced that Jet Asphalt was the low bidder to provide asphalt for road surfacing in Queens and that Mount Hope Asphalt Corporation was the low bidder to provide asphalt for the same purpose in the Bronx. Both companies were affiliated, through officers and shareholders, with Lizza Industries, which in 1984 had been convicted of racketeering because of bid rigging on state contracts. On learning of these affiliations, the City scheduled Board of Responsibility hearings for both Jet and Mount Hope. In late 1987, before the date of the hearings, both companies withdrew their bids.

The second lowest bidder on the Queens job, Rason Asphalt, replaced Jet Asphalt. However, the owner of Rason also owned Hendrickson Brothers, Inc., a company which was then appealing a $7.8 million verdict in a civil bid-rigging case brought by the State Attorney General. When a Board of Responsibility Hearing was scheduled for Rason, it, too, withdrew its bid.

For the Bronx job, the second lowest bidder, Plaza Materials, succeeded Mount Hope. However, Plaza was affiliated with

Yonkers Contracting Corporation, which had been indicted for bid rigging. When Plaza Materials refused to meet with the Department of General Services to discuss this affiliation, Plaza was removed from consideration for the job.

Having lost the two lowest bidders on both jobs, the City was forced to take emergency measures by contracting outside the competitive bidding system. Hudson Materials of Kearney, New Jersey, agreed to provide asphalt to the Bronx, and Metropolitan, a subsidiary of Edenwald Contracting Company, contracted to provide asphalt to Queens.

The City then called for bids for new contract jobs in Queens and the Bronx; Metropolitan was low bidder for both. Metropolitan, then being required to furnish a huge amount of asphalt to the City, could no longer provide asphalt to its parent organization, Edenwald. Edenwald then turned to Jet Asphalt and Mount Hope, which sold to Edenwald the amount Edenwald would have purchased from Metropolitan. (This is virtually the same amount that Jet and Mount Hope would have sold to the City in the first instance.) Thus, Jet Asphalt and Mount Hope Asphalt profited to the same degree as if they had contracted directly with the City.[56]

Failure to Utilize Debarment Procedures
The City has not vigorously sought to debar contractors who perform their public contracts incompetently or fraudulently.[57] Under Board of Estimate regulations, the City has the authority to hold a Board of Responsibility hearing on the "responsibility" of a low bidder. A unanimous vote of nonresponsibility by the three member board debars the contractor from all City contracts for three years; a majority vote debars for one year. From November 1985 to July 1988, the Board of Responsibility held only thirty-three responsibility hearings and debarred only twenty contractors, an insignificant number given the tens of thousands of contractors doing business with the City.

Since the poor performer resolution was enacted in 1985,[58] only one firm appears to have been debarred as a poor performer. Since May 1986, agencies must rate all contractors using a form developed by the Office of Construction. This must be done half-way through a job, and again at job completion. The

Office, which keeps a computerized record of all evaluations, estimates that it has approximately 3500 evaluations of about a thousand contractors. Approximately five percent are ratings of "marginal" or "unsatisfactory." There are plans for the Office of Construction's database to be made accessible through VENDEX, but an agency is not required to refuse to do business with a company that has received an unsatisfactory rating.

Conclusion

The City and all who live and work in it are the victims of waste, fraud and abuse in public works programs. The City's development and infrastructure needs are enormous and acute—schools, jails, office buildings, homeless shelters, housing, pollution control plants, recreational facilities, tunnels, bridges and roads must be built to meet basic individual, social and economic needs. Creating and maintaining public works, including the "built environment" itself, is one of the central roles of government. When public works programs are riddled with fraud, waste and abuse, costs proliferate, quality deteriorates, delays increase, and the capacity to respond to critical infrastructure needs declines. In short, the quality of life for New Yorkers is severely threatened. In turn, these problems generate overwhelming political pressure to start, maintain, and complete public works projects at any cost. This kind of political and administrative environment breeds fraud, waste and abuse.

New York City's public works projects are especially vulnerable to fraud because of problems endemic to their administration. These projects are underfunded and underadministered. In addition, they suffer from layers of well-intentioned "reforms" from previous generations—reforms that sought to implement broader social goals as well as to prevent corruption. Ironically, poorly thought out strategies for preventing corruption have only made the problem worse.

FOOTNOTES

1. See e.g., Carol Bellamy (New York City Council President) and Harrison J. Goldin (New York City Comptroller), *Our Costs Runneth Over: Cost Overruns on New York City's Lump Sum Capital Contracts* (February 1981); Office of the New York State Comptroller, *Reforming the Contract Process in New York City* (Report 17-87, September 11, 1986); C. D. Rappleyea, *Building Confidence: The Need for Public Works Contract Reforms* (Albany, N.Y.: New York State Assembly, March 1987); State of New York, Senate, Committee on Investigations, Taxation, and Government Operations, *Schools for Scandal: A Staff Report on the New York City Board of Education's Mismanagement of School Construction, Repair, and Renovation* (September 23, 1987); Institute of Public Administration, *Contracting in New York City Government: Final Report and Recommendations* (New York: I.P.A., November 1987); Task Force on Capital Financing and Construction, *Report to the New York City Board of Education* (December 22, 1987); Citizens Budget Commission, *Implementing Capital Projects* (New York: March 1988); New York City, Mayor's Private Sector Survey, *The New York City Service Crisis: A Management Response* (September 1989); Citizens Budget Commission, *Toward Greater Accountability for the Implementation of Capital Projects* (New York: CBC, November 1989); Settlement Housing Fund, *Housing New York Revisited, A Preliminary Report and Up-Date of "Evaluation of Housing in New York"* (1990); New York City Partnership, *From Schools to Skyscrapers: Building an Effective Development Process for New York City* (April 1990).

2. New York State Commission on Government Integrity, *A Ship Without a Captain: The Contracting Process in New York City* (New York: Commission on Government Integrity, December 1989) 1.

3. For a detailed description of the City's capital expenditures, see City of New York, *Mayor's Management Report* (New York: City of New York, September 17, 1989).

4. Until recently, the Board of Education was also a major public builder. Effective July 1, 1989, the Board of Education's responsibilities and authority for school construction were taken over by the New York City School Construction Authority.

5. The Office of Construction was established pursuant to Mayoral Executive Order No. 24, July 27, 1978. Among other duties, the Office was charged with 1) establishing procedures for all agencies with respect to the planning, design, processing, implementation and execution of all construction projects; 2) managing major construction projects when so directed by the Mayor; 3) requiring all agencies to prepare and submit periodic reports on the progress of all construction projects; 4) identifying all construction projects that have experienced serious delays and directing the agency involved to take appropriate action; 5) serving as a liaison with the New York City construction industry; and 6) seeking ways to increase the willingness of private contractors to do construction for the City.

The mission statement for the Office suggests wide-ranging authority and responsibility. However, the Office has had no comprehensive plan encompassing the City's vast capital construction program. Lacking a focus on the broad issues of policy and priorities, the Office has dealt mainly with interagency disputes and the promotion of development, rather than with improving the integrity and efficiency of City construction projects.

6. The Koch administration attempted to consolidate supervision of the City's capital program under a Deputy Mayor for Policy and Physical Development. The focus, however, was not on centralized planning or overarching policy development, but on discrete projects perceived by the Mayor's Office to be of critical importance.

7. See Steven G. Somlo, Counsel and Assistant Secretary, New York State Public Authorities Control Board, "Public Authorities in New York State" (unpublished manuscript, Albany, New York, 1988); and William J. Quirk and Leon E. Wein, "A Short Constitutional History of Entities Known as Public Authorities," *Cornell Law Review* 56 (1971): 521.

8. Until certain provisions of the November 1989 New York City Charter Revision take effect on September 1, 1990, construction contracts of $15,000 or less can be awarded without competitive sealed bidding, but they have to follow the rules and conditions prescribed by the Board of Estimate. New York, N.Y., Charter § 342 (1986).

Construction contracts of more than $15,000 have to be awarded by competitive sealed bid to the lowest responsible bidder. New York, N.Y., Charter § 343 (1986). The Board can waive the competitive sealed bidding requirement in a "special case," but neither the Charter nor applicable case law defines what constitutes a "special case." In practice the Board has waived competitive sealed bidding when departmental procurement requirements could not be specified in enough detail ahead of time to make competitive sealed bidding practicable. Institute of Public Administration, *Contracting in New York City Government: Final Report and Recommendations* (November 1987) 24.

Consultant, technical and personal service contracts (including consulting engineers) of more than $10,000 are not required to go through the competitive bidding process, but have to be approved by the Board after a public hearing. New York, N.Y., Charter § 349 (1986).

9. The Wicks Law is not codified in a single section. It is found in the N.Y. Gen. Mun. Law, § 101 (McKinney 1986); N.Y. Fin. Law, § 135 (McKinney 1989); and N.Y. Pub. Hous. Law, § 151-a (McKinney 1989).

10.

> External reviews and approvals now required during the project cycle have grown over time to the point where they are estimated to add, at a minimum, one to 1½ years to the average project cycle—at a cost to the City of an estimated $165 million per year, based on an assumed inflation rate of 5 percent per year. (If state or federal funds are involved, or a new site must be acquired, and environmental and land use reviews are needed, additional years may be added to the project cycle).

Mayor's Private Sector Survey, 39.

11. Mark H. Moore and Margaret Jane Gates, *Inspectors-General: Junkyard Dogs or Man's Best Friend?* (New York: Russell Sage Foundation, 1986) 17-18.

12. Fraudulent conduct is often accompanied by official corruption. Government employees may be bribed to approve overcharges and unjustified change orders, or rewarded in some other manner to facilitate the bribegiver's receipt of a benefit to which he is not entitled. For instance, in *United States v. Galucci*, 87 CR 490 (S.D.N.Y. 1987) and *United States v. Spring*, 87 CR 491 (S.D.N.Y. 1987), defendants bribed City officials to turn a blind eye toward the theft and resale of some pipe owned by the City. (Having dealt systematically with official corruption in Chapter 4, however, this chapter focuses only on fraud.)

13. "The president of one... [construction company], which had sued the City of New York over 80 times, boasted in an affidavit submitted in March 1985:

> I consider myself particularly savvy in legal matters. For better or for worse, I have led [my company] through literally scores of lawsuits involving complex, multi-party construction projects. [My company] has been a party to dozens of lawsuits involving the Board of Education, the City of New York, Department of General Services, Transit Authority, Department of Parks and Recreation, Facilities and Development Corp., Dormitory Authority of the State of New York, Metropolitan Transit Authority, among others. . . .

The affidavit is a testament to the irrelevance of good will to success in the field of public construction." John Grubin, " 'No-Damage-For-Delay' Clauses: Fair or Foul?—the Owner's Perspective," unpublished paper presented at the Fourth Annual Meeting of the American Bar Association Forum Committee on the Construction Industry (1988) 6.

14. For example, contractors can claim that cost overruns were the result of delays caused by the City when, in fact, they were caused by subcontractors. The New York State Court of Appeals addressed this problem in *Corrino Civetta Constr. Corp. v. City of New York*, 67 N.Y.2d 297, 502 N.Y.S.2d 681 (1986). The court made it more difficult for contractors to collect damages from the City by strictly enforcing the "no damage for delay" clause in all City construction contracts.

In *Corrino Civetta*, the contractors had failed to complete work in a timely fashion. In an effort to collect the balance of payment for work already performed, the contractor sued, alleging delay caused by the City. The court denied recovery because of the "no damages for delay" clause, holding that the only exceptions to the clause are: (1) delays caused by the [City's] bad faith or its willful, malicious, or grossly negligent conduct, (2) uncontemplated delays, (3) delays so unreasonable that they constitute an intentional abandonment of the contract by the [City], and (4) delays resulting from the [City's] breach of a fundamental obligation of the contract." *Corrino Civetta* at 686.

While *Corrino Civetta* makes it more difficult for contractors to avoid the "no damages for delay" clause, the exceptions will continue to provide opportunities for litigation.

15. State of New York, Commission of Investigation, *The Co-Op City Repair Program* (March 1983) 3.

16. *United States v. Steiner*, 86 CR 507 (S.D.N.Y. 1986).

17. *United States v. Bragaglia*, 86 CR 361 (S.D.N.Y. 1986).

18. *United States v. Brolawski*, 86 CR 593 (S.D.N.Y. 1986).

19. *United States v. DeMeo*, 86 CR 703 (S.D.N.Y. 1986).

20. *United States v. Guerrerio*, 86 CR 1061 (S.D.N.Y. 1986).

21. In 1989, the U.S. Supreme Court threw the legality of such programs into grave doubt in *City of Richmond v. J.A. Cronson Co.*, 109 S.Ct. 706 (1989), when it held unconstitutional a city program providing that general contractors would only qualify for public construction contracts if their bids included thirty percent for minority contractors. The Court held that such programs were not permissible unless they represented a direct effort to remediate previous discrimination.

New York State, but not New York City, has a minority-based enterprise requirement for public construction projects. The City has a locally based enterprise (LBE) program that seeks to award ten percent of its contracts to those firms qualifying as LBEs. To be certified as an LBE a firm must (1) be located within New York City, (2) have annual gross receipts of $500,000 or less ($1.5 million for firms engaged in heavy construction), and (3) have done at least twenty-five percent of its business in economically distressed areas of the city *or* employ economically disadvantaged persons for twenty-five percent of its workforce. New York, N.Y., Local Law No. 49 (1984). Since the LBE program is not specifically racially-based, it would presumably survive the *Richmond* decision.

22. New York State Commission of Investigation, *Investigation of the Building and Construction Industry: Minority Business Enterprise Programs* (1984).

23. *United States v. Gelb*, 87 CR 104 (E.D.N.Y. 1987).

24. *People v. Mikuszewski*, Ind. No. 4959/86 (N.Y. County 1986). The federal and state MBE requirements were applicable here because these contracts involved federal and state funds.

25. See Julian E. Lange, "Pricing Public Construction," *The Construction Industry, Balance Wheel of the Economy*, eds. Julian E. Lange and Daniel Quinn Mills (Lexington, Mass.: Lexington Books, D.C. Heath & Co., 1979) 37-58.

26. *People v. Durante Construction Corp.*, Ind. No. 7098/87 (N.Y. County 1987).

27. See Thomas E. Abernathy IV, "Bidding Problems and Award of Contracts," *Design and Construction Contracts: New Forms, New Realities* (Chicago: American Bar Association, Real Property, Probate and Trust Law Section, 1988) 173-248; Michael F. Albers and Robert L. Meyers III, "Current Methods for Contractual Arrangements," *Construction Contracts and Litigation*, 1988-1989 Real Estate Law and Practice Court Handbook Series (New York: Practicing Law Institute, 1989) 11-209; Kenneth W. Cushman, Bruce W. Ficken, Kenneth I. Levin and William R. Sneed III, "The Contractor and Subcontractor as Claimants," *Construction Contracts and Litigation*, 1988-1989 Real Estate Law and Practice Court Handbook Series (New York: Practicing Law Institute, 1989) 397-601.

For more general sources, see Donald P. Arnavas and William J. Ruberry, *Government Contract Guidebook* (Washington, D.C.: Federal Publications, 1986); James F. Donnelly and Andrew K. Gallagher, *The Law of Federal Negotiated Contract Formation* (Rockville, Md.: GCA Publications, 1982); W. Noel Keyes, *Government Contracts under the Federal Acquisition Regulations* (St. Paul: West Publishing Company, 1986); Eugene McQuillin, "Contrasts in General," *The Law of Municipal Corporations*, 3d ed., ed. by Ray Smith (Chicago: Callaghan, 1990) Vol 10, 241–554, Vol. 10A, 1–193; Dennis J. Riley, *Federal Contracts, Grants and Assistance* (Colorado Springs: Shepard's/McGraw Hill, 1983); Steven G. Stein, *Construction Law*, vol. 1 (New York: Matthew Bender, 1988).

28. See e.g., N.Y. Pub. Bldgs. Law § 8 (McKinney 1946 & Supp. 1990); N.Y. Pub. Auth. Law § 1209 (McKinney 1982 & Supp. 1990); N.Y. Rapid Trans. Law § 17 (McKinney 1942); New York, N.Y., Charter § 312 (1989). Small purchase contracts and emergency contracts (unforeseen danger to life, safety, property or a necessary service) are usually exempted from the competitive bidding requirements.

29. "The competitive bidding laws, which predate the American Civil War, were a major reform of the public procurement process. They were enacted to deter government officials from giving business to friends and associates and to prevent fraud by government employees who award contracts for public works and procurement." Attorney General Robert Abrams, *Bid-Rigging in the Competitive Bidding Process: A Report to the Legislature* (Albany, N.Y.: New York State Department of Law, 1985) 1.

30. Institute of Public Administration, *Contracting in New York City Government: Final Report and Recommendations* (New York: November 1987) 38.

31. Most New York City construction contracts provide that:

> The Contractor agrees to make no claim for delays in the performance of this contract occasioned by an act or omission to act of the City or any of its representatives, and agrees that any such claim shall be fully compensated for by an extension of time to complete performance of the work as provided herein.

The unwillingness of courts to enforce this clause may be changing. See *Kalisch-Jarcho v. City of New York*, 58 N.Y.2d 377, 461 N.Y.S.2d 746 (1983); *Corinno Civetta Constr. Corp. v. City of New York*, 67 N.Y.2d 297, 502 N.Y.S.2d 681 (1986). In 1989, the Law Department succeeded in obtaining summary judgment in the largest delay claim ($26 million) ever brought against the City. City of New York, *Mayor's Management Report* (New York: City of New York, September 17, 1989) 599.

32. See, e.g., New York State, Division of the Budget, *Fiscal Implications of the Wicks Law Mandate* (May 1987); New York State Facilities Development Corporation, *Construction Cost Study of Community-Based Facilities* (prepared by EBASCO Services Inc., 1986); City of New York, Office of the Mayor, *Wicks Law Repeal—A Public Construction Necessity* (September 1984); New York State, Division of the Budget, *Study of Public Construction Laws and Procedures* (1977); New York State Assembly, Standing Committee on Local Government, Sub-Committee on Bidding and Purchase Contracts, *The Multiple Contract System and Competitive Bidding Requirements* (February 1971).

33. See *General Building Contractors of New York State v. County of Oneida*, 54 Misc. 2d 260, 282 N.Y.S.2d 385 (Oneida County 1967).

34. Lange, "Pricing Public Construction," 50.

35. Many other states and the federal government once had multiple contracting requirements for public construction. These requirements have been repealed at the federal level, and repealed or substantially modified in most states. Only Ohio and Pennsylvania have multiple contracting statutes as restrictive as New York's Wicks Law. Private developers almost never resort to multiple contracting, since they find it costly and inefficient. See Committee on Municipal Affairs, the Association of the Bar of the City of New York, *The Wicks Law: Repeal It Now* (1986).

36. *Forest Electric Corp. v. State of New York*, 52 Misc.2d 215, 275 N.Y.S.2d 917, 919-20 (Ct. Cl. 1966).

37. City of New York, Office of the Mayor, *Wicks Law Repeal—A Public Construction Necessity* (September 1984).

38. See New York Building Congress, *Building New York City for the 21st Century* (April 1990). Other reports documenting the complexity of the public construction process and recommending its reform include: City of New York, *The Report of the Mayor's Blue Ribbon Panel on Building Plan Examination and Review* (August 1986); New York City, Board of Education, Office of the Inspector General, "The Board of Education of the City of New York, Division of School Buildings: A Review of Management Controls, Conclusions and Recommendations," (May 19, 1987); and *How Does New York City Work? The Major Processes of City Government: Report of the New York City Charter Revision Commission* (April 1989).

39. City of New York, Mayor's Office of Operations, "Capital Program Accelera-

tion Project: Work Methods Improvement for NYC Engineers, Phase I, Department of Transportation, Division of Bridge Design," (1987) 3.

40. The above cited study of bridge design indicated that Phase I work (investigation and primary design) required twenty-nine months. A major reason for this was poor initial work by consultants, requiring much of the work to be redone.

41.

> Effective contract management depends in large part on the ability of oversight entities to go back, after the fact, and determine who made crucial procurement decisions and why those particular decisions were made. The possibility (or the threat) of this kind of post-award review is a much more cost-effective deterrent to corrupt practice than a cursory pre-review of every contract. City-wide guidelines for limited competition contracting are necessary in order to make post-award compliance reviews possible.

Institute for Public Administration, *Contracting in New York City Government*, 36.

42. One example is the Comptroller's unrealistic requirement that engineering audits be performed on every payment request. The effect is perfunctory engineering audits and delayed progress payments.

43. A Building Congress Report on public construction noted, "The primary consequence is that project managers, department heads, chief engineers and even commissioners are more and more reluctant to use professional discretion because they expect to be challenged by legions of the City's own lawyers and auditors. The price for avoiding the appearance of impropriety has been to discourage and chill the professionals and to greatly slow the work." New York Building Congress, ii.

44. Citizens Budget Commission, *Toward Greater Accountability for the Implementation of Capital Projects* (November 1989).

45. Larry Rohter, "Arts High School Still Incomplete," *New York Times*, 25 September 1985, late ed.: A1; Larry Rohter, "Koch Orders Arts School Inquiry after New Study on Design Flaws," *New York Times*, 1 October 1985, late ed.: A1; Larry Rohter, "High School for Arts: Long History of Flaws," *New York Times*, 22 October 1985, late ed.: B1; Susan Daley, "City Takes Over High School Project," *New York Times*, 14 March 1986, late ed.: B4.

46. Mary Connelly and Carlyle C. Douglas, "Rink Resurrected: Trump Triumphant," *New York Times*, 16 November 1986, late city final ed.,: Sec. 4, 6.

47. See footnote 1, *supra*.

48. According to a representative of the bank consortium that finances most of the private developers in this program, the private renovations have been on time and within budget because the developers must put up some of their own money and a letter of credit; penalties are imposed if the renovations are late or over budget. See Alan Finder, "Plan to Redo Apartments Is $50 Million over Budget," *New York Times*, 14 March 1990: B1, 6.

49. Settlement Housing Fund, 33.

50. *Id.*, 34.

51. *Id.*, 38.

52. *Id.*, 42.

53. *Id.*, 43.

54. *Id.*, 45.

55. Tom Robbins, "City's 2.1M to Shady Firm," *Daily News*, 26 June 1989: 23.

56. These events are partially recounted in Michael Arena, "Pavers Avoid Probe," *Newsday*, 6 September 1987, New York ed: 3.

57. Unlike New York City, which at least has had the authority to debar contractors through the Board of Responsibility, New York State's debarment options are completely inadequate. The State Department of Transportation was found to have no "authority to commence any sort of proceeding for the purpose of punishing an irresponsible bidder or debarring such a bidder from submitting bids in the future." *Callanan Industries v. White*, 118 A.D.2d 167, 503 N.Y.S.2d 930, 933 (3d Dept. 1986). The authority to debar must be conferred upon state agencies in express terms by the Legislature. *Id.* at 933.

58. New York, N.Y., Bd. of Est. Res. § 5 (November 14, 1985).

PART II

Paths to Reform

A Comprehensive Crime-Control Strategy

CHAPTER 6

Designing and implementing a comprehensive crime-control strategy

Introduction

The longevity and pervasiveness of the crime problems documented in Part I have been exposed periodically over the past century by legislative committees, gubernatorial commissions, criminal prosecutions, investigative journalists and academic scholars. That these problems are as severe today as in the past is testimony not only to their intransigence, but also to the failure to design and implement a successful reform effort. Notwithstanding the exposés, publicity and widely shared perception that the New York City construction industry is rife with corruption and even "mobbed up," neither government nor the industry has made a determined effort to change the situation.

The fitful, isolated initiatives of the past are clearly not enough. Something more – completely new and different — must be done; a comprehensive crime-control strategy must be implemented. The strategy must be more sustained, more broadly focused and more intensive than any previous initiative. It will require mobilizing personnel and expertise from many different law enforcement, regulatory and building agencies, in the execution of a coordinated plan for reform.

We recognize certain practical realities. Because of State and City fiscal constraints and a host of competing funding demands, no strategy will become a reality if it requires massive new resources. Thus, we do not base our overall plan on the creation of vast and complex new agencies but, for the most part, on leveraging currently available resources.

In any case, strategic considerations also weigh against the formation of new bureaucracies. First, creating a new agency, such
as a special prosecutor or a construction industry analog to the
New York/New Jersey Waterfront Commission, would make the
corruption and racketeering problem "belong" exclusively to
that agency, thus reinforcing the already too prevalent tendency
for other officials and agencies to view fighting corruption and
racketeering as not their responsibility. Second, creating any
new agency, whatever its responsibility, would invariably lead to
turf battles and jurisdictional disputes with those already in
existence. Finally, and ironically, reliance on a new bureaucracy
to implement a reform strategy would risk increasing racketeering susceptibility and potential by creating incentives to corrupt
the new regulators.

Thus, the far preferable initiative, on both cost and strategic
grounds, is to mobilize and integrate the energies of those governmental agencies already concerned with the construction
industry. Merely requiring these agencies to focus on whether
and how their operations contribute to racketeering susceptibility and potential would substantially advance this comprehensive crime-control effort.

No single law enforcement, regulatory or building agency can,
by itself, effect the fundamental reforms necessary to reduce the
systemic criminality cataloged in Part I. However, if these agencies joined in a comprehensive crime-control strategy, a whole
much greater than the sum of its parts would result. This synergism[1] could have a profound and lasting impact on reducing corruption and racketeering.

Thus, we propose that the Governor and Mayor mandate the
establishment of a network among several currently existing
agencies, and a very few and modest new ones, with the relationships, responsibilities and accountabilities described in the
remainder of this chapter.[2] Each agency would thereby contribute to a reduction in corruption and racketeering; and each
would also be better able to accomplish its respective primary
goals of moving public works projects forward on time and
within budgets, protecting workers' rights and attracting a
greater pool of honest, competent and competitive companies to
the City's public and private construction projects.

In this chapter, we set forth our comprehensive crime-control strategy. First, we delineate its goals and objectives. Next, we outline the methods that it must employ, offer principles for its implementation, and propose a blueprint for the roles that various government agencies could play.

Defining a Comprehensive Crime-Control Strategy

To be truly comprehensive, the crime-control strategy must involve the efforts of many different government agencies, including law enforcement and the numerous local and state agencies that have regulatory and operational roles in the construction industry. These agencies know the New York City construction industry firsthand, and have often experienced the consequences of corruption and racketeering.

A strategy is a plan based on an informed understanding of the problem, organized around short- and long-term objectives that will achieve the ultimate goal. A comprehensive crime-control strategy must be institutionalized by means of an authoritative and permanent mandate; it cannot depend on one or more officials' discretion and *ad hoc* policy choices.

Institutionalization is crucial for two reasons. The first is psychological. Cynicism is one of the greatest impediments to reforming the industry. If industry participants believe that current government initiatives are merely a politically expedient and temporary response to the most recent flurry of exposés and, like its predecessors, will soon dissipate, they will not commit themselves to a reform agenda. Those who cooperate with, benefit from, or turn a blind eye to the industry's criminal elements, will bet on the racketeers, not on the government. Honest contractors, who feel they must "go along to get along," will consequently offer little, if any, help or encouragement to government reform efforts. Only by institutionalizing the crime-control effort—only by convincing the industry that the effort will be continuous and permanent—can we encourage honest businesspeople to come forward with complaints, information, and assistance.

The second reason is practical. Reform of such a seemingly intractable problem cannot be achieved by the short-term implementation of any single plan. No quick fix can eliminate corruption and racketeering. Lasting reform must be an evolving process, involving defined and interrelated roles for the diverse public and private participants in the industry. Such a process requires a mandate from the Governor, the Mayor and the Legislature.

The Goals and Methodology of a Comprehensive Crime-Control Strategy

At the most general level, the goal of a comprehensive crime-control strategy must be to reduce corruption and racketeering in the New York City construction industry significantly and permanently. To accomplish this goal requires achievement of more specific subgoals, including: 1) purging Cosa Nostra from critical positions in labor unions, construction firms and supply companies; 2) removing and deterring other criminals who prey on the industry; 3) reducing the governmental corruption associated with the regulation of public and private construction and the building of public works; and 4) reducing fraud in public works programs. A successful attack on the systemic criminality in each of these areas requires the reduction of racketeering susceptibility and potential. Such a reduction can be achieved only through a combination of deterrence, incapacitation, opportunity blocking and altered economic incentives.[3]

By definition, deterrence is created by convincing industry participants that corrupt payoffs and other crimes carry a substantial risk of exposure and significant punishment. Traditionally, law enforcement agencies have borne the full weight of implementing a deterrence strategy by threatening arrest and prosecution, and by creating the Construction Industry Strike Force in December 1987, Governor Cuomo has already institutionalized a construction-specific agent of law enforcement deterrence.

Deterrence, however, should not be exclusively a law enforcement responsibility. All government agencies with a role in the construction industry must contribute to the effort to expose and punish wrongdoing. First, they can increase the risk of detection by identifying bribes, frauds and other crimes. Second, they can refuse to do business with corrupt firms, a deterrent as, or more, potent than the threat of incarceration. Businessmen may fear the loss of business more than the loss of liberty because they believe, realistically, that substantial prison terms are reserved for notorious racketeers, and, equally realistically, that even if individuals are incarcerated, their companies usually continue business-as-usual. Therefore, two of the highest priorities of a comprehensive crime-control strategy must be: first, to identify to operating agencies those contractors and suppliers involved in systemic criminality; and second, to empower those agencies to exclude such companies from public contracting.

As a social-control strategy, incapacitation aims to make it impossible for criminals to engage in illegal activities by separating racketeers from their corrupt firms, or otherwise denying them the means to engage in criminal activities. While incarceration is the most obvious incapacitation strategy, labor and corporate racketeers can also be cut off from their unions and businesses. Civil RICO suits can remove corrupt officials from their organizations and, in appropriate cases, place those organizations under court-appointed receiverships. Agencies involved in public works and in regulating the construction industry can identify targets for such suits, and can provide information that could lead to the imposition of effective remedies.

Opportunity blocking is a less-developed strategy, but one that is extremely effective when properly designed and implemented. It seeks to change the social, economic, physical or organizational environment so that particular crimes become impossible, or at least very difficult, to carry out. A simple example of opportunity blocking is preventing theft from bus drivers by requiring that exact fares be placed in secure fare boxes which even the driver cannot open. More sophisticated examples include steps taken by some federal inspectors general to design administrative procedures and checks that prevent fraud in government spending programs, and the hiring by banks and other corporations of private investigating and security firms to carry out loss-prevention audits and security-conscious reforms of operating procedures. Later in this chapter, we will propose that general or prime contractors undertaking public construction be required to retain private investigating auditing firms which will, among other tasks, design, implement and monitor compliance with opportunity blocking strategies.

Changing economic incentives to give people less reason to reach out to racketeers and other corrupt figures is the most complex and undeveloped social-control strategy. Nevertheless, it offers the possibility of the most far-reaching reform.[4] If, for example, the process of obtaining construction permits, progress payments or change orders were made more expeditious, fair and equitable, the incentives to pay bribes to those in a position to move the process along would diminish, and corruption would be reduced. Similarly, if we could diminish the economic benefits contractors achieve by the bribery of corrupt unionists, the contractors would have less incentive to make payoffs to union officials.

Principles Underlying the Design and Implementation of a Comprehensive Crime-Control Strategy

Understanding the Causes and Dynamics of Corruption and Racketeering

The development of a comprehensive crime-control strategy requires comprehensive intelligence about contemporary crime patterns, as well as sophisticated economic and social analysis of why these patterns have persisted for so long. Intelligence information will tell us what crime groups are exerting influence over what unions, construction companies and suppliers; what cartels are in operation; and what public works projects are hemorrhaging money through fraud, waste and abuse. While creating intelligence bases is a common and well understood skill in law enforcement, sophisticated and comprehensive analysis of these databases is much less so. By such analysis, intelligence data is conceptualized into descriptive and explanatory reports which identify the means, incentives and opportunities that make possible, indeed probable, systemic corruption and racketeering. Such an analysis is critical to designing reforms that are effective because they address causes rather than symptoms.

OCTF's Construction Industry Project has been engaged in this kind of intelligence gathering and analysis for the last four years, utilizing investigations, staff research, consultants and workshops on each of the industry's principal crime problems. OCTF has relied not only on its own specialists, and on others in law enforcement, but has also consulted scholars from relevant disciplines and experts from inside and outside the industry. The resulting analysis fuels the proposals that follow.

Creating a Synergism
To achieve comprehensive reform, a few assumptions must be accepted. First, government agencies must become more crime conscious and crime resistant. This requires communication and working relationships between and among existing law enforcement, regulatory and building agencies. Second, these newly defined relationships and responsibilities should not distract these agencies from fulfilling other responsibilities. Rather, they can further crime-control goals by collecting and passing along information already available to them and by carrying out their present duties in a way that supports crime-control efforts. The regulating and building agencies must realize that a reduction in corruption and racketeering will enable them to accomplish their own goals. No building operation can be efficient if the system is rife with corruption. Similarly, it is impossible to play an effective regulating role if the regulatory environment is laced with the opportunities, incentives and norms of bribery.

The creation of this interagency synergism would thus require the following: 1) insuring that agencies relating to the New York City construction industry are aware of the dynamics of corruption and racketeering; 2) involving them in the formulation of strategies to counter that criminality; 3) inducing or requiring the implementation of these strategies; and 4) utilizing the enormous resources devoted to public construction as a means to influence directly and indirectly the conduct of private construction.

A Proposed Organizational Structure
for the Formulation and Implementation
of a Comprehensive Crime-Control Strategy
We need to design and institutionalize a coordinated attack on corruption and racketeering using the methods described above. This task has at least three prerequisites: 1) the collection of information about crime problems from all relevant sources, and its dissemination to appropriate agencies; 2) the design of pre-

ventive law enforcement, regulatory, and/or operational strategies; and 3) the implementation of these strategies. To fulfill these prerequisites the efforts of law enforcement officials must be coordinated with those of policymakers in operating agencies. This coordination should enhance the ability of all agencies involved to accomplish their respective missions, while respecting their need to operate independently.

This is not a simple proposition. The designing of a system that enables law enforcement officials to distribute relevant, non-privileged information to non–law enforcement agencies is itself a challenge. Through the use of such investigative tools as electronic surveillance, grand juries, informants and undercover operations, law enforcement is in the best position to identify corrupt individuals and organizations and discover the patterns and dynamics of corrupt activity. Traditionally, the intelligence developed from criminal investigations has been used only in criminal prosecutions. Indeed, a number of statutory constraints prevent the use of such information for any other purpose.[5] Nevertheless, we believe that law enforcement can do much more to share general and generic information about the nature of the problems and criminal schemes. Government agencies vulnerable to corruption and racketeering could then use this information to structure their operations so that opportunities and incentives for criminal exploitation would be reduced. Furthermore, even without disclosing confidential information, law enforcement agencies should use their intelligence bases to design and advocate crime-prevention strategies. These strategies should be communicated to appropriate regulatory agencies for refinement and implementation.

Organized Crime Task Force

For the last four years the Organized Crime Task Force, both through its Construction Industry Project and its participation in the Construction Industry Strike Force, has been intensely studying, investigating and prosecuting corruption and racketeering in the New York City construction industry. This experience convinces us that a statewide law enforcement-based research and analysis unit must be the "nerve center" of a comprehensive crime-control effort. Only law enforcement has the capacity to gather intelligence about criminal conduct by using traditional means of research as well as electronic and physical surveillance, subpoenas, informants and covert operations. Such a rich intelligence base needs to be analyzed and utilized in planning law enforcement strategies, setting priorities, choosing investigative targets, shaping remedies and designing opportunity-blocking and incentive-altering strategies for operating agencies.

To a large extent, OCTF's Construction Industry Project has been functioning as such a research and analysis unit. This *Final Report*, and the *Interim Report* that preceded it, are the unit's primary work product. OCTF currently has an analytic capacity in its teams of attorneys, accountants, investigators and tactical analysts, and in the consultants it has drawn from academia and industry. Nonetheless, the time and energy of OCTF's teams are almost entirely consumed by their criminal investigations and prosecutions, and the agency has a very limited in-house research and analysis division. We propose the creation of a permanent unit, staffed by individuals possessing the rich variety of skills and disciplines required to carry out its critical mission.

The principal function of OCTF's Research and Analysis Unit would be to obtain information about systemic criminal activity in the industry from the Construction Industry Strike Force, from the rest of OCTF's investigations, and from as many law enforcement and non–law enforcement sources as possible; to refine, collate and store that information in retrievable information systems; and to use that information to develop analytical reports and to design preventive countermeasures for use by non–law enforcement agencies. Indeed, this unit should have the analytic capacity to carry out studies similar to this report.[6]

Construction Industry Strike Force (CISF)

The CISF, established by the Governor as a joint venture of OCTF and the New York County District Attorney's Office, has concentrated for the past two years on the investigation and prosecution of corruption and racketeering in the New York City area construction industry. It has obtained a number of important indictments and convictions, thus significantly bolstering conventional deterrence. In addition, it has developed productive working relationships with a large number of law enforcement agencies with jurisdiction over labor and corporate racketeering, with most of the New York City building and regulatory agencies, and with several of the public authorities with large capital projects. As a result of this work, it now has a reservoir of experienced staff with knowledge of and expertise in New York City's construction industry.

OCTF and the New York County District Attorney's Office have agreed to support the New York City School Construction Authority Inspector General's Office by assigning two CISF teams of lawyers, investigators, accountants and analysts—one from each office—to investigate corruption and racketeering in the $4.3 billion school construction program. OCTF is now forging a similar Strike Force venture with the Port Authority of New York and New Jersey. Through this kind of collaboration, law enforcement will be in a better position to identify and prosecute construction-related crimes, and two important building agencies will be better able to protect themselves from victimization.

Office of Construction Corruption Prevention (OCCP)
While CISF and OCTF's Research and Analysis Unit will generate intelligence and develop anticorruption and antiracketeering strategies, a mechanism outside of law enforcement is needed to refine and implement these reforms. Thus, we propose the creation of an Office of Construction Corruption Prevention (OCCP), whose primary responsibility will be to utilize intelligence, information and industry knowledge (much of which will be collected by OCTF's Research and Analysis Unit) to design and implement regulations or procedures that bolster deterrence, further incapacitation, block opportunities and reduce racketeering susceptibility and potential. We envision, for example, the standardization of procedures related to contracting, invoicing, job classifications and record keeping by government agencies and by contractors and subcontractors working on government projects.

While OCCP will be new, we propose that, like the Construction Industry Strike Force, it be staffed jointly by and draw its authority from two already existing bodies. In OCCP, resources and expertise of the Office of Construction[7] and the Department of Investigation (DOI)[8] may be redeployed to address crime in the construction industry more effectively. The Director of OCCP should be jointly appointed (and removable) by the heads of both agencies, thus giving the office some degree of operational independence.

The marriage of DOI and the Office of Construction in this new agency is just the kind of synergism that is needed. DOI, the agency charged with investigating corruption in all City agencies, has also developed substantial expertise in crime prevention. Furthermore, through its Inspectors General, DOI is in the best position to monitor implementation and compliance with OCCP regulations and procedures.

The Office of Construction is the City's construction troubleshooter. It functions as a liaison between the construction industry and City bureaucracies. Its main goal is to expedite construction by reducing bureaucratic obstacles. Thus, it can serve as a "rationalizing body" to reduce uncertainty and promote stability in the construction process.

OCCP will be able to combine the powers of DOI to obtain City building agencies' books, records, audits and other information, with the power of the Office of Construction, to impose rules and regulations on those same agencies. We propose that the imposition of regulations and reforms proposed by OCCP require the approval of both DOI and the Office of Construction. This would insure that OCCP's proposals serve the interests of reducing corruption and racketeering without impeding the building process. We anticipate that at least one agency will receive comments on proposed reforms from those industry groups and government agencies likely to be affected.

Although an operating agency could reject an OCCP proposal outright, such a rejection should be forwarded to the Mayor in writing. Thus accountability would be insured, and the reasons for rejection made public. OCCP should also be empowered to hold periodic public hearings on corruption and racketeering in the construction industry. These hearings would: 1) generate information about systemic problems; 2) require public and private officials to detail their strategies for reducing the level of illicit activity within the industry; and 3) insure that the public climate which fosters such change continues to exist.

Certified Investigative Auditing Firm (CIAF) Program

While DOI oversees mayoral building agencies, it lacks adequate personnel to monitor the large number of New York City public works projects ongoing at any one time. Adhering to the principle of leveraging scarce government resources, we recommend in Chapter 8 a new type of private sector initiative, the adoption of a Certified Investigative Auditing Firm (CIAF) program to augment DOI's monitoring capabilities.

CIAFs would be independent firms, licensed by DOI, with the investigative, auditing, loss prevention, engineering and other skills necessary to oversee on-site construction activity and record-keeping practices. The principal contractor on public works projects in excess of $5 million would be required to employ a CIAF, with a minimum of two percent of the project cost dedicated to funding the CIAF's operations. The use of CIAFs should produce savings sufficient to justify their cost. (While CIAFs might discourage criminal conduct that actually reduces the cost of construction or provides other monetary benefits to individuals and enterprises, we do not—nor should we— calculate those figures into the equation.) But even if the legitimate savings were less than two percent of the project price, the social benefit derived from the reduction of corruption and racketeering would justify the expenditure.

The CIAF would serve as a private inspector general, hired by general or prime contractors on large public construction projects to insure compliance with relevant law and regulations (including those issued by OCCP), and to deter, prevent, uncover and expose unethical or illegal conduct. The CIAF would play the same kind of role that lawyers, accountants and investigators have increasingly performed for public and private corporations desiring protection against intentional or inadvertent violations of laws and regulations. For example, in 1983 the GPU Nuclear Corporation retained an independent investigator to conduct an inquiry into the generating station at Three Mile Island. The investigator's report was filed with the Nuclear Regulatory Commission and released to the public. The Tennessee Valley Authority authorized a similar investigation to evaluate the structure and performance of its Nuclear Safety Review Staff as an in-house investigative unit. Based on the investigator's findings, the Nuclear Safety Review Staff was replaced by a new organization.[9] Similarly, the Alaska Pipeline Commission retained an attorney/private investigator to look into cost overruns on the state's oil-and-gas pipeline. This investigation documented $1.5 billion in cost overruns. When, as a result of the investigation, the Commission filed suit against the major oil companies, the investigating attorney worked on the case. In yet another example, a lawyer/investigator team retained by Dayco Corp. (now DAY International) uncovered $13 million worth of employee fraud.[10]

A final example involves participants in mergers and acquisitions who, before completing a transaction, must exercise "due diligence" in ensuring that all the representations made by other participants are in fact true. In many instances, outside investigators are hired to perform this function by examining areas of potential problems concerning the participants or the transaction itself. To do this, the investigator may examine environmental impact studies, check compliance with Security and Exchange Commission regulations and verify compliance with numerous other relevant standards and regulations.

Office of Union Members Advocacy (OUMA)

A comprehensive crime-control strategy for the City's construction industry must also include an effective antidote to labor racketeering. In Chapter 7 we will set forth a number of proposals to implement such a strategy. We specifically propose the promotion of union democracy as a means for increasing union resistance to racketeering. If rank-and-file union members can make their elected officers responsive to the membership's actual needs and best interests, racketeers will no longer be able to sell out the rights of union members by soliciting bribes or extorting money from contractors.

To promote union democracy, we will propose the creation of an Office of Union Members Advocacy (OUMA), within the State Consumer Protection Board, to act as an ombudsman in advancing the rights of construction union members. OUMA would pay particular attention to elections and to job referral procedures—two areas often subverted by racketeers to punish those who seek to assert their rights or who dare to challenge corrupt practices. OUMA would be authorized to conduct investigations and to undertake or support litigation and advocacy before the State Department of Labor and other appropriate bodies.

In carrying out its duties, OUMA would necessarily acquire significant information on corruption and racketeering in the construction unions. Thus, OUMA and the Research and Analysis Unit of OCTF should work closely together in fulfilling their respective missions.

State and City Tax Enforcement Agencies

In Chapter 8 we will describe the strategic value that sustained, rigorous tax enforcement in the construction industry can play in a crime-control initiative. This goal requires long-term, institutionalized cooperation between CISF and both the Revenue Crimes Bureau of the State Department of Taxation and Finance and the Audit and Enforcement Division of the City Department of Finance.

CISF's attack on corporate racketeering and on Cosa Nostra members and associates would be greatly assisted if both state and local tax agencies mounted initiatives focusing on construction industry tax frauds. The tax revenues derived from a construction-specific initiative might well cover the personnel costs associated with it. Moreover, the tax agencies' efforts to audit construction companies, to increase tax compliance, and to recover monies from tax evaders would also provide investigative leads for CISF, since most corporate racketeering is accompanied by falsification of corporate books and tax fraud. This is an excellent example of how enhanced agency coordination and cooperation could help to reduce systemic criminality in the construction industry through better development of existing resources.[11]

Involvement of Other Institutions

The roles, responsibilities and interrelationships of the five agencies discussed above should provide a basis for involving many other government agencies in the comprehensive crime-control strategy. OCCP, because it is to be comprised of both DOI and the Office of Construction staffs, will be responsible for obtaining information from and involving all of the City's operational agencies conducting public works and regulating construction.

Similarly, CISF will maintain and expand working relationships with all investigative and prosecutorial agencies—federal, state, and local—whose responsibilities touch on construction-related crimes.

Similarly, in fulfilling its responsibility to analyze the information provided by the CISF, OCTF's Research and Analysis Unit will necessarily involve government agencies, universities and research institutes.

FOOTNOTES

1. *Webster's New Collegiate Dictionary* (G & C Merriam Co., 1981) defines "synergism" in a manner highly appropriate to its use here: the "cooperative action of discrete agencies such that the total effect is greater than the sum of the effects taken independently."

2. These agencies, and the relationships between and among them, are depicted in Figure 1.

3. See generally, Franklin Zimring and Gordon Hawkins, *Deterrence: The Legal Threat in Crime Control* (Chicago: University of Chicago Press, 1973); Alfred Blumstein, Jacqueline Cohen and Daniel Nagin, eds., *Deterrence and Incapacitation: Estimating the Effects of Criminal Sanctions on Crime Rates* (Washington, D.C.: National Academy of Science, 1978); and Ronald Clarke, "Situational Crime Prevention," *Crime and Justice: An Annual Review of Research*, vol. 4, eds. Norval Morris and Michael Tonry (Chicago: University of Chicago Press, 1982).

4. For proposals on how such reforms have been proposed to reduce racketeering in the carting industry, see the RAND/OCTF Study: Peter Reuter, *Racketeering in Legitimate Industries* (Santa Monica, Calif.: RAND Corp., 1987) 92-93.

5. For example, New York Criminal Procedure Law §§ 190.25(4) and 700.65 restrict dissemination of information obtained through grand jury investigations and court-ordered electronic surveillance.

6. Although the basic research on the history and socioeconomic and structural causes of corruption and racketeering in the New York City construction industry is complete with this *Final Report*, more specific reports that would focus on particular subindustries, unions, suppliers, contractors and crime problems remain to be done.

7. Established by Executive Order No. 24 in October 1978, the Office of Construction has as its mandate the facilitation of construction in the City, including the reduction of inefficiency and fraud with respect to public construction. Its primary goal, which is to promote and expedite construction, includes streamlining procedures to avoid delays in the commencement and completion of projects. The Office also acts as an ombudsman in the construction industry, and serves as a sounding board for developers, contractors and suppliers with complaints about and suggestions for reforming governmental regulation in the industry.

   This office, with its jurisdiction over construction in New York City, has amassed information concerning contractors and construction projects. The Office of Construction is thus well-situated to work with other agencies in reforming construction procedures, regulations and codes, and to be an advocate for efficiency and competitiveness as well as for integrity.

8. The New York City Department of Investigation (DOI) is a mayoral agency whose duty is to increase the government's accountability to the public. Part of its function is to uncover corruption and criminal activity, and to design, through its loss prevention unit, systems that reduce fraud, waste, abuse and criminal activity in government operations. One of the operating units in the Department of Investigation is the Corruption Prevention and Management Review Board. Its function is to review operations in agencies and develop standards to prevent corruption. Association of the Bar of the City of New York, Committee on Municipal Affairs, "Report on the New York City Department of

FIGURE 1

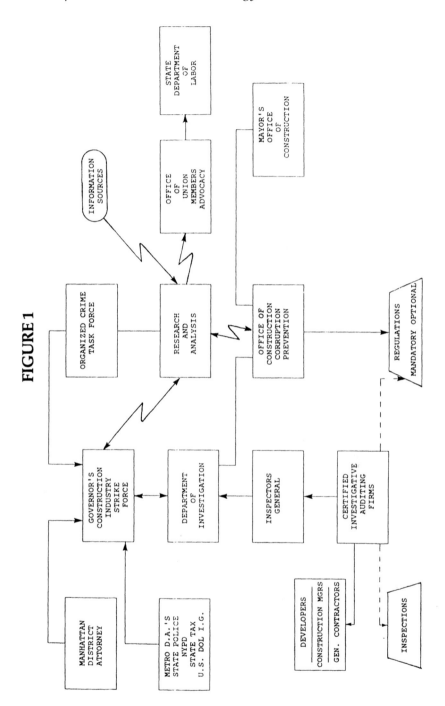

Investigation," *The Record* 43 (December 1988): 958.

DOI is required to perform investigations ordered by the Mayor, the City Council and the DOI Commissioner. Its jurisdiction, which extends beyond City agencies and employees, includes anyone doing business with the City. To carry out its investigations, DOI has the power to subpoena witnesses and hold hearings. See New York, N.Y., Charter §§ 803 and 805 (1989).

In 1986, the Inspector General program was brought into the Department of Investigation. Each City agency has an Inspector General who investigates corruption and other criminal activity within the agency and reports his or her findings directly to the DOI Commissioner. Because the Inspectors General carry out their investigations free from the interference of agency heads, they have considerable independence.

Recent changes in DOI include additional resources (including money and personnel), broader responsibilities for the Inspectors General and the Department as a whole, and, most importantly, a new emphasis on prevention of corruption. In addition, as of January 1988, the Commissioner, each agency head, and the agency's Inspector General are required to develop annually a "comprehensive anti-corruption program," whose success is evaluated at the end of the year. See Executive Order No. 105, December 26, 1986.

New methods intended to improve the recording of critical information, as well as a series of procedures designed to provide careful scrutiny of progress in ongoing investigations, have also been implemented, thus facilitating the processing of information and the conduct of investigations.

9. Eric Lindeman, "White Abolishes NSRS as TVA's Independent Investigative Branch," *Inside the N.R.C.* 8 (28 April 1986): 6.

10. Jennifer Hall, "Private Eye Lenzner Goes International," *Legal Times* 10 (6 July 1987): 4.

Our CIAF concept has already been adopted in *United States v. Salerno*, 86 CR 245 (S.D.N.Y. 1986), in which one of the defendants, Edward J. Halloran, was ordered to forfeit to the United States his interests in Certified and Big Apple concrete companies, owners of all but one of the batching plants located in Manhattan. In *Salerno*, the Court authorized the sale of Halloran's interests to the "Quad Companies," whose principals are John Quadrozzi and Michael DiBenedetto. At the same time, the Court appointed Bart M. Schwartz, of Kroll Associates, as a monitor to "oversee the activities of Quadrozzi, DiBenedetto and the Quad Companies" and gave Schwartz "full authority, without prior notice, to audit the financial affairs and business operations" of Quad. (Order of U.S.D.J. Mary Johnson Lowe, dated April 4, 1990).

11. Likewise, the Department of Labor's Fair Labor Standards Act enforcement unit should target the New York City construction industry for audits; ERISA enforcement should also give special attention to the industry as well.

CHAPTER 7

Attacking labor racketeering

Introduction: The Menace of Labor Racketeering
Labor racketeering is the most serious crime problem in the New York City construction industry because it is so pervasive, has so many victims, and is the catalyst for the commission of so many other kinds of crimes. It victimizes employers and employees, loots pension and welfare funds, mocks the federally guaranteed right to union democracy, stifles economic competition, and subverts the collective bargaining process. It is the wedge by which Cosa Nostra has pried its way into the industry.

As a result of labor racketeering, many honest workers do not run for union office, attend union meetings, insist on their contract rights, file grievances or speak their minds. Many legitimate businessmen refuse to do business in New York City or are driven away. Because labor racketeering makes public works cost more to undertake, some are not undertaken at all, or are carried out in a less ambitious manner or on a smaller scale. Through labor racketeering, corporate racketeers allocate contracts among themselves and exclude those outside their "clubs" from bidding for work.

As explained in Chapter 2, two characteristics of the New York City construction industry create the racketeering susceptibility that accounts for the prevalence of labor racketeering in many of its trade unions. First, in New York City, union officials often control the supply of construction workers on major projects. They determine who gets workers, which workers they get, how much the workers are paid, and what happens on the job site. Whoever controls labor can extort contractors by threatening labor problems and can solicit bribes from them in exchange for the ability to avoid or violate collective bargaining agreements.

Second, construction trades unions are themselves highly susceptible to influence and control by racketeers. Ironically, the same factors that create the need for construction unions explain their vulnerability to labor racketeering. Construction work is cyclical, seasonal and casual; job security does not exist. Unions bring together construction workers who are scattered on hundreds of diverse sites. But precisely because workers are so dispersed, legitimate opportunities for leaders to emerge from the rank-and-file or for solidarities to develop are extremely limited. Although strong unions can prevent exploitation by employers, they also present opportunities for exploitation by union officials. In a highly unionized construction industry such as New York City's, workers' economic survival depends on the good will of their union officials. These officials are generally responsible for assigning stewards to the job sites and for supervising the hiring hall which assigns workers to jobs and determines who gets such perquisites as overtime, easy work and no-show jobs. Workers also depend on the honesty of union officials who serve as trustees of employee benefit funds.

Once racketeers obtain control of a union, their control over rewards and punishments is so great that honest reformers find it almost impossible to remove them. The racketeers' dominance over the union's institutions gives them control over communications, budget, administrative apparatus, and pension and welfare funds. They can control meetings and rig elections. They can intimidate opposition candidates, deny them jobs, block access to accurate mailing lists, and promote propaganda and disinformation through union newsletters. Even if a rank-and-file opposition mounts a successful challenge, corrupt forces in the district council or international union can squelch the "uprising" by recognizing new locals or by placing the rebel local under international union trusteeship.

Three general strategies have been suggested to make the construction industry less susceptible to labor racketeering. The first would be to weaken the construction unions' "monopoly" over labor by encouraging competition in the supply of labor. According to this view, the existence of alternative supplies of nonunion labor would lessen the leverage corrupt union officials have over both contractors and workers. We have considered and rejected the idea of recommending that the State and City encourage open shop (nonunion) construction. First, construction unions have made immense contributions to their members' economic well being and to New York City's building industry. Second, this strategy would be counterproductive, because it would penalize the very workers whose resistance to domination by racketeers needs to be strengthened. In any case, such an approach would surely fail to be adopted, given that New Yorkers have historically provided strong legislative and social support for organized labor, especially in the construction trades.

A second strategy would be to increase regulation and supervision of the construction trades' collective bargaining process, thereby reducing abuses that result in featherbedding, no-show employees and indefensible work practices. States, however, are severely circumscribed in pursuing this strategy by the federal preemption doctrine, which bars states from regulating those fields that the national government has reserved for federal regulation. Federal preemption places states and local governments confronted by serious labor racketeering in an extremely difficult position. The federal government has established a comprehensive collective bargaining system designed to protect and enhance the rights of workers. However, when racketeers pervert this system by corruptly using the power of unions for personal gain, the federal regulatory agencies charged with addressing racketeering in labor-management relations have, at least in New York City's construction market, proven either unwilling or unable to meet their responsibilities. Nonetheless, because of the preemption doctrine, affected state and local governments to a large degree are denied the ability to take their own countermeasures.

The third and most promising strategy is to nurture, encourage and support union democracy. In essence, labor racketeering involves the exploitation of rank-and-file workers for the benefit of corrupt union officials and employers. By paying off union officials, corrupt employers can ignore the rights of their employees as guaranteed in collective bargaining agreements. Corrupt labor officials who find it profitable to trade their members' economic rights for cash and other bribes do not hesitate to blacklist those with the temerity to complain. Thus, with continued irony, unions that enhance the rights and interests of workers have, in the hands of racketeers, become vehicles for exploiting workers.

As far back as the 1940s, the American Civil Liberties Union and other reformist groups argued that unions which respect their members' rights, which have fair and competitive elections, and which make the leadership accountable to the rank-and-file, will be resistant to racketeer domination.[1] Indeed, Congress adopted this strategy for attacking labor racketeering when it passed the Landrum-Griffin Act in 1959.

The power wielded by construction union officials makes it very difficult for honest workers to assert their economic interests and regain control of their unions. Government policy must therefore give highest priority to assisting honest workers in obtaining their rights and wresting control of their unions from racketeers. We recommend that: 1) the federal government better enforce the union democracy laws now on the books; 2) New York State create a state advocate to promote construction workers rights; and 3) law enforcement continue to bring criminal and civil actions to remove racketeers from construction trade unions.

Enforcing Existing Laws

Three major federal laws have been enacted to regulate labor union activities. These are the 1935 National Labor Relations Act (popularly known as the Wagner Act),[2] which set forth the foundation of the collective bargaining system; the 1947 Labor-Management Relations Act (popularly known as the Taft-Hartley Act),[3] which sought to limit the power of unions; and the Labor-Management Reporting and Disclosure Act of 1959 (popularly known as the Landrum-Griffin Act),[4] which sought to reduce corruption within unions and to guarantee certain democratic rights to union members. Union members are also affected by a fourth statute, the Employment Retirement Income Security Act of 1974 (popularly known as ERISA),[5] which was designed to protect pension and welfare funds.

The Wagner Act

The Wagner Act recognized the right of workers to band together to bargain collectively with their employers as to wages, hours and working conditions. It created the National Labor

Relations Board (NLRB) to regulate the collective bargaining process and to settle disputes related to that process. Because the focus of the Act was the employer-employee relationship, the rights of workers within their unions was largely overlooked.

The Taft-Hartley Act

The Taft-Hartley amendments of 1947 added unfair labor practices to the list of activities prohibited under the Wagner Act. Among other things, it prohibited discrimination or coercion against union members for their intraunion political activities. The Act also prohibited consideration of a member's union political activities when referring workers for jobs from the hiring hall. While this Act has been the most important weapon for litigants challenging unfair hiring hall practices, it has three substantial limitations.[6]

First, the Act vests enforcement authority in the General Counsel of the NLRB; a decision not to issue a complaint in a particular case is unreviewable by the Board or the courts.[7] If the General Counsel files a complaint with the Board, private counsel for the complaining union member is allowed to intervene, but only to a limited degree.

Second, the NLRB's remedial authority is circumscribed by the requirement that its orders not be punitive.[8] Thus, relief is likely to be prospective only—for example, cease-and-desist orders may be issued, designed to prevent future hiring hall abuses. Furthermore, such orders may be directed only against the union generally, and not individually against any offending officials. Thus, if a union officer was found responsible for discriminating against a "dissident" with respect to job referrals, the officer could not be held personally liable for the dissident's monetary losses; damages could only be awarded against the union treasury.

Third, the Board's orders are not self-enforcing. If a union officer refuses to comply voluntarily, the Board must enforce its order in a federal circuit court of appeals via a contempt proceeding. Further delays are inevitably occasioned by lengthy appeals.[9]

The Landrum-Griffin Act

By the 1950s, it had become apparent that some unions were dominated by racketeers who were utilizing their power to exploit both employers and the union rank-and-file. In 1959, in the wake of the McClellan Committee hearings on labor racketeering, Congress passed the Landrum-Griffin Act.[10]

Title I, known as the union members' Bill of Rights, guarantees union members certain essential democratic rights: the right to nominate candidates for union office; the right to vote in union elections; the right to participate in union meetings; the right to free speech and assembly; the right to hold secret ballot elections on dues increases; and the right to sue the union. It also provides that a union cannot discipline a member without bringing specific charges and providing the "accused" an opportunity to mount a defense.

Title I rights are enforceable only through a private action filed by the aggrieved union member, who must pay all counsel fees and other litigation expenses. Although a court may order compensation for a successful litigant, such compensation cannot be counted on. Thus, in order to enforce Title I rights, a union member generally has no alternative but to hire a lawyer at his own expense, and thereby undertake litigation against an organization with vastly superior resources.

Title II, Trusteeships, describes the circumstances in which a national or international union may impose a trusteeship upon a district or local union. (Ironically, corrupt officials at the national level often use this tactic when a dissident group gains control of a local). A union member wishing to challenge such a trusteeship has two choices. First, the member can file a complaint with the Department of Labor. If the Department agrees, it may bring a civil action against the parent union. Second, the member may institute a private civil action challenging the trusteeship.

Title IV sets forth rules designed to assure fair election of union officers. Enforcement of these rules is exclusively the responsibility of the Department of Labor; individuals denied the right of free union elections must convince the Department to commence a law suit. Historically, the Department has been reluctant to bring such suits. An aggrieved union member can bring a challenge to the Department only after the election has been held and only after exhausting internal union remedies. If, after three months, the union has taken no action, the complainant can file a complaint with the Department of Labor. In *Hodgson v. Steelworkers Local 6799*,[11] the Supreme Court further limited these lawsuits by holding that the Secretary of Labor can sue only on those issues that the member attempted to correct through the union's internal proceedings.

The Department of Labor's inability or unwillingness to vigorously enforce Title IV undermines the efficacy of its remedies.[12] The erratic quality of its enforcement is attributable to a significant degree to the incompatibility of the Department's enforcement and regulatory functions. The Department's primary mission is to resolve labor-management problems. This necessarily requires good working relations with high-ranking labor officials, and makes investigating and enforcing the complaints of rank-and-file dissidents against top labor officials at best awkward and, at worst, a conflict of interest.[13]

Title V, Financial Safeguards, imposes fiduciary standards on union officers and employees. A union member may bring a cause of action against union officers on behalf of the union in a federal district or state court. Under this section, persons who violate the fiduciary requirements may be held either civilly or criminally liable.

Because of these various limitations, the Landrum-Griffin Act has not lived up to its promises.[14] Accordingly, we recommend that the Act be amended to strengthen its protection of membership rights. Some suggestions are:

- Relieve the Department of Labor of its Landrum-Griffin enforcement responsibilities and turn those responsibilities over to a specialized, independent enforcement agency or to the Justice Department.[15]
- Make Title IV's election provisions enforceable either by filing a complaint with the government enforcement agency or by bringing a private suit.
- Make preelection remedies available to complainants in election cases.
- Revise the criteria for voiding elections so that an election can be overturned if either: 1) purely technical violations could have affected the election's outcome, or 2) the violations, regardless of their effect on outcome, were so egregious that they vitiated the democratic character of the election process.

- Require unions to elect business agents, now sometimes an appointive position, thus depriving corrupt union officials of the ability to appoint another corrupt union member to this important and powerful position. Also, the position of business agent is currently categorized as a union employee or representative, making the business agent eligible to serve as a union officer as well. The business agent should be reclassified as a union officer, thus disqualifying anyone from serving in two positions—business agent as well as union officer—at the same time.

- Grant union members standing in federal court to contest the legality of those union elections supervised by the Labor Department. At present, the Department is the sole judge of an election's fairness, even though it has supervised the election.

- Make attorneys' fees more readily available for private intervention in Title IV suits. Because legal fees are uncertain in election cases, it is difficult to obtain counsel even in a meritorious suit.[16]

ERISA

The Employee Retirement Income Security Act of 1974 (ERISA) was designed to bring order and stability to private pension and benefit plans, and to prevent the looting of these funds through fraud and embezzlement.[17] Although a major advance over the patchwork of state regulations which had previously governed pension funds, ERISA has not provided adequate oversight, monitoring or enforcement. The result is that some union pension and welfare funds are a cash reservoir for racketeers. Current federal monitoring and enforcement of pension and welfare funds is too insubstantial to provide an effective deterrent to fraud and theft. If the funds were better protected against corrupt predators, racketeering potential would be reduced.

ERISA includes regulations covering four basic areas: reporting and disclosure, fiduciary standards, participation and vesting, and joint and miscellaneous tax matters. Responsibility for administering and enforcing the Act is divided among the U.S. Department of Labor, the Internal Revenue Service, the Pension Benefit Guarantee Corporation, and the U.S. Department of Justice.

The statute requires that each fund submit an annual report, with an accountant's financial statement. This report is filed with the Internal Revenue Service, which eventually forwards it to the Labor Department. It is mainly through review of these annual reports that the Labor Department is expected to detect breaches of the fiduciary standards mandated by the Act, and to refer any possible criminal violations to the Department of Justice.[18]

It has become clear that the above regulatory scheme has been a failure, and that the Labor Department has proven incapable of detecting the improper use of funds by trustees and administrators.[19] Some of the reasons for this are built into the Act itself: 1) the reports require insufficient data; 2) the independent audits that accompany the reports are too limited; 3) the reports arrive too late to be timely employed;[20] 4) the Department has only a fraction of the personnel needed for monitoring and enforcement; 5) the civil penalties that may be imposed for breach of fiduciary responsibility are not severe enough to deter fraud.

The Labor Department's Office of Labor Management Standards (OLMS) monitors and enforces the unions' compliance with the Landrum-Griffin Act, and its Office of Pension and Welfare Benefits Administration (OPWBA) monitors and enforces the funds' compliance with ERISA. To implement and enforce the Act, OPWBA has only 300 agents nationwide, mainly auditors and investigators. Falling within their purview are approximately 900,000 private pension plans containing an estimated two trillion in assets, designed to provide the retirement income for approximately 42 million people.[21]

While ERISA Section 103 requires that plans with 100 or more participants file an independent auditor's report annually, many of these audits are superficial; accountants have no incentive to delve below the surface of the materials presented by the administrator or trustees who hired them. There are several reasons for this:

1) Although these audits are conducted in accordance with generally accepted accounting procedures conforming to standards established by the American Institute of Certified Public Accountants, they are based upon financial statements presented by plan administrators. Such audits are, by definition, limited in scope.[22]

2) The Department of Labor, under administrative authority granted by ERISA, permits that assets held in trust in such government regulated industries as banking, insurance, and savings and loan institutions be excluded from the independent audit report. It is left to the discretion of the fund administrator to

include or exempt these funds from the audit.

3) An auditor has little incentive to uncover wrongdoing by the plan administrator or trustees since they hired the auditor and will decide whether or not to hire the same auditor again next year. Furthermore, nothing prevents the administrator from hiring as the independent auditor an accountant regularly retained by the fund for other purposes. Such an obvious conflict should be prohibited.

The degree to which the auditing effort needs to be expanded, and the effect, once again, of federal preemption without adequate federal follow through, can be assayed by examining the role played by the New York State Insurance Department's Welfare Fund Unit in the days before passage of ERISA, which usurped the State's monitoring role. Before ERISA, a state auditor reviewed each fund report *annually*. Standards were developed for reasonable administrative expenses (approximately ten percent), and trustees were questioned if expenses ran higher.[23] The Insurance Department performed an audit on each fund as often as necessary and "at least once every five years," as required by statute.[24] The Insurance Department billed the pension or welfare fund for the costs of the audit.

In 1974, just prior to passage of ERISA, the State Insurance Department's Welfare Fund Unit employed sixty persons, mostly auditors, to monitor 1,600 employee benefit plans. By comparison, the New York area office of the Department of Labor's Pension and Welfare Fund Benefits Administration today has only sixteen auditor-investigators to monitor 100,000 plans. Plan administrators and regulatory personnel who have observed monitoring procedures under both the New York State Insurance Department and under ERISA believe that New York State did a more timely and thorough job at no cost to the state.

A substantial enlargement of ERISA enforcement through mandatory audits conducted by a monitoring agency is essential. We recommend that this be undertaken outside the U.S. Department of Labor[25] in a manner similar to that used by New York State before the passage of ERISA. This would require a greatly increased auditing and investigative staff, for which the benefit funds could ultimately pay through a fee structure. To test this, a model program could be set up for the state of New

York which, if successful, could then be expanded to cover other states as well.

Creating an Advocate for Union Democracy

The rights of union workers provided by Landrum-Griffin and other federal (as well as state and local) laws are often not exercised. Unionized workers are not always aware of their rights, and they lack representation to assist in enforcing them. It is a sad commentary on the low regard paid to the civil rights of rank-and-file union members that, with the exception of the Association for Union Democracy (AUD),[26] no civil rights organization is devoted to vindicating their statutory rights. Therefore, we recommend establishment of a New York State Office of Union Members Advocacy (OUMA) to assume responsibility for asserting and advancing the rights of individual construction workers as well as construction workers as a class.

An appropriate home for such an office is the State Consumer Protection Board, which is now responsible for advocating the rights and interests of consumers on a number of different issues.[27] The Consumer Protection Board has scored a number of impressive victories on behalf of consumers' rights. Staffed by a small group of activist lawyers and investigators, the proposed office should be authorized to undertake investigations, litigation and advocacy. It would be authorized to assist construction workers by:

1. educating union members of their rights under the law;

2. receiving, compiling, and analyzing complaints from union members about the operation of their unions;

3. assisting groups of workers to obtain counsel and legal assistance for bringing litigation and enforcement proceedings before relevant state and federal agencies and courts;

4. monitoring elections and job referral systems in order to identify corrupt practices;

5. providing information to law enforcement in general and to the Construction Industry Strike Force in particular;

6. providing information to OCTF's Research and Analysis Unit and to the Mayor's Office of Construction Corruption Prevention, both of which we proposed in Chapter 6;

7. submitting reports to the Governor and the State Legislature about

the status of labor union members' rights in the New York City construction industry;[28] and

8. recommending legislation based upon its investigations, analyses
and reports.

Two areas of union activity should command OUMA's special
attention—union elections/referenda, and hiring halls. As to the
first, racketeers have traditionally maintained control over
unions by subverting the voting processes through electoral
intimidation, manipulation and fraud. Thus, the proposed
agency should closely monitor elections and referenda in suspect unions in order, where appropriate, to build a documented
record of election fraud. The record could ultimately be used as
the basis for federal court action to obtain appropriate remedies,
including court-appointed monitors to restore democratic
practices.

As to the second, the State Department of Labor should adopt
regulations requiring all construction unions to file a certified
statement of procedures which demonstrate that their hiring
halls, or other formal or informal job referral systems, operate
fairly. OUMA should then monitor unions' job referral procedures to determine whether they conform to the certified documents filed with the State Department of Labor. Where OUMA
finds either that the documents set forth procedures inadequate
to protect the rights of union members, or that the unions are not
acting in conformity with the filed procedures, OUMA should
take appropriate action to ensure adoption of fair procedures.
Such action might include pursuing unfair labor practice claims
before the NLRB, notification to and education of the union
membership as to the flawed hiring system, or advocacy of alternative hiring systems (for example, publicly administered hiring
halls which provide job referral services to the union's members). Where appropriate, OUMA should support civil actions in
federal court to have illegally run hiring halls placed under
trusteeship.

The Office of Union Members Advocacy should also develop
a program for informing construction union members of their
rights.[29] A better informed and educated union rank-and-file
would be more resistant to the exploitative tactics of labor racketeers. Section 105 of the Landrum-Griffin Act requires unions to

inform their members of the provisions of the Act, but this section has been largely ignored for three decades.[30] Thus, on every major New York City job site, OUMA should distribute literature describing Landrum-Griffin and other workers' rights and avenues of redress.[31] We also recommend that the State Department of Labor require unions to submit a copy of every collective bargaining agreement covering construction jobs in New York City; the State Department of Labor can then provide access to the contract to every construction trades union member.

Removing Racketeers from the Construction Unions

Unfortunately, in urging union democracy as an antidote to labor racketeering, we are not starting with a clean slate. Cosa Nostra already controls or strongly influences many construction unions; nonsyndicate racketeers control several others. The rank-and-file members of these unions need substantial law enforcement and other governmental assistance in removing racketeers, which is a precondition to the possible effectiveness of many union democracy reforms.[32]

There are very few historical examples of racketeer-dominated unions being returned to the control of honest union members; none of these examples have involved unions which had at one time been controlled by Cosa Nostra. To our knowledge, with one possible exception,[33] no such examples exist in the history of the racketeer-dominated New York City construction industry. Honest rank-and-file union members cannot be expected to defeat labor racketeers without powerful assistance. That assistance must come from the government, particularly from law enforcement agencies.[34]

The Role of Law Enforcement

Ultimately, only law enforcement, through investigation and analysis, can identify and document which New York City construction unions are influenced and controlled by racketeers. Only law enforcement can create a credible deterrent against labor racketeering. In appropriate cases, it must be prepared to use civil as well as criminal remedies to place racketeer-ridden unions under court receivership. In such cases, law enforcement must work with the court-appointed trustees to foster union democracy in the previously captive unions.

In addition, law enforcement must press for resources for itself and for other agencies contributing to the comprehensive crime-control strategy. It must play the role of educator, raising the consciousness of elected officials, the media and the public, about the reality of labor racketeering, and dispelling misconceptions about racketeer-infested unions and their leadership.

Law enforcement must cooperate with the proposed OUMA to accomplish union democracy objectives. It should forward to OUMA information concerning indictments and convictions of construction union officials, as well as other public record information relevant to OUMA's task. In addition, it should make information concerning both labor and corporate racketeering available to the general public.

To play this crucial antiracketeering role, the law enforcement effort must be focused and sustained. Law enforcement must maintain a constant presence in the New York City construction industry. Honest workers, union officials and contractors must know that they can count on law enforcement to respond to complaints of corrupt practices and that, if they cooperate with investigations and prosecutions, law enforcement will be available to provide future protection.

Increasing the Effectiveness of Court-Ordered Union Trusteeships
Under federal and state racketeering laws, prosecutors can charge those associated with Cosa Nostra or other criminal enterprises with conducting the affairs of a labor union through a pattern of racketeering (or criminal) acts.[35] Prosecutors may also bring civil suits against them and the unions they capture or corrupt, seeking the removal of labor racketeers from union positions, injunctions against racketeers having any contact with the union, and the appointment of a receiver or trustee to supervise the reorganization of the union.[36] In the last several years, RICO suits have resulted in at least five such court-appointed receivers.[37]

Each court-appointed union receiver, monitor, or trustee operates under the trial judge's order of reference. The monitorship can be tailormade to the exigencies of the situation, the goal being to purge the racketeers and return control of the union to its rank-and-file. The monitor's powers can be as broad or narrow as the judge desires. The judge can authorize a trustee to supervise an election, monitor daily operations, or take total operational control of the union and its pension and welfare funds for a limited period of time.

Court-ordered union trusteeships offer an opportunity for controlling crime by restructuring the operation of the union or ending its relationships with the racketeers who have controlled or influenced its operations.[38] A single racketeering suit can join together as defendants an entire clique of mobsters and corrupt union officials. If successful, it can enlist the federal (or state) courts in a long-term alliance seeking to reorganize and revitalize the heretofore racketeer-dominated union.

The success of a trusteeship depends on the terms of the trusteeship and on the trustee's determination and ability to reorganize and revitalize the union. In turn, the trustee's success depends on his or her ability to involve honest union members in their union, so that the union can eventually be handed over to a viable and legitimate administration.[39] This poses an enormous challenge. Rank-and-file apathy has long been a fact of life in U.S. labor unions;[40] the problem is unquestionably greater in a union that has been held under the dictatorial rule of labor racketeers for many years. Even if the racketeers are removed from such unions, honest rank-and-file union members will have had no experience or expertise in union politics or administration. Perhaps, even more importantly, they may be too cynical, apathetic or frightened to become actively involved in union affairs. While the racketeers may be formally excluded from the union's management, they are still likely to maintain informal, but potentially powerful, relationships with those "old guard" members remaining in union office and with the employers who tolerated or encouraged their prior corrupt conduct. Thus, they can continue to exert their influence:

> Indeed, a strong case can be made for the proposition that the indifference of satisfied union members is a stronger inducement to corruption than the heavy-handedness of union leaders. One of the more disturbing lessons of American trade unionism is that morally dubious activities on the part of economically effective leaders is so seldom a cause of membership revolt. "I've got mine," a Teamster said in Detroit. "Why shouldn't Hoffa get his?"[41]

Our analysis is meant to be realistic, not pessimistic. It will take a long time and much hard work to reorganize and revitalize a racketeer-dominated union. During the remedial phase of the litigation, the law enforcement agencies must not drop out of the case. If racketeers attempt to stymie the trusteeship, additional orders or indictments must be sought. [42] The trustee and his or her staff must work with labor relations and union democracy specialists to change the climate in the union, create new organs for political participation, and educate a new generation of officials. New structures, such as court-supervised hiring halls, may be necessary to break the lock of the corrupt regime. [43]

It is useful to remember that judicial efforts to remedy unconstitutional conditions in prisons, jails, mental hospitals and schools did not proceed without great difficulties and setbacks. Plaintiffs and judges would have preferred an "easier way" to bring institutional operations and conditions to a constitutionally acceptable level. In some cases, it has taken years for court-appointed masters to bring about school desegregation or to assure the rights of prisoners, mental patients or students. Ultimately, however, in almost every case the rule of law and judicial authority have triumphed.

It is critical that union trusteeships have ample funding and authority. Trying to implement court-ordered union trusteeships without adequate support and funding is a recipe for disaster. It is unrealistic to expect one full-time (much less one part-time trustee) to monitor or reorganize a union with thousands of members and a long history of racketeer domination. [44] In addition to administrative support, a trustee needs a staff comprised of investigators, auditors and labor relations specialists. Serious thought must be given to the source of funding to support the trustee and the necessary support staff. The union trusteeships established so far have been supported by the affected union locals or international. But this has posed a number of problems. Locals experiencing an organizational crisis typically have financial problems, [45] thereby sharply limiting the range of the trustee's activities. In the Teamster Local 560 case, in addition to the herculean task of removing and deterring racketeers, the trustee had to assume responsibility for running the union, including negotiating and enforcing collective bargaining agreements.

Clearly, a more substantial financial base for the trusteeships of union locals has to be found. One possibility is to require the international union to pay the cost of a viable trusteeship on the grounds that the international failed in its responsibility in the first instance to protect the local's members from the predatory activities of racketeers; it may well have been accepting dues from the corrupt local for years without having made any effort to counter the corruption which it knew or should have known existed.[46]

Research and analysis is needed on the successes and failures of the first generation RICO union trusteeships before it will be possible to make confident recommendations for the structure and operation of future trusteeships. It may turn out that different models will be appropriate for different situations. One general principle which seems to hold true in all cases is that the trustee should endeavor to turn as many appointed union offices as possible into elected offices. Racketeers flourish on pork-barrel appointments. The more offices that are filled through elections, the greater the possibility that rival union leaders will emerge with separate constituencies and power bases.

A great deal of attention needs to be given in each case to how a trusteeship might ultimately be designed and implemented if it is successfully to reform the racketeering susceptibility of a particular union. The fashioning of an appropriate trusteeship should not be left to a hasty settlement put together to avoid, or at the end of, a long trial. Existing trusteeships must be carefully studied and analyzed by law enforcement organizations, aided by labor relations and other academic specialists. Grant applications should be made to criminal justice funding agencies, such as the National Institute of Justice, for funds to carry out relevant research and analysis.

A Center for Union Democracy
In addition to a law enforcement-led effort to study union trusteeships, we recommend the establishment and support of a private sector Center for the Study and Advancement of Union Democracy. Such a center would provide invaluable assistance to the government and the courts as the effort to fulfill the promise of union democracy expands and matures. It would conduct

research, hold seminars, build a library, identify possible union trustees, and hold training sessions for trustees and their staff. A Center for the Study of Union Democracy, for which the Association for Union Democracy could well serve as a nucleus, could be funded by private philanthropic foundations. We recommend that the Governor, the Mayor, and leaders of the law enforcement community provide whatever assistance they can in making such a center a reality.

An Enhanced Role for the National Labor Relations Board

In 1985, the President's Commission on Organized Crime recommended new legislation making it an unfair labor practice to conduct or control union affairs through a pattern of racketeering activity, or for an employer to recognize or bargain with a union so tainted.[47] Under this proposed legislation, the U.S. Attorney General, in cooperation with the NLRB General Counsel, would control the filing, investigation, prosecution and settlement of these new unfair labor practice charges. On finding racketeer domination, the NLRB could decertify the union, appoint a trustee-conservator to preserve union assets and represent the employees, and debar from union office and functions for ten years any individuals found to be involved with organized crime. This is an excellent recommendation, which we enthusiastically support. In addition, we believe that the NLRB should have the option of taking over hiring halls or other particular union functions.

This report emphasizes that all too often local, state and federal agencies have abjured their own responsibility for responding to corruption and racketeering on the ground that it is "somebody else's problem." Under the National Labor Relations Act, the NLRB has two functions: the prevention and remedying of unfair labor practices and the resolution of questions of employee representation. Unfortunately, the NLRB has historically refused to withhold recognition from alleged racketeer-dominated unions on the ground that racketeering is outside its jurisdiction.[48] Although the NLRB recognizes its role in overseeing and regulating the collective bargaining system, it seems oblivious to the inescapable conclusion that such a system cannot operate as intended or in a healthy or efficacious manner when union leadership is comprised of or controlled by racketeers. Corruption and racketeering must be recognized as an NLRB problem and responsibility.

Conclusion

Labor racketeering is the gravest crime problem afflicting New York City's construction industry. The problem is all the more serious because of Cosa Nostra's direct or indirect role in a majority of the critical trade union locals. The key strategies for reform lie in strengthening federal enforcement of existing labor laws and in supporting the forces and processes of union democracy in every way possible. The most important structural reform would be to remove enforcement authority from the Department of Labor. The key to strengthening union democracy lies in assisting the rank-and-file to vindicate their own rights. The establishment of a state OUMA would be an important step toward this end. However, union democracy will not have a chance in mob-dominated unions. Thus, law enforcement must continue its efforts to purge the racketeers. This can best be accomplished by strengthening RICO and OCCA trusteeships over unions proved to be racketeer-dominated.

FOOTNOTES

1. *Democracy in Trade Unions* (New York: American Civil Liberties Union, November 1943); *Democracy in Trade Unions: A Survey, with a Program of Action* (New York: American Civil Liberties Union, May 1949); *A Labor Union "Bill of Rights," Democracy in Trade Unions: The Landrum-Griffin Act* (New York: American Civil Liberties Union, March 1963).

2. National Labor Relations Act of 1935, ch. 372, 49 Stat. 449 (codified as amended at 29 U.S.C. §§ 151-69 (1982)).

3. Labor-Management Relations Act of 1947, ch. 120, 61 Stat. 136 (codified as amended in scattered sections of 29 U.S.C.).

4. Labor-Management Reporting and Disclosure Act of 1959, Pub. L. No. 86-257, 73 Stat. 519 (codified as amended in scattered sections of 29 U.S.C.).

5. Employee Retirement Income Security Act of 1974, Pub. L. No. 93-406, 88 Stat. 829 (codified as amended in scattered sections of 5, 18, 26, 29, 31 and 42 U.S.C.).

6. See Barbara J. Fick, "Political Abuse of Hiring Halls: Comparative Treatment under the NLRA and the LMRDA," *Industrial Relations Law Journal* 9 (1987): 339. See also Robert M. Bastress, "Application of a Constitutionally-Based Duty of Fair Representation to Union Hiring Halls," *West Virginia Law Review* 82 (1979): 31.

7. See Michael C. McClintock, *NLRB General Counsel: Unreviewable Power to Refuse to Issue an Unfair Labor Practice Complaint* (Arlington, Va.: Carrollton Press, 1980).

8. *NLRB v. Strong*, 393 U.S. 357 (1969); *Local 60, United Brotherhood of Carpenters v. NLRB*, 365 U.S. 651 (1961).

9. For an example of how a union can delay compliance with such an order, see the *Kuebler* case described in Chapter 2, footnote 20.

10. For a general discussion of the Act, see Janice R. Bellace and Alan D. Berkowitz, *The Landrum-Griffin Act: Twenty Years of Federal Protection of Union Members' Rights* (Philadelphia: Industrial Research Unit, The Wharton School, University of Pennsylvania, 1979); Clyde Summers, Joseph Rauh, and Herman Benson, *Union Democracy and Landrum-Griffin* (New York: Association for Union Democracy, 1986).

11. 403 U.S. 333, (1971).

12. When Congress enacted the National Labor Relations Act in 1935, it recognized that an impartial enforcement agency was needed to deal with unions and employers. Congress did not select the Department of Labor to enforce the NLRA; it instead created the National Labor Relations Board. When Congress passed the LMRDA in 1959, it should have recognized that whatever agency enforced the Act had to remain impartial towards union leaders, on the one hand, and rank-and-file members, especially dissidents, on the other. Unfortunately, Congress lacked the foresight to provide for such an impartial enforcement agency. Instead, it gave a large measure of the enforcement power and responsibility to the Department of Labor. That oversight remains the primary obstacle to effective enforcement of the LMRDA.

Herman Benson, "Union Democracy and the Landrum-Griffin Act," *Review of Law and Social Change* 11 (1982-83): 172-73.

13. The Department of Labor's Office of Labor Racketeering (OLR) is the exception that proves the rule. Precisely in order to shield the Office from the kind of inherent conflict between cooperating with and investigating organized labor, OLR was placed under the Department's independent Inspector General. Nevertheless, the Office has always faced an uphill battle within the Department for resources and support.

14. See Edgar N. James, "Union Democracy and the LMRDA: Autocracy and Insurgency in National Union Elections," *Harvard Civil Rights-Civil Liberties Law Review* 13 (1978): 247; Paul Levy, "Electing Union Officers under the LMRDA," *Cardozo Law Review* 5 (1984): 737; Dennis Kuhn and Charles Zech, "Labor Law and the Political Process in Labor Unions: Leviathan versus Voter Responsive Democracy," *Labor Law Journal* 37 (1986): 259; and Note, "The Limitations Period for Title I of the LMRDA: Protection of the Union Member's Civil Rights," *Indiana Law Review* 21 (1988): 587.

15. We urge the U.S. Senate's Permanent Subcommittee on Investigation to hold hearings on this issue and, if its conclusions are similar to ours, to draft legislation to resolve the problem.

16. Benson, "Union Democracy and the Landrum-Griffin Act," 153; Joseph Rauh, "Twenty-Five Years of Landrum-Griffin," *Union Democracy and Landrum-Griffin*, eds. Clyde Summers, Joseph Rauh and Herman Benson, (New York: Association for Union Democracy, 1986) 14-15; Note, "Union Elections and the LMRDA: Thirteen Years of Use and Abuse," *Yale Law Journal* 81 (1972): 409.

17. The authors of the bill were in part responding to Cosa Nostra's control over the Teamsters Union Central States Pension and Welfare Fund, and to the more general threat that labor racketeers pose to union members' pension and welfare funds.

18. ERISA § 404(a)(1)(B), 29 U.S.C.A. § 1104(a)(1)(b) is a codification of the common law rule that a fiduciary must act with the care, skill, prudence and diligence under the prevailing circumstances that a prudent man acting in a like capacity and familiar with such matters would use in the conduct of an enterprise of a like character and with like aims. See also Kirk F. Maldonado, "Fiduciary Responsibilities under ERISA," *The Labor Lawyer* 2 (1986): 819.

19. See e.g., testimony of Jeffrey N. Clayton, Ian D. Lanoff and Robert A.G. Monks, former Administrators of the Labor Department's Office of Pension and Welfare Benefits Programs (now called the Pension and Welfare Benefits Administration), before the United States Subcommittee on Oversight of Government Management of the Committee on Governmental Affairs, in *Hearings on the Department of Labor's Enforcement of the Employee Retirement Income Security Act [ERISA]*, 99th Cong., 1st sess. (Washington, D.C.: GPO, 1985) 4-94.

The Subcommittee's findings included the following:

Despite the millions of workers and retirees dependent on ERISA-covered pensions, as well as the huge monetary stakes involved, the Subcommittee found that enforcement of ERISA has not been a high priority of the Federal Government. Rather, the Department of Labor's implementation of the law has been characterized by grossly inadequate resources, longstanding deficiencies, frequently changing and inconsistent leadership, and shifting enforcement strategies.

With less than one percent of plans being audited each year by the Department of Labor, the chances of the Department detecting violations of ERISA are minuscule. The lack of meaningful oversight of pension plans and their fiduciaries could jeopardize the pension protections established by ERISA.

United States, Senate, Subcommittee on Oversight of Government Management of the Committee on Governmental Affairs, *A Report on the Department of Labor's Enforcement of the Employee Retirement Income Security Act (ERISA)*, 99th Cong., 2d sess. (Washington, D.C.: GPO, 1986) 4.

See also Office of the Inspector General, U.S. Department of Labor, *Semiannual Report* (October 1, 1988-March 31, 1989) 1-5; and Office of the Inspector General, U.S. Department of Labor, *Semiannual Report* (April 1-September 30, 1989) 1-2, 11-13.

20. An electronic data processing system now being implemented within the Department of Labor should cause these reports to be available within a reasonable period after they are filed.

21. United States Department of Labor, Pension and Welfare Benefits Administration, Research Office, Washington, D.C.

22. If the expectancy is that audits will serve as compliance audits, then the audit required under existing law cannot be found adequate because that is not the audit's objective. An audit is designed to provide reasonable assurance—not a guarantee—that the financial statements do not contain material misstatements. But such an audit is not designed to measure or confirm compliance with ERISA or with the full body of regulatory requirements applicable to covered plans.

See Andrew J. Capelli, Chairman, Employee Benefit Plans Committee of the American Institute of Certified Public Accountants, "Statement on Federal Statutes, Regulations, Reports, and Oversight of Private Pension Plans under ERISA," submitted to the Employment and Housing Subcommittee of the Committee on Government Operations, United States House of Representatives, August 2, 1989.

23. By contrast, the President's Commission on Organized Crime cited the case of a small dental fund where sixty-eight percent of the money went to administration and thirty-two percent went to benefits. President's Commission on Organized Crime, *Organized Crime and Labor-Management Racketeering in the United States, Record of Hearing VI, Chicago, Illinois* (Washington, D.C.: GPO, April 1985) 521, 599.

24. In September 1984, New York's insurance law was recodified. The Article which had previously governed these funds, Article 3-A, became Article 44 (N.Y. Ins. Law §§ 4401-14 (McKinney 1984)). The law remains essentially the same.

25. Section 805(b) of the Comprehensive Crime Control Act of 1984 amends ERISA and chides the Secretary of Labor for past failure to act against racketeering. Underlying passage of Section 805 was Congress' conclusion that the bane of employee benefit plans and unions was not only the loopholes which §§ 801 through 804 address, but also laxity by the Department of Labor. See Danielle Panter, "The Changes Accomplished by the Labor Racketeering Amendments of the Comprehensive Crime Control Act of 1984," *Labor Law Journal* 36 (1985): 744.

At hearings leading up to passage of the act, Senator Sam Nunn stated that "on the Teamsters investigation, it was almost as if the Labor Department—and I say almost because I never did find anything this direct. But it was almost as if they said, 'anytime you fellows investigating out there get anywhere near organized crime, back off, we'll find a way to exclude that.'" United States, Senate, Subcommittee on Labor of the Committee on Labor and Human Resources, *Labor Management Racketeering Act of 1981: Hearings on S. 1785*, 97th Cong., 2nd sess., 10 (Washington, D.C.: GPO, 1982) 29. Senator Nunn attributed this problem to a misconceived sense that "if you root out corruption in organized labor, you offend organized labor" (37).

26. AUD operates on a meager budget, with extremely modest outside funding. Nevertheless, it plays a vigorous and crucial role in advising union grievants and dissidents, publishing an informative newsletter (*Union Democracy Review*), sponsoring conferences, and keeping the issue of workers' rights alive. AUD is a model for the Center for the Study of Union Democracy which we recommend in this chapter, and itself might well be the nucleus of the proposed Center.

27. We are not the first to see the advantage of expanding the jurisdiction of an office which has already proven its effectiveness as an advocate. See *Insuring Our Future: Report of the Governor's Advisory Commission on Liability Insurance* (1986).

28. While it is, of course, appropriate to be concerned about the rights of members of all unions, we recommend that, at least in the beginning, the Advocate's responsibility be limited to the New York City construction industry's trade unions. This experiment in union democracy could thus be tested by concentrating OUMA's resources on this single, troubled area.

29. Section 104 of the Landrum-Griffin Act (codified at 29 U.S.C. § 414) requires labor organizations to provide, on request, copies of collective bargaining agreements to members covered by such agreements. Few rank-and-file union members are aware of their rights or of the Secretary of Labor's responsibility for enforcement.

Another frequently ignored provision is § 201 (codified at 29 U.S.C. § 431) which requires labor organizations to adopt and to file copies of their constitutions and by-laws and various financial reports. While labor organizations are required to make such information available to members, many unions ignore this requirement.

30. The U.S. Department of Labor takes the position that it has no responsibility or authority for enforcing § 105, and that enforcement of this section can be accomplished only through private legal actions brought by union members. Assuming that this interpretation is correct, we propose that the law be amended to authorize Department of Labor enforcement.

31. More specifically, we make the following recommendations, which are closely based on those of the Association for Union Democracy: the U.S. Department of Labor should adopt a regulation that, within ninety days of its adoption, requires all labor organizations to certify to the Department of Labor that they have informed their current members of the provisions of the Landrum-Griffin Act in accordance with § 105. Thereafter, all new members of labor organizations shall be informed of the provisions of the Act within ninety days of their entry as members. This regulation would specifically require labor organizations to inform their members of the conditions under which they may obtain copies of collective bargaining agreements, constitutions, by-laws and financial reports as specified in the Act. Labor organizations should be required to comply with this regulation by mailing to the home of each member the full text of the Act printed in a minimum type size of 10 point. Alternatively, a summary of the Act, prepared by the U.S. Department of Labor and in a form authorized by it, could be printed in the union's newspaper or mailed to each member.

32. As a recent law review note explains, "The Landrum-Griffin Act cannot achieve its goal of union democracy in a union captured by corrupt leadership. ...Union officials intent on using the union for illicit purposes and personal gain through embezzlement, fraud and kickbacks, will not respond to members who desire to clean up their unions." Eric Tilles, "Union Receiverships under RICO: A Union Democracy Perspective," *University of Pennsylvania Law Review* 137 (1989): 929, 940.

33. In the 1960s, Frank Schonfeld, after several electoral defeats, was finally able to win election to the top position in a corrupt Painters Union, but the corrupt regime was able to seize power back from Schonfeld six years later. Schonfeld then fought on alone, without the backing of any government agency. The story is partly told in *Schonfeld v. Raftery*, 275 F.Supp. 128 (S.D.N.Y.), *aff'd*, 381 F.2d 446 (2d Cir. 1967).

34. We note that one New Jersey developer has mounted a challenge to alleged racketeering by carpenter and cement mason union locals and eleven concrete contractors by filing a civil RICO suit seeking both treble and punitive damages from and injunctive relief against three business agents and all eleven contractors. *Johnston Development Group v. Carpenters Local Union No. 1578*, 89 Civ. 566 (D.N.J. 1989).

35. The federal Racketeer Influenced and Corrupt Organizations Act (RICO) is set forth at 18 U.S.C. §§ 1961-68. New York's Organized Crime Control Act (OCCA) is contained primarily in N.Y. Penal Law Article 460. Under RICO, defendants need not be members of a criminal enterprise to be guilty of racketeering. Under OCCA, however, only those employed by or associated with a criminal enterprise may be charged. Nevertheless, the legislative history makes clear that OCCA meant to include within the meaning of the term "criminal enterprise" not only traditional criminal syndicates such as Cosa Nostra families, but also captive labor unions whose leaders demonstrate a shared criminal purpose. See Donnino, Practice Commentary to P.L. Article 460. (McKinney 1987).

36. Under RICO's provisions, a civil suit can be brought without instituting a criminal proceeding; see 18 U.S.C. § 1964 (a). Under OCCA, a prior criminal conviction is required; see N.Y. CPLR § 1353(1) (McKinney Supp. 1990).

37. *United States v. Local 560, International Brotherhood of Teamsters*, 581 F.Supp. 279 (1984), *aff'd*, 780 F.2d 267 (3d Cir. 1985), *cert. denied*, 476 U.S. 1140 (1986); *United States v. Local 6A, Cement and Concrete Workers*, 86 Civ. 4819 (S.D.N.Y. 1986); *United States v. The Bonanno Organized Crime Family*, 87 Civ. 2974 (E.D.N.Y. 1987) (trusteeship over Teamster Local 814); *United States v. Local 30/30B, United Slate, Tile and Composition Roofers*, 87 Civ. 7718 (E.D.Pa. 1987); *United States v. International Brotherhood of Teamsters*, 708 F.Supp. 1388 (S.D.N.Y. 1989). For a discussion of the advantages and disadvantages of using RICO in union corruption cases, see Garth L. Mangum, "RICO *versus* Landrum-Griffin as Weapons against Union Corruption: The Teamster Case," *Labor Law Journal* 40 (February 1989): 94.

38. For a discussion of the common law and statutory precedents for judicially supervised reform of labor unions, and an evaluation of leading examples of union reform litigation, see Michael J. Goldberg, "Cleaning Labor's House: Institutional Reform Litigation in the Labor Movement," *Duke Law Journal* (1989): 563. Goldberg discusses in detail several of the union trusteeships cited in the previous footnote.

39. See Tilles, 929.

40. See Seymour Lipset, Martin Trow and James Coleman, *Union Democracy*, (Garden City, N.Y.: Free Press, Anchor Books, 1962). See also Herman Benson, "The Fight for Union Democracy," *Unions in Transition*, ed. Seymour Lipset, (San Francisco, Cal.: Institute for Contemporary Studies Press, 1986) 323-70; William Leiserson, *American Trade Union Democracy*, (New York: Columbia University Press, 1959); J. Edelstein and Malcolm Warner, *Comparative Union Democracy*, (New Brunswick, N.J.: Transaction Books, 1979); Clyde Summers, "Democracy in a One-Party State: Perspectives from Landrum-Griffin," *Maryland Law Review* 43 (1984): 93.

41. John Hutchinson, *The Imperfect Union: A History of Corruption in American Trade Unions* (New York: E.P. Dutton, 1970) 374.

42. Efforts by the court-appointed administrator, investigating officer and elections officer to monitor and supervise the International Brotherhood of Teamsters have been plagued by dilatory union tactics. Contempt proceedings against the union are pending in Chicago, Cleveland and Newark. See generally, "Teamster Battling Supervision Is Held in Contempt," *New York Times*, 10 December 1989, late ed.: I, 4; Ann Hagedorn, "Carberry's Corruption Fight Shifts Focus to Teamsters," *Wall Street Journal*, 14 July 1989, eastern ed.: B1.

43. Another option is to seek NLRB supervision of the hiring hall, as was done in the case of Operating Engineers Local 138 on Long Island in 1962.

44. Court-appointed prison special masters often have substantial staff support, and their task—to monitor a public institution's progress toward constitutional compliance—is far less challenging than that of a union trustee faced with reorganizing a sprawling union local consisting of thousands of members, dozens of racketeers and hundreds of contracts.

45. In the Teamsters Local 814 case, *United States v. The Bonanno Organized Crime Family*, 87 Civ. 2974 (E.D.N.Y. 1987), the federal judge's order stated that "every effort should be made to minimize costs incurred by the court-appointed trustee and to preserve the fiscal solvency of Local 814 and the Local 814 funds." See Consent Judgment with Local 814, Local 814 Executive Board, Local 814 Funds, Ignatius Bracco and Vito Gentile, October 8, 1987, 14.

46. While a federal court's equitable and remedial powers are very broad, federal legislation would probably be needed to implement this idea.

47. President's Commission on Organized Crime, *The Edge: Organized Crime, Business, and Labor Unions* (Report to the President and the Attorney General) (Washington, D.C.: GPO, October 1985) 318.

48. See Lee Modjeska, "The NLRB and the Mob," *Labor Law Journal* 37 (1986): 625.

CHAPTER 8

Attacking corporate racketeering

Introduction

Because corrupt labor union officials have been the most prosecuted racketeers in the construction industry, they are also the
most visible. Businessmen, however, have been no less culpable.
Much of the industry's labor racketeering occurs when contractors seek an illicit competitive edge by either bribing union officials to avoid collective bargaining contracts or by using them to
form and discipline contractor or supplier cartels. Such conduct
is appropriately described as "corporate racketeering."[1] Corporate racketeering includes the corrupt domination of markets;
bid rigging; bribery of public, union and other officials; false
invoicing and other billing frauds; frauds on union pension and
welfare funds; tax evasion; and the manipulation and falsification of business records to support these and other crimes.

Types of Corporate Racketeering:
A Hypothetical Account

Consider the case of an ambitious young contractor with a concrete pouring company in New York City. For a few years he has
carried out jobs by himself, or with a small workforce he employs
on a job-by-job basis. His business has grown steadily. Like other
contractors he knows, he occasionally cuts costs by using inferior
concrete, by paying less than the prevailing wage, and by paying
off City inspectors in the rare instances when his noncompliance
is detected. In violation of his collective bargaining agreement,
he often employs nonunion labor to work alongside his union
employees.

After a few years, his success comes to the attention of the
union local representing concrete workers. Suddenly, he finds
that the union hiring hall is sending him workers who lack skills

201

and motivation; his jobs are plagued by accidents, mistakes and delays. The shop steward sent by the union is causing constant problems—refusing to work, directing "rule book" slowdowns, insisting on literal compliance with technical and commonly overlooked worksite requirements, and protecting no-show workers. Eventually, a union business agent reaches out to the contractor, promising to help straighten things out. The fee for his help is one percent of the contract price and two dollars per cubic yard of concrete poured.[2] As soon as the young contractor pays off the business agent, his labor problems subside and his contracts get back on track. As he gets to know the business agent better, he learns that, by "playing it smart," many of his competitors are able to avoid contractual obligations, including overtime and employer contributions to union pension and welfare funds. They may even avoid maintaining a union shop. He too starts making periodic payments to various business agents to gain this competitive edge.

To obtain cash for his proliferating payoffs, the young contractor learns a number of cash generating schemes. For example, he arranges for his supplier to give him an invoice showing delivery of fifty-five yards of concrete when only fifty yards are delivered. He gives the supplier a check for the full amount and takes back a cash "refund" of the overpayment for the five yards not delivered, minus a one percent "administration fee."[3] Thus, the contractor obtains cash to use for payoffs and an invoice to document falsely a tax-deductible business expense. Another way that he meets his growing need for cash is to make out and cash checks to fictitious workers on his payroll; to facilitate cashing, he uses a local check-cashing operation that asks no questions.

The young contractor starts bidding for larger projects. Failing to win any of these bids, he begins to suspect that a "fix" is in. When he is low bidder on one contract, the union business agent tells him to withdraw his bid because the contract has already been allocated to another firm. The business agent explains that there is a club of contractors who cooperate in rigging bids and allocating jobs.[4] The union assures cooperation; anyone who challenges the system would soon be without workers or critical supplies.[5] In response to his request for club membership, the business agent further explains that such decisions are not in his hands. "The shots are being called by some 'wise guys' (Cosa Nostra members)," he is told. "You have to know somebody to get yourself fixed up."

The young contractor has seen mob figures at various construction sites and, on a few occasions, has had drinks with one of them. He now asks his underworld acquaintance for help. The acquaintance says he will see what he can do. After a time, the acquaintance tells him that he can be of some help, and that the contractor will be allowed to pour concrete on a $1 million project in the Bronx. He tells the young contractor how much to bid and what he must kick back. This job leads to others, and soon the young contractor, his business thriving, is working in a *de facto* partnership with racketeers. The racketeers secure him work, take their cut up front, and occasionally ask him to put a no-show worker on the payroll or to pay someone for nonexistent materials or services. On occasion, he is told to put in a complementary bid on a contract that has been fixed for another mob-supported company.

He comes to know mob "fixers," who have "hooks" into the unions covering many of the trades on which he is dependent— teamsters, carpenters, concrete workers, wirelathers and other specialties. Sometimes he is told to use certain subcontractors and to buy his materials from certain suppliers at predetermined, inflated prices. He encounters few problems from ancillary unions or contractors. It seems to him that the mob controls every part of the construction industry. Over time, he makes a great deal of money, for himself and for the mob. When one of the mob's favored companies is tied up by a criminal investigation, more business is shifted to his firm. Finally, he becomes a member of the cartel which apportions among its members all concrete construction jobs over two million dollars. However, only one firm is permitted to take the biggest jobs (those over $12 million).[6]

After several years of prospering as a member of the inner circle, his Cosa Nostra connection informs him that he must take in a silent partner and accept a back seat in running his company. He is told to accept whatever changes his new partner makes, including a reduced share of the profits and loss of control over the books. Still thinking of himself as essentially a legitimate and independent businessman, he refuses. Thereafter, his work diminishes rapidly, as he is underbid on every major contract he seeks. In a short time, he realizes that firms in the inner circle have made the final compromise; the club is comprised of firms owned or controlled by the mob itself.[7] He remains now on the periphery of the industry, performing what small jobs he can still get, and still paying the business agent for labor peace.

Only a tiny fraction of the tens of thousands of developers, contractors and suppliers in the New York City construction industry have become as deeply involved in corruption and racketeering as the hypothetical contractor described above. As the level of criminal activity escalates, the number of companies involved decreases. In essence, we are describing a pyramid, with many firms engaging in the kind of corruption discussed at the beginning of the story, and fewer firms being involved at each successive level as the story goes on. While only a very small number of contractors actually become partners of Cosa Nostra, a large number engage in labor payoffs, cash-generating schemes and bribing public and labor officials. Even developers and contractors who insulate themselves from payoffs, frauds and other corrupt activities accept such criminality as an unalterable fact of life.

Why Corporate Racketeering Thrives in the New York City Construction Industry

Because of the highly competitive nature of the construction industry (and low barriers to entry), there are powerful incentives for and pressures on corporations to gain a competitive edge.[8] The opportunity to circumvent the collective bargaining agreement by operating wholly or partially nonunion, to pay less than union scale, and to avoid making mandated employer contributions to health and welfare funds, may provide such an edge. Paying straight time rather than an overtime premium can mean the difference between modest and huge profits; it can sometimes mean the difference between bankruptcy and prosperity. The ability to purchase supplies for less than one's competitors (because of a tie-in with a mob-connected seller) may mean the difference between winning or losing a multimillion dollar contract. The ability to pay off a building inspector to overlook problems or simply to expedite an inspection can save hundreds of thousands of dollars in interest charges. The ability to count on the union's job referral system for good workers and labor peace may be the difference between survival and success on the one hand, and failure and extinction on the other. Cosa Nostra has flourished in the New York City construction industry for so many decades because of its unique ability to provide businesses with a competitive edge.

Strategies to Combat Corporate Racketeering

A number of characteristics of New York City's construction industry create substantial incentives for contractors and suppliers to engage in corruption and racketeering. These characteristics contributing to racketeering susceptibility principally include the fragility of the construction process, the high cost of delay, the power of unions, and the balkanization of collective bargaining among the many unions and employer associations. To a large extent, these characteristics are "givens" which cannot be eliminated. However, law enforcement, government and the industry itself can take action to affect some of these "givens" in a way that will reduce corporate racketeering.

We recommend three basic strategies to combat corporate racketeering: 1) opportunity blocking that makes it more difficult for contractors to make illegal payoffs; 2) stimulating competition in order to counteract monopolization and cartelization; and 3) increasing the risks and costs of criminal activities.

Opportunity Blocking: Using Certified Investigative Auditing Firms to Deter Payoffs and Make Them Easier to Detect

If law enforcement officials could better trace the flow of money from general contractors to specialty contractors, suppliers and consultants, they would be in a much stronger position to detect patterns of corrupt activities, identify key corrupt and racketeering figures, and block the means by which Cosa Nostra receives its money. If contractors had to account fully and accurately for their revenues and expenditures, law enforcement and other government agencies would be able to take some of the profits out of corporate racketeering. Racketeers could be forced to forfeit their ill-gotten gains and pay taxes owed in an industry where millions of dollars of taxes are evaded annually.

Adoption of the Certified Investigative Auditing Firm (CIAF) requirement on public construction projects (see Chapter 6) would make it substantially more difficult for contractors and suppliers to engage in corruption and racketeering. The building and business activities of the general contractors for which the CIAFs would work, as well as the activities of the subcontractors and suppliers of the general contractors, would all be under constant scrutiny by the CIAFs. Schemes for generating cash, difficult for an outsider to detect, would be apparent to CIAF auditors; the benefits obtained by bribes to labor officials or construction inspectors would likewise be apparent. Contractors who heretofore felt they had no alternative but to make payoffs might resist shakedowns with the now credible claim that payoffs would be detected.

CIAFs would also help deter and detect corruption in the work site inspection process. In Chapter 9, we will propose that much of the inspection workload now undertaken by the Department of Buildings be assumed by independent architects and engineers hired by contractors and builders. This form of self-inspection would be bolstered by CIAF monitoring. CIAFs would also be responsible for designing and monitoring loss-prevention strategies in conjunction with the Department of Investigation, the Office of Construction and the proposed Office of Construction Corruption Prevention.

CIAFs should initially be required only for public construction projects in excess of $5 million, with two percent of the contract price being allocated for their funding. The results of this initiative should be carefully monitored and—if successful and where appropriate—extended to the private sector.

Such a requirement would not be unprecedented.[9] Federal and state regulations which mandate expenditures of private funds for oversight exist in almost all sectors of the economy. For example, the Securities and Exchange Commission (SEC) requires that publicly held corporations comply with extensive regulations and procedures including registration of securities, making public certain financial information, and maintaining certain records and reports.[10] In order to assure compliance, the SEC requires public corporations to hire certified public accountants to provide periodic audits. Likewise, state liquor authorities monitor the accounts and operations of dram shops. One of the most heavily monitored of all industries is casino gambling, where government inspectors, funded by casino owners, are assigned to scrutinize books and records, the operation of the gaming tables, and virtually every phase and aspect of the business. Another example is the hazardous waste disposal industry.[11] State permits are required for such activities as the transportation, treatment, storage or disposal of the waste material. Detailed reports, tests and evaluations must be continuously supplied to the regulatory agency as a condition for obtaining and maintaining the permit. A permittee must agree to provide access to the premises by government inspectors at any reasonable hour for the purpose of inspecting facilities, operations or records, or of taking samples of waste materials. In certain cases that require close, ongoing government scrutiny, "environmental monitors"—employees of the regulatory agency whose salary and expenses are borne by the permittee—are assigned to a particular facility or operation to assure strict compliance with rules and regulations.

CIAFs must be independent and institutionally free to expose corrupt activities. At the same time, they must be useful to project managers and protective of business and trade secrets. General and prime contractors must be encouraged to use CIAF services as management tools without fearing that discoveries of improper practices could be used by competitors or by potential litigants in suits against the construction company. We therefore would require the CIAFs to be certified and licensed by DOI, which would have sufficient power to mandate appropriate conduct. The CIAFs would provide reports to the Inspector General of the agency supervising the public works, as well as to the general or prime contractors who employ them. Such reports, however, must be protected from public disclosure by the CIAF or any government agency. Such secrecy provisions would not apply to transmittal of information to law enforcement personnel, in particular the OCTF Research and Analysis Unit. Thus the information obtained by a CIAF could be used to 1) analyze current industry trends; 2) develop approaches and strategies for new investigations; and 3) provide the bases for more effective

OCCP regulations. CIAFs could further play a critical role in monitoring the "self inspections" by independent architects and engineers.

While we are convinced that development of the CIAF program would be valuable in controlling corruption and racketeering, we are also aware that potential problems and unresolved issues exist. Clearly, some contractors might seek to hire the least aggressive or least competent CIAF, and some CIAFs would find it in their long-term interest to be accommodating to those who offer the prospect of future work. Nevertheless, similar concerns have not made ineffective SEC regulations involving corporations' relationships with privately retained certified public accountants.[12] If inappropriate patterns of hiring occur, DOI might require that a contractor use a particular or randomly selected CIAF. While we also believe the use of CIAFs might prove beneficial in private construction, the need to have sufficient experience in the public sector in dealing with these unresolved issues convinces us to propose restricting its application initially to public construction.

Stimulating Competition

Corporate racketeering has stifled competition in many sectors of the construction industry. Numerous contractor and supplier clubs and cartels allocate contracts. Even the perception of racketeering operates as a barrier to entry for new firms uncertain about how to conduct business in an atmosphere notorious for labor and corporate racketeering. Under these circumstances, every effort should be made to foster and encourage as much business competition as possible. The more competition, the more difficult it will be for racketeers to establish and maintain cartels, clubs, and collusive bidding. Thus, we offer the following recommendations to foster more competition.

Better Utilization of Civil and Criminal Antitrust Remedies

The federal and state antitrust laws aim to deter and punish price fixing, collusive bidding and illegal cartels. In addition to fines and jail terms, the antitrust laws provide that injured parties can sue for three times their losses. Recently, the federal government has effectively used the antitrust laws to attack bid rigging among road contractors throughout the country.[13] Nevertheless, neither federal nor state antitrust enforcement has been systematically deployed against business crime in the New York City construction industry.[14]

New York State's Donnelly Act[15] generally follows federal antitrust statutes. It prohibits all contracts or combinations which tend or are designed to eliminate or stifle competition, effect a monopoly, artificially affect prices, restrict production, or in any way control the market to the detriment of the general public. It empowers the state, political subdivisions, public authorities and individuals to bring civil suits seeking treble damages plus costs and attorneys' fees. The statute contains criminal provisions with maximum punishment for individuals of up to four years incarceration, plus fines of up to $100,000. Corporations can be fined up to $1 million. The State Attorney General may also bring an action to restrain and prevent violations of the Act.

Given that the New York City construction industry is so rife with price fixing, collusive bidding and cartels, there ought to be a major antitrust initiative specifically focused on it.[16] Unfortunately, county district attorneys' offices do not have antitrust expertise, perhaps because antitrust activity is often seen more as a civil than a criminal matter. Moreover, there seems to be a widely shared misconception in law enforcement circles that only the Attorney General can bring an antitrust action. In actuality, the Donnelly Act allows any district attorney to bring a criminal antitrust charge, but gives the Attorney General the authority to intervene.[17] It is, perhaps, from this right of intervention that the erroneous assumption has evolved that the Attorney General's jurisdiction is exclusive.

There are occasions where the prohibition of business practices having some anticompetitive features would itself have broad economic implications. In such cases, a consistent statewide policy is appropriate, and may be established and maintained only by permitting intervention by the Attorney General. In such cases, it is sensible to give the Attorney General this right and to suffer its negative effect on the initiative of the district attorneys. But where, as in the construction industry, racketeering influence and the actions of criminal enterprises result in collusion, cartels and other anticompetitive behavior, no such concerns pertain. In such cases we recommend that the county district attorneys, along with OCTF, be encouraged to enforce the state antitrust law and that, accordingly, the right of intervention not apply.

Public Benefit Corporations

The City and State should take every possible action to encourage construction and supply firms to enter those specialty markets within the New York City construction industry which are dominated by racketeering and corrupt companies. Unfortunately, there are some sections of the industry where corrupt firms are the only ones capable of providing certain supplies or services. When the City is faced with the unpalatable alternative of either dealing with racketeers or not completing the job, it must be creative and aggressive in encouraging competitive alternatives. One possible way might be to create some form of public sector option, such as a public benefit corporation.[18] Where geophysical factors contribute to the racketeer's monopoly or cartel, the City should seek to use eminent domain powers to break the corrupt monopoly.

The City's response to Cosa Nostra's monopoly over concrete production was a step in the right direction, even though the actual implementation of the City's plan has been the subject of substantial criticism. In 1986, New York City sought bids from contractors willing to supply the City's concrete needs in Manhattan. More than 300 companies nationwide were contacted. An agreement was reached with the West 57th Street Concrete Corporation (West 57th).

The City agreed to clear and renovate a Manhattan site for the new concrete plant at a cost of $2 million, and to provide West 57th with a five year rent-free lease. West 57th agreed to construct the concrete plant and to supply all the City's concrete needs, through direct purchases by contractors working on City projects, for a period of five years at a fixed price of $68.85 per cubic yard. West 57th could sell any concrete in excess of the City's requirements to the private market at a price no higher than that of the fixed public price. While this was not structured as a public benefit corporation, the idea was similar.[19]

Shortly thereafter, the dominant concrete producers filed suit to block the creation of this plant. The court supported the new concrete plant saying that "there was clearly a rational basis for the City...to conclude that a monopoly existed in the concrete industry," and that "it was the duty of the City to take action."[20]

West 57th experienced many difficulties in commencing business. It failed to secure the necessary financing for the new plant, and therefore failed to become fully operational. In September 1987, the City allowed the company's owner to sell out to F.E.D. Concrete Company. By early 1990, the plant, under new management, was producing enough concrete to fulfill the City's needs. Meanwhile, however, the market price of concrete has fallen to levels below the agreed fixed price. As a result, the City is paying West 57th more than the market price for the concrete. The City argues, however, that the market price would not have fallen without the threat of competition from West 57th. Overall, the City's initiative, even if not executed as effectively as it might have been, was an important precedent that should be expanded upon in the future. It represents a valuable experiment in using publicly fostered competition as an antidote to corporate racketeering.

Encouraging More Firms to Enter the New York City Construction Market
Many firms are deterred from doing business in the New York City construction market by the perception that they will be shipwrecked on the twin shoals of City building regulations and Cosa Nostra racketeering. Thus, every effort should be made to rationalize and modernize the building code and the City's administrative apparatus which enforces it. This topic is dealt with at length in Chapter 10.

To encourage new firms to enter the New York City construction market, there must be an aggressive program by City building agencies to recruit a larger pool of contractors into the public construction market. In November 1988, the New York Building Congress provided such a forum by hosting a two-day conference entitled "Rebuilding New York." Commissioners from all mayoral, building and several state agencies, and the chief executive officers from a number of authorities with large capital construction programs (such as the Battery Park City Authority, the Port Authority, the Dormitory Authority and the Metropolitan

Transit Authority) were invited to describe new business opportunities. The conference sought to attract firms not currently competing in the public sector. More than 200 firms attended, thirty percent of which were from out of town. This kind of outreach is necessary if the City hopes to promote the competition that will be necessary to break the cartels in certain sectors of the construction market.

New firms must be assured protection from unlawful economic retaliation by those seeking to limit the number of contractors competing for public works projects. We believe that the comprehensive crime-control strategy set forth in Chapter 6 will go far toward providing that protection and support.

Fostering and protecting competition should be one of the highest priorities of the proposed Office of Construction Corruption Prevention (OCCP) and the Construction Industry Strike Force (CISF). OCCP should work closely with OCTF's Research and Analysis Unit to identify those sectors of the industry marked by clubs and cartels, mount an aggressive outreach program through the Office of Construction to encourage new companies to enter those sectors, and mobilize law enforcement and building agencies to protect those new companies from unlawful economic retaliation.

Bolstering Deterrence

Historically, to the extent that corruption and racketeering in the construction industry were conceptualized as crime problems, they were mostly thought of as a "mob" problem or a "labor racketeering" problem. While the mob and labor racketeers play very important roles, and while the mob is involved in corporate racketeering, it is important for a comprehensive crime-control strategy to focus on ordinary construction businesses whose cooperation or accommodation (whether willing or unwilling) makes these criminal conspiracies possible.

A comprehensive crime-control strategy cannot make significant progress as long as developers, contractors and suppliers perceive little risk and few costs in making payoffs and in cooperating with or accommodating mobsters and racketeers. Law enforcement must incapacitate, punish and deter corporate racketeering. Existing laws and resources must be used more vigorously against corporate offenders, sanctions must be enhanced, and certain reforms of substantive and procedural criminal laws effectuated.[21]

More Vigorous and Even-Handed Use of Labor Bribery Statutes
Payments made to and received by labor officials are illegal in New York, either as bribes as defined in Penal Law Article 180, or as prohibited financial transactions in Labor Law §§ 723 and 725.[22] Under the Penal Law, it is unlawful to confer, or offer or agree to confer, any benefit on a labor official in order to influence the exercise of the official's duties. Giving or receiving a bribe is a felony, punishable by up to seven-years' imprisonment.

Historically, prosecutors have targeted bribe recipients rather than bribe givers, partly on the theory that the bribe receiver, who is violating a fiduciary obligation, is generally more culpable, and partly because bribe givers, when apprehended, often claim that they were victims of extortionate demands—that is, that the bribes paid were not given voluntarily, but in response to threats of economic harm. New York law, unlike federal law, provides that coercion is an absolute defense to bribery. Such a policy is wrong when the "threat" is to enforce the legitimate terms of a collective bargaining agreement or to require a nonunion contractor to sign one. In such situations, the "threat" may be a real one, deserving punishment as the crime of coercion. Nonetheless, the contractor who "succumbs" to the threat—by paying money to avoid a legitimate obligation—has achieved an improper result. There must be a credible deterrent to contractors making such payments; they must perceive a real likelihood of risks and costs—and not just benefits—associated with responding to such demands by paying the corrupt union official rather than calling law enforcement.

Both bribe giving and bribe receiving require proof of a *quid pro quo*—an understanding that the giver of a benefit will get something in return. The Labor Law also makes it unlawful for an employer to give, or for a labor official to receive, anything of value, but it does not require proof of a *quid pro quo*. The giving or receiving of such unlawful gratuities is punishable as a misdemeanor by no more than one year of incarceration. Because they are misdemeanors, unlawful gratuities are rarely prosecuted in state court (except as a sort of "lesser included" offense of a concurrent charge of bribery), regardless of the size of the unlawful payment.

The explanation for the difference in treatment of bribes and gratuities is obvious: the former are, by definition, necessarily and explicitly corrupt, while the latter are more in the nature of a conflict of interest. However, even with gratuities, the corrupt purpose is implicit, and once the payment reaches a certain amount, its corrupting effect is inevitable, even if the *quid pro quo* cannot otherwise be established beyond a reasonable doubt. Congress recognized this when it amended the Taft-Hartley Law to make payments exceeding $1,000 felonies, with or without proof of a *quid pro quo*.[23] We recommend that New York's Labor Law be amended in the same way.

The Penal Law provisions prohibiting labor bribery and bribe receiving also do not differentiate according to the amount of the bribe. Obviously, the size of the bribe is some measure of the benefit the bribe giver expects to receive. The legislature recently recognized this gradation of culpability in the context of official corruption. A 1986 amendment to the Penal Law made bribes over $10,000, paid to and received by a public servant, a C felony punishable by up to fifteen-years' imprisonment. Bribes below $10,000 are left as D felonies punishable by up to seven-years' imprisonment.[24] A parallel change should be enacted, making violation of Penal Law Sections 180.15 and 180.30 a C felony when the amount of the bribe exceeds $10,000.

Two more changes in the law are necessary if bribery of and bribe receiving by a labor official are to be effectively and even-handedly prosecuted. The first change is in New York's accomplice corroboration rule, which severely restricts the ability to prosecute bribery transactions. Under this rule, neither the bribe giver nor the bribe receiver can be convicted on the testimony of the other unless independent corroboration of such testimony exists.[25] The second change concerns New York's transactional immunity law, which precludes the prosecution of any person who has received immunity during his appearance before a New York grand jury, even when the case against that person is built on evidence entirely independent of his testimony.[26] Taken together, these two statutes often impede prosecution of all persons identified in an investigation as party to a corrupt conspiracy.

One example of the many problems created by New York's immunity law arises when a cooperating witness's corrupt activities are uncovered independently of, and after, the witness's grand jury testimony. New York's broad immunity law will likely prevent prosecution of the witness based on the new evidence. Taking the safe road of not calling the witness before the grand jury means foregoing the witness's useful testimony. Using the witness, on the other hand, means prosecution of only one side of the corrupt transaction at the expense of prosecuting the other. Giving prosecutors these two bare choices may harm an investigation, no matter which decision is made.

Typical of the problems created by the accomplice corroboration rule are those that arise when a union official agrees to cooperate only after he is indicted or convicted for bribe receiving. The contractors who have bribed him cannot be prosecuted based upon his accomplice testimony unless corroboration of his allegations exists. Such corroboration may be impossible to develop, however, because the prior disclosure of his indictment may make covert investigation of the contractors impossible.

Together, these two statutes often have the practical effect of requiring an early, irrevocable decision to prosecute the bribe giver or the bribe receiver, even when it later appears that the other choice should have been made, or both otherwise could—and should—have been prosecuted.

Neither of these sets of problems exist in the federal system, or in those of most other states, since the immunity given to a grand jury witness in these jurisdictions is "use" immunity, rather than New York's transactional immunity. Furthermore, juries are simply warned to be wary of accomplice testimony, but are not, as in New York, precluded from relying on it to convict.

The New York State District Attorney's Association has long advocated changing New York's immunity and accomplice corroboration statutes. Because of the obstacles they create in prosecuting union (and official) corruption in the construction industry, we firmly endorse the association's proposals.

More Effective Tax Enforcement

Corruption and racketeering among construction and supply companies is rife with cash payoffs, money laundering and tax evasion. Consequently, massive violations of corporate, partnership, individual and sales taxes occur. Practically every type of corporate racketeering results in violations of state and local tax laws.[27] For example, a contractor's cash payroll scheme generally includes a failure to withhold federal and state taxes and to report cash wages; employees thus evade income tax by under-reporting their true wages. Payoffs to organized crime also involve tax crimes, since many companies falsely record these bribes on their books as tax qualifying business expenses, and the recipient of payoffs is not likely to report them as income. The strategic use of tax laws against Cosa Nostra members and other racketeers should be given higher priority; historically, such prosecutions have been a major law enforcement tool.

One potential jurisdictional hurdle affecting the ability of New York City-based prosecutors to pursue tax cheats needs legislative attention. Prior to 1985, state law provided for jurisdiction over a defendant charged with tax fraud either in the county of his residence or in the county in which he received any income, as well as the county where the return was or should have been filed. In 1985, the state legislature, while amending the statute for unrelated reasons, failed to reenact that jurisdictional provision. As a result, all prosecutions under the state tax law must now take place in Albany County, where every New York State tax return is deemed "filed."[28] There are obvious problems with such a long distance presentment. The tax crime prosecutions likely to arise in the context of corruption and racketeering will generally be part of much larger prosecutions in New York City. If the tax counts can be prosecuted only in Albany County, they will likely never be brought by the New York City District Attorneys. On the other hand, the Albany County District Attorney, even if of a mind to prosecute, will face severe logistical problems, such as securing attendance of downstate witnesses who would be required to testify in two separate proceedings. We therefore recommend that the legislature reenact the former jurisdictional provision with retroactive application.

Developing and Utilizing More Potent Sanctions
The sanctioning of businessmen and corporations for wrongdoing has been a much neglected subject. Judges who daily sentence murderers, rapists, and other violent street criminals tend to view businessmen—even corporate racketeers—as inappropriate candidates for prison or even large fines.[29] In one particularly egregious case, a paving contractor pleaded guilty to an eighty-two count indictment and admitted to having defrauded three City agencies of at least $342,000. The court sentenced the defendants to probation, imposed a $75,000 fine, and failed to order restitution.[30] Tougher sanctions are necessary.

SEEKING CORPORATE DISSOLUTION WHERE APPROPRIATE
Some contracting firms which do business in the New York City construction industry are so corrupt and/or so closely tied to Cosa Nostra that they should simply be dissolved. The State Attorney General can petition for dissolution of a domestic corporation where the corporation is engaged in illegal conduct or carries on its business in a persistently fraudulent manner.[31] While the Attorney General does not have the power to dissolve a foreign corporation, its authority to do business in New York can be revoked.[32] Similar sanctions can be imposed on partnerships and other businesses using assumed names.[33] Article 13-B of the New York State Civil Practice Law and Rules (CPLR) also allows dissolution of a corporation or other entity controlled partially or entirely by a person convicted of a violation of the State's Organized Crime Control Act (OCCA), where dissolution is necessary to prevent a further OCCA violation.[34]

MAKING MORE EFFECTIVE USE OF FORFEITURE LAWS
(i) Civil Forfeiture
New York's general civil forfeiture law, Article 13-A of the CPLR, provides potentially powerful remedies against corporate racketeers. Article 13-A allows prosecutors to obtain the forfeiture of the "proceeds of a crime," which is any property obtained through the commission of a felony.[35] Thus, in the hypothetical example with which this chapter began, the savings in wage and benefit payments resulting from labor bribery and the earnings from bid rigging are forfeitable. Moreover, since Article 13-A

allows recovery of a money judgment equal in value to the proceeds,[36] the recovery can come out of any of the contractor's
property; it is not necessary to identify the specific tainted proceeds.[37]

More significantly, Article 13-A permits prosecutors to obtain
the forfeiture of the "instrumentality of a crime," which is any
property whose use contributes directly and materially to the
commission of a felony.[38] Thus, in the hypothetical example at
the beginning of this chapter, the systematic use of the corporation for labor bribery, tax evasion and organized crime-related
bid rigging and job allocation schemes would render the company itself forfeitable.[39]

The remedies created by Article 13-A are civil and remedial,
and are not subject to the procedural requirements of the criminal law. For example, the standard of proof is, with certain exceptions, proof by a preponderance of the evidence, far less than the
criminal law's standard of proof beyond a reasonable doubt.[40] A
forfeiture action for corporate racketeering such as is set forth in
the hypothetical case must be grounded upon a criminal court
conviction,[41] but the forfeiture action may be commenced—and
corporate assets frozen—even prior to indictment.[42] Moreover,
the scope of the forfeiture action may be broader than the prosecution—it may encompass the entire common scheme or plan of
misconduct.[43]

Current law discourages prosecutors' use of civil forfeiture
remedies by inhibiting the flow of information for civil forfeiture.
Although corporate racketeering cases are thoroughly developed only in the grand jury, the law is unclear as to whether
grand jury materials could be made available for civil forfeiture
actions.[44] Moreover, district attorneys have no subpoena power
to conduct a parallel civil forfeiture investigation or to gather
information outside the scope of the grand jury's usual concerns,
such as information relating to defendants' assets. Laws explicitly enabling prosecutors to use grand jury materials for Article
13-A civil forfeiture cases and authorizing prosecutors to subpoena information outside of the grand jury are needed. The
Governor's 1989 Program Bill, introduced in the Assembly,
would so provide.

(ii) Criminal Forfeiture

A corporate racketeer prosecuted for an OCCA violation may face criminal forfeiture of the sources of influence over the corporation, the interests acquired or maintained in the corporation, and/or the interests derived from investing criminal proceeds in the corporation. Separating the corporate racketeer from the source of the power he misused and from the interests in the enterprise he employed are obviously necessary components of a deterrent strategy.

OCCA has been law for only slightly more than three years, and only a handful of OCCA prosecutions have as yet been instituted.[45] In part, this is because cases already developed that were suitable for OCCA prosecution had been referred, before OCCA was enacted, to federal prosecutors. Significant lead time was thus necessary for the development of new cases of sufficient significance to warrant the use of OCCA. There is, however, another explanation for the relatively few OCCA prosecutions. As was the case with RICO, it has taken state and local prosecutors some time to become comfortable with the complexities of OCCA and to realize the benefits of seeking OCCA's criminal sanctions in appropriate cases. OCTF has been aiding county district attorneys by holding seminars to explain the law and its uses. Prosecutors should be encouraged to seek these sanctions, including criminal forfeiture, in appropriate cases.

Just as law enforcement, in appropriate situations, should seek court-ordered trusteeships against racketeer-controlled labor organizations, they should also seek trusteeships against racketeer-controlled construction, supply and transport companies. These remedies can now be obtained under New York State's OCCA law. While law enforcement agencies are considering whether forfeiture or dissolution are appropriate remedies in particular cases, they must also face the fact, incredibly enough, that sometimes racketeer-controlled companies are the only ones providing a certain construction supply or service. In such circumstances, continuing the company under the auspices of a court-appointed trustee is preferable to destroying it.

PROCEEDING AGAINST SURETY BONDS

The City should proceed against the surety on a contractor's performance bond where the contractor's fraud has caused an agency financial damage. This would not only make the City whole for its loss, but would also serve the cause of deterrence. The resulting increase in insurance rates can be a significant cost for the contractor; if he is unable to obtain insurance, it can be devastating.

Conclusion

Corrupt businesses play a major role in labor racketeering by paying off union officials to ignore collective bargaining provisions and to provide the muscle to control clubs and cartels. To generate cash for such payoffs, corrupt businesses falsify business records, using schemes which involve massive tax evasion. Strategies to move against corrupt businesses include much more vigorous antitrust and tax enforcement, and more severe criminal punishments, sometimes including corporate dissolution and civil and criminal asset forfeiture. A successful attack on business crime also requires certain substantive and procedural criminal law reforms. Encouraging economic competition should also be considered an important anticorruption and racketeering strategy. Where that proves impossible, the public sector should consider setting up public benefit corporations.

FOOTNOTES

1. When using the term "corporate," we are referring to all business entities operating in the construction industry without regard to legal form (i.e., partnerships, joint ventures, associations, etc.).

2. See the testimony of Stanley Sternchos, president of Technical Concrete Construction Corp. and Vanderbilt Biltmore Construction Corp., Record at 6506-07, *United States v. Salerno*, 86 CR 245 (S.D.N.Y. June 23, 1987).

3. Although a few prosecutions have identified a small number of firms whose only business is providing false invoices, the practice of supplying inflated invoices is most often carried out by otherwise legitimate suppliers seeking to accommodate their regular customers.

4. At trial in *United States v. Salerno*, Stanley Sternchos testified that:

    ...Scopo told us that there were other contractors—he called them club contractors—who were allowed to do this larger work over two million dollars...in exchange for...these jobs.....These large superstructure contractors...would be paying...2% to the wiseguys who ran the club.

    Record at 6527, 86 CR 245.

5. At trial in *United States v. Salerno*, Louis Corbetta, president of Corbetta Construction Co., testified that in 1980, as an out-of-town contractor, his company had prepared a $29 million bid for the superstructure and slab-on-the-ground concrete at the Javits Center. The day before the bid was to be submitted, Corbetta was visited by another contractor who told him that he "was acting as a messenger for a group" who wanted Corbetta to submit a complementary bid because the job had been set up for Nasso/S & A Concrete Co., which was going to bid $31 million. Ultimately, Corbetta submitted no bid and Nasso/S & A obtained the contract. Record at 5497, 86 CR 245.

6. See *United States v. Salerno*, 85 CR 139 (S.D.N.Y. 1985), known as the "Commission Case."

7. In an electronically intercepted conversation between two private carting owners, Lucchese Crime Family Soldier Salvatore Avellino and his associate Emedio Fazzini, Avellino described how the family planned to use its control of a union and the employers association to squeeze all but its own favored companies out of the Long Island private carting industry.

    AVELLINO: It's gonna [start with] 50-60 of us [companies]...We're gonna knock everyone out, we're gonna knock everybody out, absorb everybody, eat them up, or whoever we, whoever stays [are] only who we [are] allowing to stay in there.

    FAZZINI: You got big plans.

    AVELLINO: Well, isn't that the truth.

8. See Casey Ichniewski and Anne Preston, "The Persistence of Organized Crime in New York City Construction: An Economic Perspective," *Industrial and Labor Relations Review* 42 (1989): 549. [Symposium issue: "Attacking Corruption in Union-Management Relations."]

9. The U.S. Supreme Court has explicitly found a lessened expectation of privacy inherent in the operations of private businesses that are "closely regulated." See *New York v. Burger*, 482 U.S. 691 (1987).

10. The Securities Act of 1933 gives the Securities and Exchange Commission the authority "to prescribe the form and forms in which required information shall be set forth, the items or details to be shown in the balance sheet and earnings statement, and the methods to be followed in the preparation of accounts, in the appraisal or valuation of assets and liabilities, in the determination of depreciation and depletion, in the differentiation of recurring and non-recurring income." 15 U.S.C.A. § 77s(a) (West 1981).

11. See, e.g., N.Y. Comp. Codes R. & Regs. tit. 6, §§ 360, 361, 364, 370-74 and 380 (1989).

12. For example, if a corporation subject to SEC regulations discharges a CPA, the SEC must be notified of the discharge and the reasons therefore must be related. See Changes in and Disagreements with Accountants on Accounting and Financial Disclosure, 17 CFR 229.304 (1988).

13. One investigation of road and highway construction conducted by the U.S. Department of Justice, Antitrust Division, encompassed twenty-three states, including New York, and resulted in 378 criminal prosecutions involving 328 corporate defendants and 309 individuals. Charges have included violation of Section 1 of the Sherman Act and false statements to government agencies. Over ninety percent of these defendants have been convicted, resulting in fines totaling more than $65 million and aggregate jail sentences of more than sixty-one years actual incarceration. State governments, as a result of these prosecutions, have been able to recover millions of dollars in overcharges. Prices paid for road construction projects have also declined ten percent as a result of the elimination of bid rigging, resulting in millions of dollars of additional savings.

14. Some instances where antitrust actions have been directed at construction industry criminality include:

State of New York v. Amfar Contracting Corp., 83 Civ. 2598 (S.D.N.Y. 1983), alleged a conspiracy to allocate via bid rigging virtually every major highway and sewer project on Long Island. In this case, the State won a $7.8 million judgment against several highway contractors.

State of New York v. Transit-Mix Concrete Corp., 84 Civ. 4194 (S.D.N.Y. 1984) charges nineteen companies and several individuals with monopolization of ready-mix concrete.

People v. Cedar Park, 85 Civ. 1887 (S.D.N.Y. 1985) and *State v. Century-Maxim Construction*, 86 Civ. 8128 (S.D.N.Y. 1986) charges eight construction firms with bid rigging.

In *People v. DiNapoli*, 35 A.D.2d 28, 312 N.Y.S.2d 547, 549 (1970), *aff'd*. 27 N.Y.2d 229, 316 N.Y.S.2d 229 (1970), the defendants pleaded guilty to violations of § 340 and § 341 of the General Business Law arising out of the submission of rigged bids to Consolidated Edison Company of New York for construction work.

15. Donnelly Antitrust Act, N.Y. Gen. Bus. Law §§ 340-47 (McKinney 1988).

16. See Attorney General Robert Abrams, *Bid-Rigging in the Competitive Process: A Report to the Legislature* (Albany, N.Y.: New York State Department of Law, 1985).

17. N.Y. Gen. Bus. Law § 347 (McKinney 1988) provides that "The attorney general may prosecute every person charged with the commission of a criminal offense in violation of the laws of this state, applicable to or in respect of the practices or transactions referred to in this article.... A district attorney shall give reasonable notice to the attorney general of intention to prosecute under this article and the attorney general may appear in any criminal proceeding brought under this article."

18. Another possible tactic would be for government to itself undertake construction of its public works projects. For example, in Great Britain, since the late nineteenth century, many local governments have had a "direct labour organization" constituting a public sector construction force to undertake all building of housing and other public works, paving roads, and maintaining the infrastructure. One justification for the direct labor organizations is that they serve as a benchmark against which the cost and performance of private contractors can be compared.

19. For recommendations regarding creation of a public benefit corporation as one means of reducing racketeering in the Long Island carting industry, see Peter Reuter, *Racketeering in Legitimate Industries* (Santa Monica, Calif.: RAND Corp., 1987) 92-93.

20. *Quadrozzi v. City of New York*, Ind. No. 28421/86 (N.Y. County 1987), 6-7.

21. For a brief history of organized crime in the business world, and some of the prosecutorial methods which have been used to remove organized crime from legitimate businesses, see Donald Hermann, "Organized Crime and White Collar Crime: Prosecution of Organized Crime Infiltration of Legitimate Business," *Rutgers Law Journal* 16 (1985): 589.

22. N.Y. Penal Law § 180.25 (McKinney 1988) (Bribe receiving by a labor official); N.Y. Lab. Law §§ 723(1)(e) and 725(4) (McKinney 1988).

23. The relevant section of the Taft-Hartley Act was amended by Congress in 1984. See 29 U.S.C.A. § 186(d)(i)-(2) (West 1978 & Supp. 1989). Punishment for the violation (when the value exceeds $1,000) is a fine of not more than $15,000 and imprisonment of not more than five years, or both. If the value is less than $1,000, the violation is a misdemeanor, and the fine is not more than $10,000 or imprisonment for not more than one year, or both.

24. N.Y. Penal Law § 200 (McKinney 1988).

25. New York's accomplice corroboration provision prohibits the conviction of a defendant upon an accomplice's testimony without independent corroborative evidence connecting the defendant to the crime. N.Y. C.P.L. § 60.22 (McKinney 1981). The rule's intent is to prevent a conviction based solely upon the testimony of a confederate with a motive to testify falsely. In practice, however, the rule sweeps too wide. It applies, for example, whether one or ten accomplices testify against the defendant; there would have to be independent corroboration of the ten accomplices even though the totality of their testimony conclusively established the defendant's criminal behavior. The federal, and over thirty state, rules recognize the inherent unreliability of accomplice testimony, but adopt more reasonable protections. Rather than require independent corroboration of each accomplice, these jurisdictions require the trial court to caution the jury that accomplice testimony should be rejected unless the totality of circumstances establishes its reliability. We believe this to be a more sensible and appropriate rule.

26. New York State has the broadest grand jury immunity rule in the nation. It confers "transactional" immunity on witnesses who are called to appear and give evidence before a grand jury. N.Y. C.P.L. §§ 50-20 (McKinney 1981) and 190.40 (McKinney 1982.) This means that once the witness has testified before the grand jury, he can never be prosecuted for any offense revealed in, or even remotely related to, that testimony. Moreover, this immunity is conferred automatically on any witness who testifies. Thus every witness receives immunity unless he affirmatively waives it. By contrast, federal and most state rules pro-

vide for invoked "use" immunity. This more limited immunity doctrine provides that testimony (or evidence derived therefrom) cannot be used against the witness in later proceedings; however, if the prosecution has evidence independent of that witness's testimony, the witness can still be prosecuted for the crimes to which his testimony relates.

27. See N.Y. Tax Law, §§ 1800-48 (McKinney 1987 & Supp. 1989).

28. *People v. Fioretti*, N.Y.L.J., July 12, 1988 (Bronx County 1988).

29. Notable exceptions include the sentencing of Biff Halloran, convicted of mail fraud, conspiracy (RICO), and substantive RICO offenses, to thirteen years of confinement, $266,000 in fines, plus two times the gross profits from the crimes.

30. *People v. Durante*, Ind. No. 7098/87 (N.Y. County 1987).

31. See N.Y. Bus. Corp. Law §§ 109 and 1101 (McKinney 1986).

32. "The attorney-general may bring an action or special proceeding... to enjoin or annul the authority of any foreign corporation which within this state contrary to law has done... any act which if done by a domestic corporation would be a cause for dissolution under § 1101." N.Y. Bus. Corp. Law § 1303 (McKinney 1986).

33. N.Y. Gen. Bus. Law § 130 (McKinney 1988) prohibits a business using an assumed name or a partnership from doing business under that name without filing a certificate of business with the county clerk. N.Y. Exec. Law § 63(12) (McKinney Supp. 1990) gives the attorney general the power to cancel such certificates.

34. See CPLR § 1353(1)(c) (McKinney Supp. 1990).

35. See CPLR §§ 1310(2) and 1311(1) (McKinney Supp. 1990).

36. See CPLR § 1311(1) (McKinney Supp. 1990).

37. See *Morgenthau v. Citisource, Inc.*, 68 N.Y.2d 211 (1986).

38. See CPLR §§ 1310(4) and 1311(1) (McKinney Supp. 1990).

39. A court might limit the forfeiture to protect the rights of innocent principals or shareholders or if the value of the corporation substantially exceeds the value of the proceeds. See CPLR § 1311(4)(d)(ii), (iv).

40. See CPLR § 1311(3) (McKinney Supp. 1990).

41. See CPLR § 1311(1)(a) (McKinney 1990).

42. *Id.*

43. *Id.*

44. Grand jury materials may be disclosed by a prosecutor only "in the lawful discharge of his duties or upon written order of the Court." C.P.L. § 190.25(4)(a) (McKinney Supp. 1990). Prosecutors are expressly authorized to conduct 13-A civil forfeiture actions, CPLR §§ 1310(11) and 1311(1) (McKinney Supp. 1990), and therefore disclosure of grand jury materials without a court order for 13-A actions would appear to be within a prosecutor's duties. However, the Court of Appeals has held that the Suffolk County District Attorney could not use grand jury materials without a court order in a civil RICO treble damages action. See *Matter of District Attorney of Suffolk County*, 58 N.Y.2d 436 (1983). The Court also ruled that a court order for disclosure must be based on a showing of compelling and particularized need for access, and that court-ordered disclosure is the exception and not the rule.

45. See *People v. Pagano*, Ind. No. 89-120 (Rockland County 1989); *People v. Moscatiello*, Ind. No. 8081/89 (N.Y. County 1989); *People v. Grillo*, Ind. No. 10732/88 (N.Y. County 1988); *People v. Edmonson*, Ind. No. 2849/89 (Kings County 1989); *People v. Nicoletti*, Ind. No. 89-217 (Niagara County 1989).

CHAPTER 9

Attacking official corruption

Introduction

Chapter 4 provided a historical perspective on official corruption in the regulation of public and private construction, and in the administration of public works. It emphasized that susceptibility and potential for official corruption in the construction process are high because so many public officials have the power to bestow substantial benefits or to inflict substantial costs. In addition, it pointed to such other contributing factors as low pay, poor morale and unrealistic performance standards for building inspectors; underinvestment in the administration of public works; and the failure to prohibit many types of "honest graft."

Given the long history and repetitive nature of this kind of causation, the only way to have a significant effect is to devise short- and long-term initiatives to reduce corruption susceptibility and potential, and to develop and implement corruption opportunity-blocking strategies.[1] To do so, the following must be achieved: 1) campaign finance and ethics laws must be strengthened; 2) administration of public contracts and the performance of public works administrators must be improved; 3) building codes must be reformed; 4) recruitment, pay, morale and performance of building inspectors must be enhanced; 5) certain regulatory functions must be privatized; and 6) deterrence must be increased.

Historically, powerbrokers and other high government officials have been able to engage in corrupt behavior because influence peddling and self-dealing were for the most part lawful and unregulated. The City corruption scandals of the mid-1980s led to the creation of the State-City Commission on Integrity in Government[2] and the New York State Commission on Governmental Integrity.[3] Many of the ideas and recommendations of these commissions have recently been embodied in State and municipal law, especially in the new City Charter. Thus, as the new decade emerges, New York City has some of the most progressive campaign finance and ethics legislation in the country. Since this legislation is still in the process of implementation, the need for reforms other than those discussed below cannot now be anticipated. However, over the next several years, the strengths and weaknesses of the current reforms must be carefully assessed.

Reducing Corruption Susceptibility and Potential among High Government Officials and Powerbrokers

Campaign Finance

Campaign financing presents a complex problem. Special interest groups have increasingly become major sources of funds for U.S. political campaigns at all levels. In New York City and throughout the State, real estate developers and construction contractors are among the biggest campaign contributors. Developers and contractors, whose businesses depend on public contracts, make significant campaign contributions to elected public officials. If such largess were offered as a *quid pro quo* for favorable governmental action, it would constitute the crime of bribery.[4] Usually, however, no such explicit request is intended; even if it is, it is unlikely to be proven. Developers and contractors naturally seek access to the good will of decision makers who can benefit their projects. They realistically assume that public officials who are economically dependent on, or indebted or grateful to them, will view their interests favorably. This manner of funding political campaigns and boosting political careers creates an intolerable conflict-of-interest for public officials. It also reinforces cynicism and creates a climate of corruption in which officials perceive that it is acceptable to solicit, receive and accept contributions or favors from those who do business with the City.

In 1988 and 1989, New York City completely revamped its regulation of campaign finance.[5] Indeed, the City went from one of the least regulated jurisdictions in the country to one of the most heavily regulated and progressive jurisdictions. We strongly endorse these reforms and urge that they be closely monitored to determine whether they reduce the influence of wealthy individuals and interest groups over the electoral and governing process.

The New York City Campaign Finance Act is a new law that provides for optional public funding of candidates' campaigns for City offices, and establishes a Campaign Finance Board to regulate and oversee the public funding program. To qualify for public campaign funding, the candidate must voluntarily limit the private campaign contributions he or she receives.

The five-member Campaign Finance Board is charged with administering the Act. The Board is authorized to employ necessary staff and to investigate all matters pertaining to the Act's administration. It has the power to subpoena people and documents, and to give advisory opinions in response to written requests. The Board will receive reports on campaign donations and expenditures, computerize this data, publish the names of violators and report on the program's operation.[6]

The optional matching grant funds will come from a special fund separate from the City's general fund. Candidates who desire public funding must certify their compliance with applicable contribution and expenditure limits; they must also reach a threshold of private contributions from the requisite number of contributors.

To comply with the contribution limit, candidates for mayor, president of the city council and the comptroller cannot receive more than $3,000 from any individual (or related individual) for the primary and $3,000 for the general election; candidates for borough president and city council may not receive more than $2,500. All contributions coming from a corporation and its parent, subsidiaries or affiliated corporations are totaled and treated as coming from a single source. Campaign loans, if not repaid by the date of the election, are treated as contributions. Participants in the matching grant program must also observe expenditure caps. For example, in the mayoralty election a candidate is limited to spending $3,000,000 and only certain kinds of expenditures are permissible. Violations of the campaign finance law constitute a class A misdemeanor.

While the Campaign Finance Law is a massive step forward in reducing the dependency of high government officials on big campaign contributors, the optional matching program is voluntary. A candidate can still choose to raise funds through traditional means.[7] Thus, if a candidate declines to participate in the matching program, there would be nothing to stop him or her from relying on large contributions from developers, real estate interests, contractors or unions. Nevertheless, the existence of the optional program makes it possible for political candidates to fund their campaigns without reliance on special interests and, of course, publicly to contrast their own economic and political independence with the economic and political indebtedness of their opponents.

The Campaign Finance Act marks a significant positive step toward preventing the development of a political environment that nurtures official corruption. It is much too soon to evaluate the success of New York City's Campaign Finance reform. If it does not break the link between moneyed interests and political campaigns, further reform will have to be considered.

Ethics Legislation

New York City officials have a long tradition of profiting from their official positions by capitalizing on inside information or connections, steering contracts to firms with which they are affiliated, and taking kickbacks in one form or another from City contractors. In the wake of the City corruption scandals of the last several years, both State and local lawmakers have moved to limit the opportunities for officials to profit personally from their public positions.

The 1987 State Ethics Law

The 1987 State Ethics Law[8] covers statewide elected officials, state officers and employees, state legislators and their employees and, for some purposes, political party county chairpeople.[9] Such persons are prohibited from appearing or rendering services for compensation on behalf of private clients on certain matters before state agencies, and from engaging in various business transactions with state agencies. The inclusion of political party chairpeople, whether or not they hold public office, is an important step toward limiting the influence of powerbrokers. However, in several respects, the State law needs to be strengthened. The Act does not prohibit private counseling of clients on matters before state agencies, nor does it restrict covered individuals from appearing before counties and municipalities on behalf of private clients. Penalties for violating the Act are cumbersome and weak.

The City Charter

Of the many monumental changes brought about by the new City Charter, none is more far reaching and significant than its ethics provisions.[10] Following the scandals involving corruption by elected and appointed officials, and revelations of widespread "honest graft," it is not surprising that the City Charter provides for comprehensive ethics and conflicts-of-interest legislation. If enforced, this body of law promises a significant step toward reducing the kind of official corruption that has previously undermined the moral environment of City politics and economic activity. This new legislation comprises a comprehensive web of prohibitions applicable to all elected and appointed City officials (including former officials). The prohibitions pertain to every variety of self-dealing by public servants, including the negotiating, acceptance and performance of private sector employment after leaving government. Violations of the new rules will result in criminal (misdemeanor) sanctions and administrative penalties, including termination of employment. The Charter also provides for publicizing and explaining these ethics and conflicts-of-interest rules to City employees.

The new ethics and conflicts-of-interest laws prohibit City elected officials and some appointed officials (except for City Council members) from holding high political party office, thus directly attacking the powerbroker phenomenon.[11] City Council members must disclose on the official records of the Council any direct or indirect financial conflicts-of-interest with respect to proposed legislation. No member of the Council or salaried City employee is permitted to have a direct or indirect financial interest in any business dealings with the City or its agencies. Nor can a Council member or City employee act as an attorney, agent, broker, consultant, etc., for any person, firm, corporation or other entity interested directly or indirectly in any business dealings with the City. Former City officials are barred for three years from private employment on matters in which they were involved while in City government.

In addition to extensive and detailed definitions of what constitutes prohibited conflicts-of-interest, the Charter contains broad prohibitions on public servants profiting in any way from their public positions. For example:

> No public servant shall engage in any business, transaction or private employment, or have any financial or other private interest, direct or indirect, which is in conflict with the proper discharge of his or her official duties. [12]

* * *

> No public servant shall use or attempt to use his or her position as a public servant to obtain any financial gain, contract, license, privilege or other private or personal advantage, direct or indirect, for the public servant or any person or firm associated with the public servant. [13]

Moreover, the Charter prohibits public servants from accepting any "valuable gifts" from any person or firm doing business or intending to do business with the City. Furthermore, it is an offense for any public servant to compel, induce or request any person to pay any political assessment; it is also an offense to pay such a political assessment.

The new Charter establishes a five-person Conflicts-of-Interest Board which is responsible for issuing interpretative guidelines elaborating the conflict-of-interest provisions. [14] The Board is also responsible for overseeing the publication of the rules and agency efforts to make them known to all employees. In addition, the Board provides advisory opinions on all conflict-of-interest issues covered by the Charter. The Board is the recipient for the extensive financial disclosure reports that City employees must file. Finally, the Board receives complaints of misconduct against public servants, refers appropriate cases to the Commissioner of Investigation and, where probable cause is found, holds hearings to determine whether the conflict-of-interest rules have been breached. The Board is also authorized to impose penalties when it determines that the rules have been violated. Finally, the Board is required to issue an annual report on all its activities.

The major revamping of the City's ethics legislation in the

Charter reform is a historic effort to come to grips with more than a century of honest and dishonest graft. It remains to be seen whether this impressive legal assault on the problem will produce an equally impressive change in politics as usual. Clearly, enforcement is crucial. Given the Board's extensive responsibilities, making Board membership a part-time position is unrealistic. While the Board is authorized to hire necessary staff, it seems likely that effective administration and enforcement will require a full-time commitment. In any event, the entire ethics machinery should be carefully analyzed and evaluated over the next few years so that problems and pitfalls can be quickly and accurately identified and, if necessary, administration and enforcement can be strengthened.

Improving the Administration of Public Contracts
Our recommendations to improve the administration of public works are presented in Chapter 10, which focuses on strategies to reduce fraud, waste and abuse in the public works process.

These recommendations come at a propitious moment, because they coincide with the implementation of the new City Charter. The Charter creates a Procurement Policy Board comprised of appointees who have the expertise necessary to carry out the policy making role previously held by the Board of Estimate. The Procurement Policy Board has the power to establish methods for soliciting bids or proposals and awarding contracts, and for specifying the manner in which agencies administer contracts and oversee their performance.[15] Clearly, such efforts can reduce official corruption as well as waste, abuse and fraud.

The Office of Construction Corruption Prevention (OCCP), described in Chapter 6, is designed to work closely with the Policy Procurement Board. Indeed, this type of cooperation was foreseen by and mandated in the Charter, which directs that,

> [I]n the promulgation of any rules pertaining to the procurement of construction or construction related services, the board shall consult with any office designated by the mayor to provide overall coordination to the City's capital construction activities.[16]

Reducing Corruption Susceptibility in Inspectional Services

Reforming the Building Codes
In 1988, the Corruption Prevention and Management Review Bureau of the New York City Department of Investigation issued a report finding that the present codes are inadequate and encourage corruption. The Bureau stated that "[t]he Administrative Code of the City of New York, and any related regulatory requirements, must be reviewed and amended to eliminate contradictory and unnecessary code requirements," and urged the formation of an interagency task force among the inspectional agencies to review the code and recommend specific revisions.[17] We strongly recommend that this be done. A mayorally appointed panel of architects, engineers, developers, contractors, lawyers and union officials should eliminate code requirements that are not justified by health and safety, but instead reflect the power of special interest groups or the technologies and politics of bygone eras. We believe that such costly and wasteful requirements generate incentives for corruption.

Comprehensive code reform is an ambitious undertaking, requiring technical expertise and a sophisticated understanding of present-day corruption. The federal government and various other jurisdictions have successfully tackled this problem by adopting the Model Code of the Building Officials and Code Administrators International (BOCA).[18] It could also serve as a basis for code reform in New York City.

Privatizing Inspections
While we will offer a variety of recommendations to improve the delivery of inspectional services, we also believe that the twenty year trend toward privatizing of building inspections should be continued. Privatization makes sense because: 1) inspectional resources are so inadequate that the system cannot effectively carry out its mission of protecting the public's health, safety and welfare; and 2) inspections have been marred by corruption and incompetence for so long that one cannot be sanguine about the prospects for reform. Although it may not be feasible to give the Department of Buildings the resources necessary to have its own

inspectors in sufficient numbers and of sufficient quality to do the entire job, it should be possible to alter the Department's focus so that it can, to a greater degree, play the more realistic and no less critical role of monitor and auditor of a mixed public and private inspectional system.

The privatization of building inspections is not a new idea. The 1968 Building Code Reform codified self-inspection for certain kinds of inspections on certain kinds of projects. Directive No. 14, issued in 1975 by Buildings Commissioner Jeremiah Walsh, went somewhat further:

> Where an owner or lessee responsible for performance of the work elects to do so, he may employ a registered architect or licensed professional engineer to make inspections during progress of the work and upon completion. In such case, the owner or lessee shall notify the Buildings Department of the name and address of such architect or engineer. Where any work is found not in compliance with the plans or not in compliance with applicable laws, it shall be corrected, and if not corrected, the Department shall be notified by the architect or engineer and a violation requiring elimination of the defective work shall be filed.

However, Directive 14 applies only to relatively minor renovations.

The present system of inspections in New York City does include a mixture of public and private certification. Certain aspects of construction are considered to be controlled inspections, and are the mandatory responsibilities of the builder. Other aspects, such as the final inspection on certain projects, may be conducted by the builder, at the builder's option. It is difficult to determine the degree to which there has been more self-certification in recent years than since self-inspection was first codified in 1968. The system is moving toward a still-evolving consensus concerning the most efficient way to conduct inspections. The consensus remains bounded, however, by budgetary constraints and the cooperation of the industry.

We recommend expanding the number of inspection responsibilities executed by certified architects and engineers, either by contracting out to private agencies certain inspectional responsibilities,[19] or by requiring licensed architects and engineers to certify that work they have designed and supervised meets Code requirements.[20]

Architects and engineers who are specialists in construction have such a substantial investment in their careers and state licensing, that they are unlikely to be readily bribable. For privatization to succeed, however, the New York State Department of Education, which licenses architects and engineers, must be much more vigorous and aggressive in bringing disciplinary actions in appropriate cases. Any system utilizing private inspections must also be accompanied by unannounced, in depth, random and meaningful follow-up inspections by City inspectors.[21] Monitoring and auditing by the proposed Certified Investigative Auditing Firms (CIAF) would be an additional check on both the "private" and "public" inspectional programs.

In 1974, a Mayor's Special Committee proposed that, for smaller jobs, either a City inspector could certify code compliance or the building owner could hire a certified, registered architect or engineer to inspect the job and file compliance papers with the City. On larger jobs, defined as alterations valued at more than $150,000 or new buildings with more than fifteen stories or forty-two residential units, the proposal called for mandated certification of code compliance by licensed architects and engineers in place of inspections by Buildings Department personnel. (Most of these jobs are already supervised by architects and engineers.) All architects and engineers performing official inspections would be registered with the Buildings Department. Knowing misstatements on official forms or grossly negligent inspections would constitute a crime and automatically result in the loss of registration and possible decertification, i.e., loss or suspension of the license to practice as an architect or engineer in New York State. The Buildings Department would carry out frequent and thorough spot-checks. We think this proposal could well serve as a starting point for designing an appropriate privatization model.

The proposed Office of Construction Corruption Prevention (OCCP) should have the responsibility for determining the optimum amount of privatization and how best to implement it. By drawing on information from OCTF's Research and Analysis Unit, the Department of Investigation, CIAFs and the Office of Construction, OCCP will be particularly well suited to undertake this design and implementation task.

Improving Recruitment, Pay, Morale and Performance of Building Inspectors
Corruption among inspectors charged with responsibility for enforcing the City's Building Codes has been a fact of life for many years, and has survived a succession of exposés, firings and departmental reorganizations spanning several decades. In Chapter 4, we identified the underlying factors facilitating such corruption. We believe that any meaningful attack on the problem must include improving the pay, status and morale of the inspectors in order to bolster their stake in their careers. It also requires stressing those aspects of the inspector's role that directly relate to public health, welfare and safety.

Improving Pay, Status and Morale
A critical first step in increasing corruption resistance among building inspectors is to improve the number and quality of inspectors. As noted in the *Mayor's Management Report* for 1989:

> Fiscal 1989 proved to be a difficult year for the Division because of an increasing demand for service and the loss of approximately one-third of the field staff through higher than normal attrition. The Department averaged only 65 inspectors throughout the year, 14 percent fewer than planned and 6 percent fewer than last fiscal year. Inspectors completed 126,784 inspections, 12 percent fewer than in Fiscal 1988 and 14 percent below the plan. Most of the decline was attributable to staffing problems. . . . [22]

Staffing problems, evidenced by turnover of a third of the workforce in one year, must be corrected if there is to be a professional organization capable of addressing short- and long-term corruption problems, and overseeing increased privatization of inspections.

City building inspectors earn far less than construction workers with equivalent skills. Low pay creates problems in recruitment and retention. It leads to low morale and creates vulnerability to corruption. We recommend an increase in pay, perhaps funded by increased fees for certain inspections.

Greater compensation, by itself, will not be enough. Building inspectors must be convinced that their jobs involve more than paper pushing. The inspectional corps is the guardian of the City's built environment and infrastructure; the inspectors must understand that they are protecting workers and the health, safety and welfare of the general citizenry. This sense of organizational mission cannot simply be conveyed through a directive or public relations brochure; it will require training and leadership. It will be facilitated by paring down inspectional functions to those that are clearly linked to protecting health, safety and welfare.

Establishing Realistic Performance Standards

Understandably, fiscal pressures lead budget conscious officials to establish quotas for workers, such as building inspectors, who are not closely supervised. Inspectors, however, should not interpret such performance standards, and the punishments and rewards that attend them, as a signal that "only numbers count" and that managers care more about quantity than quality. Thus, quantitative performance measures should be reviewed to assure that they are compatible with careful and thorough inspection. More importantly, nonquantitative productivity measures, focusing on the thoroughness and accuracy of inspections, should be formulated and implemented.

The 1973 recommendations of a management consulting firm, H. B. Maynard and Company, seem an excellent starting point for developing appropriate qualitative performance measures.[23] The Maynard Report recognized that a prerequisite for implementing an appropriate evaluation system is an effective "hierarchy of responsibility." Supervisors have to be capable of and committed to evaluating line inspectors' work.[24] The report recommends that each time the supervisor contacts a line inspector, the supervisor must evaluate the inspector's work and fill in quality ratings forms that note any major or minor oversights or errors.[25] The line inspector must initial the form, thereby indicating that he has seen the evaluation (and, hopefully, will learn from it). In addition, when reviewing the line inspector's paper work, the supervisor must keep track of all serious mistakes, and on a weekly basis tally such mistakes and rate each subordinate on a ten-point scale. The supervisor must, on a monthly basis, provide a quality rating to the "clerical supervisor." In turn, the clerical supervisor must evaluate the competency and quality of the supervisor's evaluations and submit to the Borough Superintendent a monthly evaluation of each supervisor.

Deterrence and Opportunity Blocking

More must be done to increase the likelihood of detecting and significantly punishing official corruption related to construction. The backbone of deterrence is investigating complaints, conducting sting operations and prosecuting and punishing violators. A strengthened whistleblower law would encourage honest employees to come forward with complaints. In addition, stronger civil sanctions, including pension forfeiture, should be available.

A Critical Role for the Department of Investigation

The main investigative and law enforcement response to official corruption will necessarily continue to be played by the New York City Department of Investigation (DOI).[26] The City Charter requires DOI to conduct any investigation referred by the Mayor or City Council and vests the agency with authority to make any other study or investigation which, in the Commissioner's opinion, may be in the best interests of the City. The Commissioner's power to study or investigate is not limited to corruption cases, but goes broadly to the "affairs, functions, accounts, methods, personnel, or efficiency of any agency."[27] DOI has significant investigatory powers, including the power to subpoena and examine witnesses under oath in private or public hearings; it also has the authority to issue public reports.

In addition to its considerable investigatory powers and resources, DOI also has the capacity to play a major role in designing anticorruption strategies. Its Corruption Prevention and Management Review Bureau (CPMRB) has for the past twenty years been charged with developing "uniform systems of control against corrupt and dishonest activities in City agencies. . . ."[28] With a mandate "to identify and correct management deficiencies. . . that provide opportunities for corruption and dishonest activities,"[29] CPMRB regularly reviews city operations for the purpose of developing anticorruption standards for particular agencies.

CPMRB's effectiveness, however, has been limited by its exclusion from the ongoing operations and investigations of DOI in general, and of the inspectors general in particular. Only after investigations have been concluded and made public through reports or prosecutions has CPMRB been made privy to the information generated by these investigations. As a result, CPMRB studies analyzing management deficiencies and proposing operational reforms are often issued only after short-term, "quick-fix" remedial steps have been taken by the corrupted agency, and long after public outrage and concern over a particular corruption scandal have abated. Thus these reports are often dated and largely ignored. DOI must better integrate the operations of CPMRB with its investigative bureaus and Inspectors General.

A second problem limiting CPMRB's effectiveness has been the absence of any institutional follow-up to or implementation of its analyses and recommendations. We have been struck by the number of thoughtful and useful CPMRB reports that have generated little public interest and led to no institutional reform. Given its own loss-prevention mandate, the proposed OCCP can play a new and critical role in employing CPMRB's work product to formulate and institute corruption prevention strategies.

Another aspect of DOI's efforts can usefully be strengthened. Through CPMRB, DOI has required each City agency to draw up an annual corruption analysis. In 1988, thirty-two such reports were received. While many demonstrated mature reflection and analysis, the majority unfortunately did not. This perhaps is not surprising, since the kind of internal corruption susceptibility audit DOI has asked for requires an expertise that operational agencies do not often possess. Thus, the demand for such reports must be supported by training. CPMRB—and OCCP—should also scrutinize these reports and generate feedback, at least for the initial years, to the agency report writers.

Another example of DOI's anticorruption efforts are the following anticorruption guidelines, issued in January 1988 to all City inspectional services:

Operational Standards:

1. All inspectional personnel must be subject to periodic rotation in assignment/location or job duties.

2. Supervision of inspectors must be adequate.

3. The reporting requirement of Operation Double Check (whereby supervisors randomly re-inspect certain sites) must be redesigned and the function maintained to insure its use as an effective

means of assisting in the identification of patterns of corruption.

4. Inspectional reports and resultant agency action must be processed in a uniformly expeditious manner.

5. Inspectional personnel must be provided with a copy of their agency Standards of Conduct and be given training in corruption recognition and avoidance.

6. All persons whose place of business or activity are subject to an inspection must be provided with written information explaining the inspectional process and that the offering of a bribe or gratuity is a criminal offense.

7. Records pertinent to the inspectional process are to be identified and secured.

Management Standards:

1. The Administrative Code of the City of New York, and any related regulatory requirements, must be reviewed and amended to eliminate contradictory and unnecessary Code requirements.

2. Criminal and administrative penalties should be vigorously pursued against those engaged in corrupt activity.

3. Agency management must make a vigorous commitment to the detection and prevention of corrupt practices and take those steps necessary, including the development of adequate controls, supervision, and reporting systems.

4. Agency management must establish a management review program for modified inspection findings.

5. Agency management must review the role of the inspectional function within the agency.

6. Proper screening and selection of persons for inspectional positions must be made.[30]

DOI has also formulated several anticorruption programs directed specifically at construction. In 1987, it formed a Capital Construction Unit, consisting of two engineers, two auditors and an architect, to investigate allegations of corruption in the City's capital construction program. This unit has reviewed policies and procedures in capital construction contracts and conducted investigations on its own and with State and federal prosecutors. So far, the unit has begun investigations into several major public construction projects, but no resulting cases have yet been made public. While the intent is excellent, the scale of the effort is inadequate. If it sets up expectations that cannot be met, it could prove counterproductive.

DOI's investigatory efforts and management reforms for reducing corruption among the inspectional services are the kind of sensible experiments in institution building that should be undertaken. Nevertheless, if these initiatives are to succeed, they must be well funded and supported. They should also be regularly evaluated (with the participation of OCCP and perhaps outside consultants as well), and terminated or changed in order to expand successful programs and to weed out unsuccessful ones.

The expansion of DOI and the increasing sophistication of its anticorruption efforts are a salutary development in the battle against official corruption in New York City. However, DOI could be even more effective if its independence were increased. DOI's independence is particularly important given the critical role this report envisions for that agency. Currently, DOI is a mayoral agency, and its commissioner serves at the Mayor's pleasure. We recommend that the commissioner serve for a fixed term of years and be subject to discharge only for cause with the concurrence of an independent body.

Encouraging Whistleblowing
In 1986, the state legislature significantly strengthened the so-called "Whistleblower Law."[31] It protects public employees from retaliatory personnel action affecting, among other things, appointment, compensation, assignment, promotion, transfer or evaluation, if such personnel action is related to a report to a governmental body by such employee of (1) a violation of a law, rule or regulation where such violation presents a substantial and specific danger to public health or safety or (2) a matter which such employee reasonably believes is true, and which such employee reasonably believes constitutes an "improper government action." Improper governmental action includes any action taken by either a public employer or employee that constitutes a violation of any federal, state or local law, rule or regulation.

While the 1986 amendments were a major step in the right direction, the Legislature refused to adopt the complete definition of "improper governmental activity" advanced by Governor Cuomo.[32] Under the Governor's proposal, the whistleblower

law would have protected an employee who reported malfea-
sance, conversion or misuse of government property, as well as
gross waste of public funds, misconduct or abuse of authority by
a public employer or employee.[33]

We recommend passage of this more expansive whistleblower
protection. It would encourage public employees to assume
responsibility for ensuring that the public is not victimized by
corrupt officials. It would also add to the deterrence of fraud,
waste, and abuse.

The problem is, of course, that while actual whistleblowers
must be protected, corrupt, incompetent or otherwise unsuit-
able employees often adopt the posture of whistleblowers to
insulate themselves from actions taken against them for meritorious reasons unrelated to their manufactured "complaints."
Thus, while we recommend effective whistleblower legislation,
we also recognize the need to deal effectively with pretenders.
In order to preserve both the functioning of City agencies and
the integrity of the whistleblowing program, procedures must be
instituted and implemented to identify and punish such individuals.

Enhancing Administrative Sanctions

For reasons deeply embedded in the civil service system, personnel law and public sector collective bargaining agreements,
administrative responses to official corruption have been inadequate and ineffective. Corrupt officials are not often prosecuted
and, if they are, they are not adequately punished. Deterrence of
official corruption would be greatly bolstered, for example, by
pension forfeiture legislation. Currently, City employees found
guilty of corruption, even of major proportions, are able to retire
with generous public pensions for the rest of their lives. This
kind of benign response contributes to the corruption-generat-
ing political environment we have noted elsewhere in this
report.

Like the New York State Commission on Government Integrity, we believe it should be recognized that "[i]n the public sector, pensions are not merely a form of deferred compensation,
they are a reward for faithfulness to duty and honesty of performance. A public servant who, by engaging in serious criminal

misconduct, abuses the power of office and violates the fiduciary duty owed to the public relinquishes any claim to a pension financed by the taxpaying citizens of this State."[34]

In recent years, Pennsylvania, Florida, Georgia, Illinois and Massachusetts have all enacted pension forfeiture statutes which recognize that loyal, honest service is an essential prerequisite to pension eligibility. In these five states, criminal misconduct related to a public employee's official duties operates to sever the employee's claim to a taxpayer-financed pension. New York State should adopt a similar position.

The options for reform of pension entitlements in New York State are significantly limited by the state constitution, which provides that:

> After July first, 1940, membership in any pension or retirement system of the state or of a civil division thereof shall be a contractual relationship, the benefits of which shall not be diminished or impaired.[35]

This provision makes it very difficult to formulate legislation which would make forfeitable the pensions of current—although not future—employees who engage in criminal activity.

For present employees, however, the City does have another option. In order to receive benefits as a member of the City's Retirement Plan A (the plan awarding full retirement benefits), an employee must give thirty days notice before retiring. If, during that period, a disciplinary hearing is held and employment is terminated for cause, the employee will not be eligible to receive Plan A benefits. (Benefits for Plan B—early retirement—vest instantly upon application, but are considerably less than those of Plan A.) Unfortunately, the City has not made an aggressive effort along these lines, and many inspectors who have been charged with soliciting and accepting bribes have retired with full pension benefits. Under the current system, they continue to receive pension benefits even after being convicted of these offenses in criminal court.

There is no difficulty, however, in beginning the reform process by passing legislation applicable to new employees. The State Comptroller has introduced such a pension forfeiture bill ("S-5026"), which provides that new employees will forfeit their publicly financed retirement benefits if convicted in state court of a felony that constitutes a breach of their official duties or responsibilities. At the same time, the bill empowers a judge to direct the payment of benefits to a convicted official's financially needy spouse or dependents, provided they had no culpability for the acts upon which the felony conviction was based.

We recommend passage of this bill, although, like the New York State Commission on Government Integrity, we believe certain amendments are in order.[36] We are particularly concerned about the standardless escape hatch which, with one hand, gives back to the corrupt employee's family the pension that is taken away from the employee with the other. We also recommend that it be amended to permit a pension to be forfeited following conviction of any crime, state or federal, that constitutes a breach of official duties.

Conclusion

Official corruption has long plagued government offices and functions in New York City. Although it is not unique to government operations involving construction, construction processes are highly susceptible to official corruption because of the leverage that so many officials have over a construction project. Moreover, the inspectional services have an almost unbroken record of corruption throughout this century. Both "honest graft" and "dishonest graft" should be eliminated from governmental processes in New York City. The new campaign finance and ethics rules embodied in the City Charter mark a historic move away from politics as usual in New York City and, if effectively enforced, can result in a major reduction in corrupt behavior.

One of the most promising approaches to attacking corruption in the building inspectorate is privatization. Routine inspections by certified engineers and architects, especially with the establishment of a CIAF program, would result in a better and more effective inspectional process. However, all government functions involving construction cannot be privatized. Much work must be done to rebuild the quality and morale of the inspectional services corps—among supervisors as well as the rank-and-file. Better training, higher pay and more responsibility are obvious and necessary reforms. Most importantly, creative ways must be found to give inspectors an enhanced sense of professionalism and a greater stake in their careers. The Department of Investigation's Inspectors General will continue to play a crucial role in ferreting out corruption and in designing systems to prevent corruption. The Department's role should be supported and its Commissioner made more independent.

A stronger whistleblower law would encourage public employees to report cases of corruption, thereby increasing the risk of apprehension. A tougher pension forfeiture statute would substantially increase the cost of corruption, thereby bolstering deterrence. A reinvigorated law enforcement commitment to official corruption would also reinforce deterrence and the rule of law.

FOOTNOTES

1. See Ronald Goldstock, "Non-Prosecutorial Strategies in Fighting Corruption," presented at the Fourth International Anti-Corruption Conference, Sydney, Australia, November 1989. (Paper No. 89-51, available at the New York State Organized Crime Task Force.)

2. The State-City Commission on Integrity in Government, *Volume 1: Reports and Recommendations* (New York: January 1987).

3. The following is a list of reports issued by the New York State Commission on Government Integrity (The Feerick Commission) that are relevant to this chapter: *Campaign Financing: Preliminary Report* (December 1987); *Ethics in Government Act: Report and Recommendations* (April 6, 1988); *Crime Shouldn't Pay: A Pension Forfeiture Statute for New York* (May 1988); *Draft of Proposed Ethics Act for New York State Municipalities* (May 1988); *Campaign Finance Reform: The Public Perspective* (July 1988); *The Albany Money Machine: Campaign Financing for New York State Legislative Races* (September 1988); *Unfinished Business: Campaign Finance Reform in New York City* (September 1988); *Restoring the Public Trust: A Blueprint for Government Integrity* (December 1988); *Municipal Ethics Standards: The Need for a New Approach* (December 1988); and *The Midas Touch: Campaign Finance Practices of Statewide Officeholders* (June 1989).

4. "The core of the concept of a bribe is an inducement improperly influencing the performance of a public function meant to be gratuitously exercised." John T. Noonan, Jr., *Bribes* (Berkeley, Calif.: University of California Press, 1984) xi.

5. See New York City Campaign Finance Board, *A Guide to New York City Campaign Finance Program* (February 8, 1990). See also Herbert E. Alexander, "Campaign Finance Reform," *Restructuring New York City Government: The Reemergence of Municipal Reform*, eds., Frank J. Mauro and Gerald Benjamin (Montpelier, Vt.: Capitol City Press, 1989).

6. State campaign finance reporting requirements will still apply. Statements listing the dollar amount of any contribution, the contributor's name and address, and the date of receipt, plus a detailed account of expenditures must be filed with the City Board of Elections. (Contributions of less than $99 may be reported in the aggregate.) N.Y. Elec. Law § 14-102 (McKinney 1978).

7. Under state law, the primary campaign contribution limit to a candidate for City office is the total number of enrolled voters in the candidate's party in the district where he is running for office, multiplied by $.05. In the general election, it is $.05 times the total number of registered voters in the district, except for the candidate's family, each of whom may contribute a sum equal to $.25 per registered voter. N.Y. Elec. Law § 14-114 (McKinney 1978). The candidate may spend as much of his own money as he chooses.

The contribution limit for a corporation to a candidate may not exceed, in the aggregate, $5,000 in any calendar year. N.Y. Elec. Law § 14-116 (McKinney Supp. 1990). However, this limitation is often avoided through additional contributions by corporate subsidiaries or affiliates.

8. Ethics in Government Act, ch. 813, 1987 N.Y. Laws 1404 (McKinney) (codified in scattered sections of N.Y. Public Officers Law, Executive Law, Legislative Law, Judiciary Law, and General Municipal Law).

9. The Act also applies to the judicial branch with respect to financial disclosures.

10. New York, N.Y., Charter §§ 2600-2606 (1989).

11. New York, N.Y., Charter § 2604(b)(15) (1989). Council members may, however, serve as assembly district leaders or hold any lesser political office.

12. New York, N.Y., Charter § 2604(b)(2) (1989).

13. New York, N.Y., Charter § 2604(b)(3) (1989).

14. New York, N.Y., Charter §§ 2602-2603 (1989).

15. New York, N.Y., Charter § 311 (1989).

16. New York, N.Y., Charter § 311(d) (1989).

17. New York City Department of Investigation, Corruption Prevention and Management Review Bureau, "Operating and Management Standards for Integrity Within New York City Agencies Providing Inspectional Services," (March 1988) 14.

18. *BOCA National Building Code / 1987: Model Building Regulations for the Protection of Public Health, Safety and Welfare*, 10th ed. (Country Club Hills, Ill.: Building Officials and Code Administrators International, Inc., 1986). The BOCA Code has been adopted and adapted with success in several jurisdictions. It has been adopted by several local governments in New York state and is the mandatory baseline code for all jurisdictions in New Jersey.

19. The Department of Buildings announced that as of March 1990 it would contract with private inspection agencies to conduct some "application" inspections heretofore performed by employees of the Bureau of Electrical Control. City of New York, *Mayor's Management Report* (New York: City of New York, February 15, 1990) 165.

20. Current City regulations permit licensed architects and engineers to certify compliance on certain classes of construction work which do not involve modification of the certificate of occupancy. New York, N.Y., Department of Buildings Directive No. 14 (1975). Administrative Code violations for nonhazardous conditions can be resolved through certifications by architects and engineers that the condition has been corrected.

21. As is often the case, historical perspective is enlightening. The New York State legislature passed the nation's first comprehensive tenement house law in 1901 in an attempt to deal with fire and disease, which were claiming hundreds of lives per year in the tenement districts. The standards set for the inspectors and their work were extraordinarily high. It was claimed that every building inspection was doubled checked!

> Each inspector's work is checked in the field, generally within twenty-four hours of the time of his inspection, and if material variations are found in his report or matters that are clearly incorrect, a complete and thorough examination is at once made and charges proffered against the inspector for making false and misleading reports.

Robert W. DeForest and Lawrence Veiller, "First Report of the New York City Tenement House Department," (1902-1903) 322.

22. City of New York, *Mayor's Management Report* (New York: City of New York, September 17, 1989) 304.

23. H. B. Maynard and Company, "Procedural Manual For Construction Inspection Division," Report Prepared for the New York City Department of Buildings, Housing and Development Administration, City of New York (June 1973).

24. The report states that, at a minimum, a building inspector must: 1) be an

expert on the Building Code; 2) be able to read blueprints and specifications; 3) know building materials and practices; and 4) be able to write accurate and complete reports.

25. A "major oversight" is defined as an important provision of the building code or regulations that could cause danger to the public, e.g., no control inspector on site, absence of a sidewalk bridge, no sheeting or bracing on an excavation, or omission of fireproofing on steel works. A "minor oversight" is a violation of the building code or regulations that would not prove hazardous to the public.

26. DOI's roots go back to the Bureau of Accounts, which was established by the Legislature in response to the scandals surrounding the Tweed Ring in 1873. See Association of the Bar of the City of New York, Committee on Municipal Affairs, "Report on the New York City Department of Investigation," *The Record* 43 (December 1988): 948.

27. New York, N.Y., Charter § 803(b) (1989). Thus, DOI has a front-line role to play in preventing and investigating frauds in public construction, the subject matter of Chapter 10.

28. City of New York, *Mayor's Management Report* (New York: City of New York, February 10, 1988) 469.

29. City of New York, *Mayor's Management Report* (New York: City of New York, September 17, 1987) 72.

30. New York City, Department of Investigation, Corruption Prevention and Management Review Bureau, "Operating and Management Standards for Integrity Within New York City Agencies Providing Inspectional Services," (January 1988). These guidelines became a mayoral administrative mandate in March 1988 after the surfacing of a corruption scandal among Department of Health restaurant inspectors.

31. See N.Y. Civ. Serv. Law § 75-b (McKinney Supp. 1990).

32. See Governor's Program Bill #220 of 1986.

33. The Governor's Program Bill, drafted in coordination with the Kings County District Attorney's Office, was modeled after the federal law, which provides such broad protection. See 5 U.S.C.A. § 2302(b)(8) (West. Supp. 1989).

34. New York State Commission on Government Integrity, *Crime Shouldn't Pay, 8.*

35. N.Y. Const., art. V, § 7.

36. See New York State Commission on Government Integrity, *Crime Shouldn't Pay.*

CHAPTER 10

Attacking fraud, waste and abuse in public construction

Introduction

Public construction projects are more vulnerable to fraud, waste and abuse than private construction projects because of the complex body of laws regulating the public construction process, the intense political pressure to begin and complete public works, and the severe administrative and personnel deficiencies in their administration. We offer recommendations in each of these areas. At the outset, however, we are mindful of one critical consideration set forth in Chapter 5. Many public contracting requirements and multilayer review procedures, originally instituted to assure fairness and prevent corruption, have instead resulted in less accountability and more corruption susceptibility. Any new reforms of the public contracting system must not unwittingly contribute to the creation of a more unwieldy, confused and costly public construction process. This would only extend the cycle of corruption.

We saw in Chapter 5 that the City has little control over its choice of construction contractors. Contract award is governed strictly by competitive bidding. As a result, competent and honest contractors cannot be rewarded with new contracts. Conversely, incompetent and dishonest contractors cannot easily be denied future contracts. Moreover, the City's cumbersome and dilatory procedures, muscle-bound bureaucracy and underfunded project administration create a business environment marked by uncertainty, confusion and financial risk—clearly an environment ripe for exploitation by corrupt contractors. Not surprisingly, many honest contractors will not bid on the City's construction contracts. In some niches of the industry, virtually

251

the only contractors who do bid are those with a record of incompetence, fraud or ties to organized crime.

Reforming Contract Letting

Thus, the first step in combating fraud in public construction is to reform the contract letting system so that the City has greater control in selecting contractors for its multibillion dollar public works program. To accomplish this, the City needs 1) the authority to prequalify bidders; 2) a strategy for increasing the size of the prequalified pool of contractors; 3) the ability and willingness to declare an unacceptable low bidder "not responsible;" 4) the authority to debar an incompetent, defaulting, or corrupt contractor from public contracting; and 5) the option to use contract letting procedures other than pure competitive bidding.

Prequalification

Prequalification procedures require contractors to submit a prequalification application detailing the firm's financial capacity, work experience, construction capability, management composition (identifying officers and principals), and all matters bearing on integrity. Proper administration of this process enables an agency to compile a list of contractors eligible to bid on its projects. In theory, prequalification eliminates unqualified and corrupt contractors before any bids are submitted, before the bidders acquire any conditional right to a contract.

The new City Charter provides a significant opportunity to institute a prequalification system for construction contractors.[1] Sections 318 and 324 permit the prequalification of prospective vendors for particular types of goods, services and construction, according to criteria to be established by a five-member Procurement Policy Board.[2] The Charter gives all agencies the authority to prequalify their vendors, and expressly provides that factors to be considered should include "past performance" and the "ability to undertake work." Unfortunately, however, the Charter does not authorize prequalification for all contracts; it limits prequalification to "special cases."

We recommend that the Procurement Policy Board, which has substantial rule making authority under the Charter, define "special cases" broadly enough to make prequalification an option in as large a percentage of construction contracts as possible. One possible strategy would be to declare projects in excess of a certain dollar threshold to be "special cases." If the courts reject this interpretation, the Charter should be amended to make prequalification an option for all significant public construction contracts.

Prequalification, however, will accomplish little if not extended to subcontractors; otherwise, a corrupt contractor or material supplier denied prequalification might nonetheless appear on the construction site as a subcontractor. Although the Charter does not expressly provide for subcontractor prequalification, it does empower the Procurement Policy Board to play a role in drafting contract language. We recommend that the Board modify existing City construction contract language to require all City construction contractors to subcontract work only to firms that have been prequalified.

It is vital that an appeal from a denial of prequalification not be permitted to suspend or delay the bidding process.[3] Contractors denied prequalification should not be permitted to enjoin agencies from putting contracts out to bid; their only relief, in the event of a successful challenge, should be to have their names placed on the prequalification list for future contracts. Otherwise, agencies will be reluctant to deny prequalification for fear of resulting delay. The Procurement Policy Board should include an anti-injunction clause in the prequalification rules. In the event this strategy fails, the Charter should be amended to provide such a prohibition.

Prequalification will only make a significant contribution to reducing fraud, waste and abuse if the prequalification process is rigorous and meaningful. City agencies must devote significant investigative resources to prequalification. Applicant firms must be thoroughly investigated; principals and major investors must be subjected to background checks. Because construction firms, especially corrupt firms, have a chameleonlike character (appearing and reappearing under different names and joint ventures), all names under which the firm and its principals formerly did business must also be investigated.

A meaningful prequalification review requires a centralized clearinghouse with information on contractors' prior histories and work experiences. Over the past several years, the Construction Industry Project has received a large number of requests from State and City agencies (and public authorities) for information on public contractors. Many requests include complaints that agencies have no other source for background information on bidders. While the City's Vendex system, managed by the New York City Office of Contract Administration, does collect some important information (e.g., debarments, poor performer ratings and bankruptcies) from all City agencies, it fails to capture other significant information indicating untrustworthiness. The City must expand the Vendex database to include convictions, indictments and agency performance ratings.[4]

The State's efforts to coordinate the collection and dissemination of information relating to contractors' responsibility is a model the City might adopt; alternatively, the City might seek inclusion within the State's system. Governor Cuomo has directed a Council of Contracting Agencies to "establish procedures to ensure the systematic collection and timely exchange of information [among state agencies] relevant to agency determinations of responsibility and reliability of bidders, contractors, and proposed subcontractors...."[5] The OCCP proposed in Chapter 6 should play a major role in designing the means to collect, store and retrieve information from all City construction agencies.

Expanding the Pool of Qualified Bidders

Prequalification of bidders is a necessary strategy for improving City public works administration and for reducing fraud, but only if a significant pool of qualified bidders actually exists. Where there are only two, three, or four firms within a particular construction niche, and each of them is subject to disqualification on integrity grounds, a City agency is faced with the untenable choice of ignoring its prequalification standards or abandoning its construction project. Ways must be found to avoid this dilemma.

The City must therefore take initiatives to expand the pool of qualified bidders on public works projects. First, the City must "sell" itself as an employer. Too many contractors perceive the City as incompetent, dilatory, unfair and as imposing unacceptable risks on contractors. The City must change this perception (and the reality) by improving its general relationship with its construction contractors and, more specifically, by improving its designs, payment and decision making procedures, and its mechanisms for resolving disputed change orders.

Simultaneously, the City must pursue aggressive outreach strategies to recruit more contractors. Perhaps an effective public relations campaign could inform local and regional contractors about the City's new procedures and capabilities for expeditious project implementation. In 1988, The New York Building Congress sponsored a conference on public construction opportunities in New York City, which was attended by many firms not presently working in New York City. This kind of event should be repeated. Perhaps special assistance ought to be provided for contractors who have never bid on a City contract. At a minimum, preferences and restrictions for hiring local contractors should be made more flexible or eliminated.

Declaring Bidders Nonresponsible

City agencies have long had the authority within the competitive bidding process to refuse to award a contract to the lowest bidder, based on a determination that the bidder is "not responsible." The courts have permitted agencies to base such a finding on a wide range of factors, including criminal convictions, indictments, pending grand jury investigations, incompetence and lack of integrity.[6] Nevertheless, agencies very rarely exercise this authority because the resulting litigation has the potential to slow, and even stop, the progress of construction projects.

A competitive bidding procedure on a major contract can consume up to five months—requests for bids must be advertised, questions answered, bids received and opened, and winning bidders notified. Once the bids are in, the low bidder has a right to be awarded the contract, subject to being found responsible. At that point, declaring the low bidder nonresponsible has been regarded, perhaps incorrectly, as tantamount to taking the contract away from the contractor. As a result, significant procedural protections are invoked. The old Charter called for a hearing before a Responsibility Board composed of the letting agency's commissioner, the Corporation Counsel, and the Comptroller.

This board voluntarily adopted extensive due process procedures which permitted the parties to suspend a public works
project for months or even a year or more. Therefore, few agencies were anxious to take advantage of this option.

The new Charter also provides for appeals from an agency
finding of nonresponsibility.[7] If these procedures are not strictly
controlled, the problems of the old Board of Responsibility will
reappear. For example, since bidders are only required to hold
their bids for forty-five days, any appeal that takes longer than
that could result in the rebidding of the entire contract. This can
set back the construction timetable by many months and result
in a still higher contract price. Just the threat of delay that is
inherent in any determination that a low bidder is nonresponsible makes the need for prequalification procedures even clearer.
It is far more efficient to eliminate a contractor with a criminal
record from the process before any bids are tendered. It is also
fairer to the contractor to move to disqualify before the expense
of preparing a bid is incurred.

Creating Alternatives to Competitive Bidding
Fraud, waste and abuse are so closely linked to the competitive
bidding system that it is natural to ask whether that system
should be abolished altogether. The main reasons for preserving
the present system are to keep public contracts equally available
to all and to protect the selection process from favoritism and
cronyism. While these justifications are entitled to some weight,
the many disadvantages of competitive bidding have become so
great that other options must be seriously explored. A number of
models are available.[8]

The new City Charter mandates competitive bidding as the
preferred method of public contracting, but it allows for a flexible
departure from standard competitive bidding in some instances,
and major departures under special circumstances. Section
313(b)(2) gives the Mayor the authority to award a contract to a
higher bidder when it is in "the best interests of the City." The
Charter seems to envision circumstances beyond those of nonre-
sponsive bids and nonresponsible bidders, since those problems
are specifically dealt with in other subsections.

We recommend that the Mayor, with the advice of the Procurement Policy Board, take full advantage of these powers. For example, where two or more bids are within a small percentage of one another, the Mayor ought to award the contract to a contractor with a proven record of solid performance on previous public works projects. Such a "plus factor" would be a fair and appropriate reward for doing a good job in the past, provide an incentive for good performance in the future, and contribute to a healthier relationship between the City and its construction contractors. If such mayoral action were required to be justified in writing, potential for abuse and corruption could be reduced.

Charter Section 312, recognizing the need for a more flexible public contracting system, permits an agency to depart from sealed competitive bidding in any "special case" where sealed competitive bidding is "not practical or not advantageous." As defined, "special case" includes a variety of circumstances, such as any situation in which "judgment is required" to evaluate competing proposals on bases other than price alone. We recommend that the Procurement Policy Board consider placing various categories of large and complex construction contracts into this category. If this interpretation is successfully attacked in court, we recommend that the Charter be amended to allow more contracting options for construction.[9]

The federal postal system's new merit-based contract system is an innovative contracting alternative that bears careful consideration. It allows contract officers to negotiate with bidders within a competitive range and award the contract to the bidder who offers the most impressive package of price, plans and proven competency. Under this system, a chief contracting officer selects an impartial panel to evaluate the major nonprice strengths and weaknesses of each bid with regard to previously selected and weighted criteria. These factors (such as past performance, resources and experience) are evaluated by a simple scoring system. Upon receipt of the evaluations, the contracting officer must award the contract to the bidder whose proposal is "most advantageous to the Postal Service." The selection must include a determination that the price is fair and reasonable, and an explanation for the basis of determination.

If the submitted bids reveal that the bidders misunderstand the scope, design or other aspects of the work to be performed, "clarification meetings" are authorized. Under this procedure, known as an "award with discussions," clarification meetings must be held with all contractors who have a realistic chance of being awarded the contract. The bidders then have an opportunity to submit a "best and final offer." Following contract award, unsuccessful bidders are notified of the number of proposals received, the name and address of the bidder receiving the award, the price of the award, whether discussions were held and a brief statement of the basis for selection.

We strongly recommend that City agencies, at least on an experimental basis, be afforded this kind of flexibility in selecting their construction contractors. Any such experimentation should be thoroughly evaluated in order to determine comparative cost and efficiency, as well as corruption and fraud potential. Once again, this is an appropriate area in which the proposed OCCP should work closely with the Procurement Policy Board.

Debarment

Debarment, the final strategy for policing the public contracting system, comes into play after a contractor has been chosen and after contract execution has, or should have, commenced. Debarment provides public builders with a means of protecting themselves from contractors who have defaulted on contracts, committed fraud, or been convicted of a crime demonstrating lack of integrity. In the past, however, City agencies very rarely utilized the debarment process.

The new Charter provides an opportunity to utilize debarment more effectively. Section 335(b)(1) provides uniform rules and procedures for the suspension and debarment of contractors from bidding on or receiving City contracts: "[u]pon the petition of the head of an agency, after reasonable notice and reasonable opportunity for the person or firm to respond at a hearing to be held on a record, the Office of Administrative Trials and Hearings [OATH] shall determine whether a person or firm should be debarred for cause from consideration for award of any City contract for a period not to exceed five years." The Charter lists five nonexclusive reasons for debarment:

1. indictment or conviction for an offense including a lack of business integrity or business honesty;

2. failure to perform according to contract specifications or time limits or a record of unsatisfactory performance on one or more contracts;

3. being in arrears in payment of taxes or a debt or contract with the City or default on a surety;

4. an agency determination of nonresponsibility; and

5. violation of provisions of Charter Chapter 13-B (which prescribes the Office of Labor Services' responsibility for enforcing a City-wide program to ensure equal employment opportunities in construction for minorities).[10]

In order to deter fraud, waste and abuse on public works contracts, City agencies must initiate this process in all appropriate cases. In the past, the City instituted debarment proceedings only after an undesirable contractor had sought to bid on a contract. This should be reformed so that the City can institute and conclude such proceedings, even when the contractor has moved to withdraw a bid and terminate the proceedings.

Repealing the Wicks Law

We strongly recommend repeal of the Wicks Law. Many previous commissions and study groups have also called for repeal on the grounds of inefficiency and high cost.[11] Our recommendation is based on the law's contribution to corruption and racketeering. If the Wicks Law were repealed, City agencies could solicit bids from general contractors rather than from multiple prime contractors. A successful general contractor could then select subcontractors by soliciting price quotations from and negotiating with specialty contractors—a process likely to frustrate collusion among specialty contractors. Moreover, because a general contractor would be committed to a contract price before negotiating with subcontractors, his or her ability to pass along the cost of an inflated subcontract would be substantially reduced, and the incentive to find alternatives to collusive bidding among specialty subcontractors substantially increased. Repeal of Wicks would further frustrate collusion among specialty contractors, since it would create incentives for a large number of new specialty contractors in a variety of trades to bid for work as a general contractor, and then to subcontract all work not within their specialty expertise.

It is notable that the Legislature provided the new School Construction Authority with a five-year exemption from the Wicks Law.[12] At the conclusion of this five-year "experiment," if not sooner, the Legislature should repeal the Wicks Law outright.[13]

Improving Contract Administration

Fictitious and padded bills, fraudulent change orders and spurious litigation impose enormous costs on the City and its taxpayers. For the reasons set forth in Chapter 5, these problems can most effectively be addressed by improving the administration of public works.

An overhaul of the administration of the City's building programs clearly requires a depth and breadth of specialized expertise beyond those contributing to this report. A number of reform initiatives, however, have recently been proposed. For example, the Institute for Public Administration has produced a valuable two-volume report on certain aspects of the administration of New York City's contractual process.[14] Among its most important recommendations are the following:

1. The commissioner of each line department should appoint at a top managerial level a chief contracting officer with extensive experience and professional commitment in contract design and management, as well as contractor selection processes.

2. There should be a sustained effort to build widespread professionalism for contracting activities among program managers by recruitment, training, and clarification of contract management responsibilities.

3. The City should develop simplified and more uniform standard bidding and contract language ("boilerplate") and information requirements. "The willingness of businesses, non-profit organizations, and individuals to do business with the City would be materially improved if the array of time delays, seemingly confusing requirements, and overly complex contract and bidding documents were reduced."[15]

4. The Mayor should develop and promulgate citywide policies and guidelines that would provide a consistent framework within which departments will operate.

5. The City should continue developing an information system that serves management information requirements as well as investigatory needs.

In addition to the recommendations of the management consulting group, the industry itself has produced a number of ideas worthy of consideration. The New York Building Congress, a private sector association representing every segment of the design, building and construction industry, completed a report in April 1990 calling for a complete overhaul of the City's administration of its public works program. [16]

A successful solution to fraud, waste and abuse on public works requires comprehensive improvement of the City's administrative capacity. Without offering a detailed blueprint for improved administration and personnel policies, we believe that the following general and specific recommendations will aid in that improvement.

Balancing the Pressure to Get the Job Done with Efforts to Control Fraud, Waste and Abuse

With commissioners and their deputies under so much pressure to bring public works projects to fruition—often without regard to cost—they are understandably reluctant to take the often difficult steps necessary to detect fraud, waste and abuse. Commissioners are evaluated by their ability to award contracts, spend or commit their capital budgets and complete their construction projects. [17] Ironically, many previous efforts to prevent corruption in the administration of public works have increased delay, and consequently, only increased pressure on commissioners to keep projects moving.

These two goals—getting the job done and controlling fraud, waste and abuse—are inherently in tension. The challenge facing commissioners and top City officials is to make these goals as compatible as possible. A well-managed public works program should not be forced to choose between building vital public works and stopping corruption. The goal must be a public works program that operates efficiently and expeditiously, while at the same time effectively controlling fraud, waste and abuse. Agencies engaged in public works programs must themselves address such problems openly and forthrightly. Solutions which can only emerge by cooperatively addressing common problems will require changes in personnel policies and in bureaucratic and budgetary incentives. Commissioners must be evaluated not only on their success in advancing building projects, but also on their capacity to reduce fraud, waste and abuse.

Building a More Positive Relationship between Public Builders and Their Contractors
Another precondition to more efficient public works projects is greater trust and a healthier relationship between City agencies and their contractors. The effort to address fraud, waste and abuse cannot succeed if public officials and the public contracting system view contractors as quasicriminals whose every action is calculated to pile up fraudulent claims against the City; nor can it succeed when public contractors view City officials as mean-spirited bureaucrats who care only about appearances and career advancement. City officials are legitimately concerned about spurious postconstruction litigation which escalates project costs to an extent that makes a mockery of the competitive bidding system. Contractors are legitimately concerned about the City's design errors, dilatory progress payments (which can force a contractor into bankruptcy),[18] and lengthy decision making. Poorly drawn designs and specifications and premature contracting do cause delays and change orders. The costs of such delays and changes should be borne by the City, not by its contractors.

Increasing Responsiveness and Accountability for Change Orders
Under the old City Charter, major change orders on New York City building projects had to be approved by the Board of Estimate. This procedure was extremely time consuming and inefficient. One of the most important responsibilities facing the new Procurement Policy Board is its responsibility under the Charter to promulgate rules and regulations for the fair and equitable resolution of contract disputes.[19] It is critical that the right solution be found. The best approach may be to foreclose disputes by inserting as many clauses as possible into the construction contract to prevent future claims against the City. By its nature, construction generates many bona fide disputes; the touchstone for their resolution should be reasonableness.

The City's current system of resolving change orders and other contract disputes has proven totally incapable of producing expeditious decisions or rulings. Contractors complain that no one is authorized to make a decision; consequently, when questions arise as to whether plans should be changed in order to take account of an unforeseen problem, an entire project can be brought to a halt for weeks or months. To the extent that this is true, it reflects an intolerable failure of administration that can only be solved by placing greater authority in the hands of project managers. We recommend that the project manager be given the power to approve all change orders up to an aggregate amount which does not exceed five percent of the original contract price; once change order approvals reach that maximum, the commissioner or agency head should be empowered to approve additional change orders. If the project manager refuses the change order request, and it involves a significant cost to the contractor, there must be some manner of expeditious appeal. One possible model is a process-oriented approach that would emphasize informal mediation and arbitration;[20] the administrative tribunal construction appeal boards that the federal government uses provide another model for careful consideration.[21] The City should experiment with these systems, and others, to determine which dispute settling mechanism works best.

Improving Supervision of Construction Projects
Agency reshuffling, auditing procedures, and controls over the construction process will not make a significant difference without a corps of construction supervisors and managers who have sufficient abilities and resources to oversee the City's construction projects.

Highly competent and highly motivated project managers are the key to a successful public works program. Each major public construction project should be assigned a project manager—an engineer on the agency staff, who would be responsible and accountable for supervising the execution of the project. The project manager's oversight should commence at the design stage and continue until project completion. This recommendation sharply contrasts with the City's present system, which divides responsibility for different phases of the construction process among various different departments. Although the current system of construction management by consultants should be maintained in appropriate situations, consultants should be directly accountable to project managers. Ultimately, however, agencies should develop a professional staff of construction experts to support project managers, rather than rely so heavily on consultant construction managers. Even where construction managers are retained, however, the project manager should in all respects function as the chief administrator on the job site, and should not delegate his authority and responsibility to consulting managers or engineers.

In order to reduce its heavy reliance on outside consultants, the City must aggressively recruit, train and employ additional resident engineers. The current starting salary of a New York City resident engineer, which is $35,000, is far below comparable compensation in the private sector and in other municipalities.[22] It is too low to attract people with the necessary technical and management skills. It makes no sense to hire unqualified or underqualified people to supervise billion dollar public works projects. To attract the best-qualified engineers as project managers, the City's salary structure must be at least comparable to those of other large cities and not vastly less than those of private engineering firms.[23]

A promising approach to this problem is the Mayor's Corps of Engineers, initiated in 1988 by the Department of Personnel. This program recruits engineering students to work for the City in the summer after their junior year of college. If, after graduation, the engineer works for the City for four years as an engineer intern, the City will pay up to $36,000 in tuition reimbursements. This creative approach might be expanded to cover other professions as well. Still, in the long run, competitive salaries are the best way to recruit and retain a corps of experienced engineers.

Improving Designs and Specifications
Many claims for change orders arise out of allegations that City designs and specifications are inaccurate and incomplete. Although some of these allegations are fraudulent and self serving, and seek to exploit the City's inability to defend itself effectively against the tidal wave of construction litigation, many such allegations are fair and accurate. We recommend development of a centralized capacity to review (and eventually prepare)

plans and specifications. Today, the City contracts out for most designs and specifications, utilizing architects on a rotation basis. An architect selection system based on rotation has many of the same defects as the competitive bidding system—that is, a particular architect has no incentive to do an excellent job, since it will not affect future opportunities. Thus, we recommend that previous performance (even those not giving rise to formal findings of "poor performance") be counted as a major factor in the award of consulting engineer contracts.

Utilization of Public Authorities
It is a telling fact that whenever a public sector building crisis becomes acute, state and local governments in New York assign the job to a public authority unfettered by the legal requirements that bind the City. For example, the Legislature recently created the New York City School Construction Authority to take over responsibility for building and renovating schools. In its findings justifying the need for a new authority, the Legislature specifically stated that the Board of Education's building capability had been crippled by "inefficient bureaucratic practices... lengthy review and approval processes, ... [and] limitations on the construction process [which] have proven to be inefficient, wasteful, and incapable of yielding quality construction on time and at reasonable cost."[24] The same legislative findings could be made in a large majority of public construction contexts.

It is widely accepted that public authorities have been more successful builders than City agencies.[25] The advantages enjoyed by public authorities are evidenced in the legislation establishing the School Construction Authority. They include prequalification of bidders, exemption from the Wicks Law, the presumption that construction managers are the preferred management tool to coordinate all trades and aspects of the construction process, and freedom from citywide requirements for multiple outside agency reviews and approvals. In the short-term, unless or until comprehensive changes can be made in the City's public works program, we recommend utilization of existing or new public authorities to carry out as many public works as possible.

Identifying and Deterring Contract Fraud

We have stressed that the City must work toward a less adversarial relationship with its construction contractors. Nevertheless, the City cannot ignore the large number of unscrupulous contractors who treat public works projects as "a racket"; these firms must be identified, punished and purged. There must be a realistic perception that the commission of fraud on a public construction project carries a significant probability of detection and punishment. This means increased emphasis on oversight, field audits, sting operations, undercover initiatives, and enhanced administrative and criminal sanctions.

Improving the Auditing of Public Works Projects

A strong auditing program is essential for taking stock of existing problems, designing preventive mechanisms and locating information in cases of suspected fraud. Good auditing contributes to good management, deterrence and the raising of victim consciousness. The principal purpose of auditing should not simply be to catch corrupt contractors and irresponsible administrators, but to provide a flow of relevant information to decision makers, so they can better manage future construction projects and, ultimately, design better construction practices and procedures. Thus we have previously recommended in Chapter 8 adoption of a Certified Investigative Auditing Firm (CIAF) program for public works projects.

Auditing ought to be defined very broadly. The *Audit Guide for the Review of New Construction Projects* prepared by the Federal General Services Administration (GSA) provides a promising model.[26] Its strategy of "process-oriented" auditing gives the auditor an important role at every stage of the construction project. Underlining the point we have been stressing, the *Audit Guide* states that the principal purposes of "process-oriented" auditing are the need to strengthen management and to expedite projects.[27] The objectives of this audit guide are to ensure that:

> (1) new construction projects are administered efficiently and economically, and (2) [the building agency] is fulfilling its responsibilities in an effective manner and is complying with existing regulations and procedures. This Guide will also seek to identify any potential weaknesses or problems in the prevention and detection of fraud, waste and abuse.[28]

In addition to recommending adoption of a process-oriented auditing program,[29] we offer the following recommendations to achieve more effective auditing.

Strengthening the Role of the Engineering Audit Officer
An engineering audit officer (EAO) is an engineer whose review is required before payment of construction invoices can be made. An EAO review requires an engineering audit of work performed and/or materials installed. Most City building agencies have a staff of EAOs who are in an important position to detect and prevent fraudulent billings. Any enhancement of the number and powers of EAOs will heighten the perception that frauds will be detected.

The current position of EAOs—as merely advisory officers in the City agencies they are assigned to audit—undermines their ability to deter fraud, waste and abuse. While there is value in having EAOs as part of management, they should be able to appeal for an "outside" review when their recommendations for addressing fraud are rejected. Thus, the EAO should be required to report in writing to the agency's Inspector General any disagreement between an EAO and an agency head concerning an EAO's determination of fraud. The Inspector General should recommend appropriate action to the Commissioner within a narrowly prescribed time frame. If the Inspector General joins the EAO's recommendation to reject an invoice on grounds of fraud, and the agency head persists in rejecting the recommendation, the agency head's written decision and the Inspector General's recommendation should be forwarded to the Commissioner of Investigation.

Because this proposal, if not carefully structured, could paralyze decision making processes, we emphasize that final responsibility for the decision to pay the challenged invoice rests exclusively with the agency head. The EAO, Inspector General and DOI opinions should be advisory only, and should not delay decision making by the agency head.

Establishing a Liaison between Engineering Audit Operations and the New York City Law Department
The Commercial and Affirmative Litigation Division of the New York City Law Department is charged with, among other things,

recovering public funds that have been lost through contract fraud, theft or other means. To carry out this responsibility more effectively, better coordination with DOI is essential.[30] The advantage of joining investigators, prosecutors and corporation counsel in pursuing allegations of fraud is that together they can exact substantially greater penalties for offenders than either could exact working alone.[31] We therefore recommend that, whenever an EAO recommends action be taken against a contractor on grounds of fraud, the EAO be required to notify the Corporation Counsel.

Improving Documenting Procedures at the Site
We have found that current documentation practices on public works projects are generally unsatisfactory for tracing how and for what money is spent, and for determining whether the City obtained the performance for which it contracted and paid. Better records need to be kept by the site supervisors who oversee major projects on the City's behalf.[32] In addition to providing better information to management in the supervision and post hoc review of construction projects, better documentation will also provide a "paper trail" which, in appropriate instances, can be of decisive importance to law enforcement and auditing agencies.[33]

Making the Surety System Work
Public contractors are required to provide a surety's performance bond in the event that they default on or cannot complete their contractual obligation. In theory, when a City agency declares a default, the surety must finish the job or make up any loss that the City incurs in hiring a replacement contractor. In practice, however, the surety is rarely called on to make good on its client's default. This reluctance to "tap sureties" stems in large part from political pressure to minimize delays. The months involved in finding a suitable substitute contractor can devastate a construction time schedule. The Procurement Policy Board should examine the surety contractual language in an attempt to restructure the contractual relationship so as to more effectively force the surety to protect the City in instances of default.

Need for Aggressive Law Enforcement Initiatives
In Chapter 5, we described some of the important investigations and prosecutions of fraud in the public construction process. However, law enforcement efforts must be enhanced. The Governor's decision to continue funding and support for the CISF assures that resources and expertise will continue to focus on corruption and fraud in the public construction process.

We are also encouraged by the Manhattan District Attorney's creation of a new Contract Investigation Unit, which will use computer analyses to expose possible patterns of corruption in the records of public contracts. In announcing the new unit, the District Attorney stated: "The mission of this unit is to develop expertise in bid rigging and other corrupt practices in the contract process involving city and state. With this expertise we won't necessarily need whistleblowers or other sources of information to find corruption."[34] We urge other district attorneys to create similar units that can join together in a city-wide assault on fraud in the public contracting process.

Conclusion
The most promising antidote to fraud, waste and abuse in public works is reform of the system of public contracting and better public administration. A City government poorly organized to carry out public works promotes delay, indecision, lack of accountability, and a culture of fraud, waste and abuse.

The City must also invest greater funds and resources in auditing public works projects, and in investigating and punishing contractor fraud, both administratively and through the courts. Similarly, incompetent contract administration facilitates unnecessary or unjustified change orders, bogus claims of all kinds, and unsafe construction. The solution is to overhaul and reform the public works process by abolishing the Wicks Law, reforming the lowest responsible bidder system, improving auditing procedures, and improving recruitment and training. Most of all, it means reforming the administration of public works. In the short run, much of the public works program should be transferred to public authorities.

FOOTNOTES

1. Our discussion of the New York City Charter's provisions with respect to pre-qualification, as well as other construction procurement activities, has been greatly guided and assisted by the work and analysis of the Construction Law Committee of the Association of the Bar of the City of New York.

2. Agencies shall maintain lists of prequalified vendors and entry into a pre-qualified group shall be continuously available. . . . [C]riteria established by rule of the procurement policy board . . . may include, but shall not be limited to, the experience, past performance, ability to undertake work, financial capability, responsibility, and reliability of prospective bidders, and which may be supplemented by criteria established by rule of the agency. . . .

New York, N.Y., Charter § 324(a) (1989).

3. A contractor who has been notified that he does not meet the criteria set forth in the invitation for bids may, within five days of the notice of the agency decision, appeal this decision to the agency head; the agency head's decision may be appealed to the Office of Administrative Trials and Hearings, whose decision will be final. New York, N.Y., Charter § 324(b) (1989). The Office of Administrative Trials and Hearings (OATH), created under the City Administrative Procedure Act, is mandated to "conduct adjudicatory hearings for all agencies of the city unless otherwise provided for by executive order, rule, law or pursuant to collective bargaining agreements." New York, N.Y., Charter § 1048(a) (1989).

4. OCTF, the State's district attorneys and federal prosecutors cannot share much of their information due to statutory proscriptions (e.g., those that prohibit disclosure of grand jury or eavesdropping information) or the needs for confidentiality (e.g., of informant information). Furthermore, staffing limitations prevent OCTF and other law enforcement agencies from sifting through their files to separate and distribute the considerable amount of public information (e.g., indictments, convictions, trial testimony, newspaper articles) that is equally available to public building agencies.

5. Executive Order No. 125 (May 22, 1989) mandates that the information gathered and made available include:

> (a) actions relating to responsibility taken by any contracting agency, law enforcement authority or the Department of Labor against bidders, contractors and subcontractors; b) debarments pursuant to express statutory authorization; and (c) summaries of pending agency reviews with the potential for adverse actions relating to responsibility against bidders, contractors and subcontractors.

6. See, e.g., *Konski Engineers P.C. v. Levitt*, 69 A.D.2d 940, 415 N.Y.S.2d 509 (3d Dept. 1979), aff'd 49 N.Y.2d 850, 427 N.Y.S.2d 796 (1980); *Picone v. City of New York*, 176 Misc. 967, 29 N.Y.S.2d 539 (N.Y. County 1941).

7. The Charter now provides two levels of review from an agency's nonresponsibility finding. Within five days of being notified of the agency's decision, the contractor may appeal to the agency head. The agency head's decision may be appealed to the mayor, whose action on the matter is final. New York, N.Y., Charter § 313(b)3 (1989).

8. See Louis F. DelDuca, Patrick J. Falvey and Theodore A. Adler, "State and Local Government Procurement: Developments in Legislation and Litigation,"

Urban Lawyer 18 (1986): 301, which summarizes developments in state and local government procurement from 1983 through 1985, with special focus on the American Bar Association's Model Procurement Code for State and Local Governments.

9. Another potentially serious legal problem looms large here as well. Section 103(1) of New York State's General Municipal Law mandates the use of competitive bidding for all public works contracts involving more than $7,000, except with respect to state or municipal exceptions provided for prior to September 1, 1953. It is possible to argue that the new Charter is merely an amended successor to the earlier charter, which predates 1953, but a court might well find that the new Charter's attempt to supplant competitive bidding is preempted. In that case, we recommend an amendment to the State General Municipal Law.

10. New York, N.Y., Charter § 335(b)(3) (1989).

11. Studies have documented the many ways in which the Wicks Law contributes to inefficiency, unnecessary cost and inferior construction. City officials have estimated that under the Wicks Law, construction costs are at least ten percent higher than they would be if all construction on a site were supervised by a single general contractor. See City of New York, Office of the Mayor, *Wicks Law Repeal—A Public Construction Necessity* (September 1984). In 1987, New York State estimated the differential at twenty percent, and concluded that repeal of Wicks would reduce statewide capital spending by more than three hundred million dollars annually. See New York State, Division of the Budget, *Fiscal Implications of the Wicks Law Mandate* (May 1987).

12. In his statement on passage of the legislation, Governor Cuomo described the Authority's exemption as "a magnificent victory for our long battle to reform the Wicks Law" and an "opportunity to measure over five years the effectiveness of construction without the requirements of Wicks."

13. The Construction Law Committee of the Association of the Bar of the City of New York has recently concluded that using the School Construction Authority's experience over the next five years may not be a fair test of "construction without the requirements of Wicks." The Committee noted that the Authority faces many hurdles unrelated to Wicks, and that the exemption from Wicks was so watered down by compromises that in effect the Committee concluded that, should the Authority not live up to the expectations underlying its creation, its failures might have nothing to do with whatever exemptions from the Wicks Law were made. Association of the Bar of the City of New York, "School Builders Unbound: A Review of the School Construction Reform Act" (February 1990).

14. Institute of Public Administration, *State-of-the-Art in Procurement: A Framework for Reform in New York City* (January 22, 1987); Institute of Public Administration, *Contracting in New York City Government: Final Report and Recommendations* (November 1987).

15. Institute of Public Administration, *Contracting in New York City Government*, 19.

16. New York Building Congress, *Building New York City for the 21st Century* (April 1990).

17. See Citizens Budget Commission, *Toward Greater Accountability for the Implementation of Capital Projects* (November 1989).

18. See, e.g., testimony described in New York State Commission on Government Integrity, *A Ship Without A Captain: The Contracting Process in New York City* (Dec. 1989).

19. See New York, N.Y., Charter § 301(b)(7) (1989).

20. The City has already taken steps in this direction by joining the Center for Public Resources, a national organization whose purpose is to encourage member organizations to use alternative resolution techniques. An Interagency Task Force on Public Dispute Resolution has been formed, and OATH has put together a list of more than sixty individuals and firms qualified to act as dispute resolution professionals. The New York City School Construction Authority has also adopted expedited mediation to resolve all contract disputes.

21. This problem has been addressed on the federal level by 41 U.S.C. §§ 601-13. Section 607 permits the establishment of agency boards of contract appeals. If an agency does not have a large number of contract appeals, two or more agencies may share the same adjudicatory panel. There are two appeal procedures: one for amounts exceeding $10,000 and a second, expedited procedure for contractors' claims under $10,000. HUD's board of contract appeals' procedures and operating rules are found at 24 C.F.R. § 20.10 (1988).

22. [T]he median City technical salary is 37 percent below similar medians among all Professional Engineers in New York City; the City median is also 14 percent below the New York State median. Faced with a 15 percent average turnover rate in the critical three to ten-year experience category, an inability to fill many technical openings, and the substantial decline in new technical graduates, it is obvious that the City must become more competitive in salary levels.

New York City, Mayor's Private Sector Survey, *The New York City Service Crisis, A Management Response* (September 1989) 41.

23. The New York City Office of Management and Budget announced the City's intention of hiring 258 resident engineers over the next ten years. See New York City Office of Management and Budget, "Capital Management Initiatives: Overview," *Ten-Year Capital Plan, Fiscal Years 1989-1998* (1988) 4.

24. New York City School Construction Authority Act, ch. 738, 1988 N.Y. Laws 1525. In signing the bill into law, Governor Cuomo stated: "Today the years of red tape and bureaucratic paralysis that have characterized school construction in the City of New York will begin to unravel."

25. "Public authorities make possible the efficient construction and maintenance of public works. . . . They can pay higher salaries and hire outside the civil service system. They can let contracts expeditiously and cut through red tape. . . . Authorities have proved time and again that with dedicated revenues and freedom from red tape, they can indeed perform more efficiently than regular city or state agencies, and without abusing the democratic process." "Public Authorities, Public Competence," editorial, *New York Times*, 22 May 1988, late ed.: Sec. 4, 28. See also, William J. Quirk and Leon E. Wein, "A Short Constitutional History of Entities Known as Public Authorities," *Cornell Law Review* 56 (1971): 521.

26. U.S. General Services Administration, *Audit Guide for the Review of New Construction Projects* (Washington, D.C.: GSA, 1984).

27. The impetus for the *Audit Guide* was the construction of a federal building in Queens in 1983-84. The federal agency's approval of 219 days of delay in favor of contractors, plus a barrage of postproject law suits, led to a wholesale review of construction auditing and management.

28. General Services Administration, 3.

29. The proposed OCCP can play an important role in reviewing and improving auditing procedures. Adoption of the proposed CIAF program will further

enhance auditing capabilities. CIAFs will not only directly perform auditing tasks, they will also participate with OCCP in reforming City auditing standards and practices, and in monitoring compliance with such reform.

30. One barrier to energetic litigation for recovery of public funds is the emphasis of DOI investigators and attorneys on criminal cases. In criminal cases, DOI personnel, especially in the Inspectors General offices, prefer to pursue allegations of fraud by prosecution as cross-designated federal or state prosecutors. Thus, once cases are before grand juries, DOI personnel are legally prohibited from sharing the evidence with the Law Department. This makes it difficult for the Law Department to defend the City in damage suits brought by contractors who are under grand jury investigation.

31. DOI's "Operation Norton," an investigation of sewer connection inspectors and plumbing contractors resulted in both criminal and civil cases. Through the latter, the City was able to obtain over $100,000 in damages, plus an agreement that the contractors would correct structural damages to sewer mains caused by defendants' actions, and a guarantee that the work would be satisfactorily completed. For a detailed description of these cases, see Chapter 4, pp. 110-111.

32. At a minimum, the following records should be kept in the field offices:
   1. Daily Log—Notes what construction activities have transpired during the day, the number of personnel employed at the site by each contractor and the number of hours worked, material shortages, labor difficulties, weather conditions, visiting officials;
   2. Blue Sheet—Indicates any specific problems with the contractor's performance or with the project's objectives; and
   3. Change orders, field orders, partial payments, contractor monthly reports, architect's plans and specifications, and the progress schedule.

33. In several of our investigations, we have been confronted with instances where it is clear that money was illegally or inappropriately expended, but it was impossible to determine who had authorized which expenditures and for what purpose. If such information were available, the ability to detect and deter fraud would be improved. The City-employed resident engineers or the consultant engineers who supervise a project on the City's behalf should keep meticulous notes in daily logs. Better computerized tracking systems would also enhance record keeping and assure standardization of costs and retrieval of information.

34. Timothy Clifford, "Corruption Fight Goes High-Tech," *Newsday*, 10 February 1989, city ed.: 22.

EPILOGUE

Corruption and racketeering have marked business-as-usual in the New York City construction industry practically since the turn of the century. By now, corruption and racketeering are firmly entrenched institutionally and psychologically. A significant percentage of the City's construction unions and a small percentage of contractors and suppliers are strongly influenced or even controlled by racketeers connected to Cosa Nostra organized crime families. A larger group, although not connected to organized crime, believe that it is necessary to pay off racketeers to obtain an edge over competitors, or that extortion and bribery are simply the price of carrying out construction in New York City.

The structure and pattern of corruption and racketeering have survived many calls for change over a long time period. Not surprisingly, there is great cynicism about the prospects for reform. This cynicism is reinforced by the long history of corruption in the government's own building inspectorate and by fraud, waste and abuse in the government's public works programs.

To bring about reform, we need to challenge and eventually dissipate this cynicism. Exhortation alone will not change this attitude. Those who constitute the industry and those who do business with it must be convinced that things can change, that reform and fair dealing are possible, and that government and the rule of law are stronger than Cosa Nostra racketeers and corrupt contractors, suppliers, public officials and building inspectors. Change will require demonstrated commitment, achievements and institution building. To alter business as usual will require extraordinary efforts by new and existing agencies and organizations.

Words and promises will not inspire and move to action an

audience that for generations has seen public attention wax and wane, and government initiatives appear and disappear. People must be convinced of the government's commitment to reform, no matter how long it takes. The implementation of the comprehensive crime-control strategy that we recommend requires the continued support of the Governor and the Mayor. Legislative support is also necessary, not just to fund this crime-control strategy and to enact the legislation we propose, although both are critical, but also to place the legislative spotlight on the construction industry. For example, public hearings would give greater visibility to the construction industry's corruption and racketeering problems by mobilizing general support and a constituency for reform. Finally, without a strong commitment by other political leaders and the support of individuals, organizations and institutions in the public and private sectors, the efforts of the last two years could come to naught.

The Governor's support has already enabled us to begin the process of building the organizational framework and momentum necessary for fundamental change. The Construction Industry Strike Force is now in place; it is the most experienced and focused investigative and prosecutorial effort ever directed against systemic crime in a particular industry. Moreover, the joint initiatives now being implemented between OCTF and both the School Construction Authority and the Port Authority are excellent examples of the kind of cooperation needed between law enforcement and government operating agencies.

The creation of the proposed Office of Construction Corruption Prevention would put into place another critical piece of the comprehensive crime-control plan. The public sector building agencies must show a strong and united commitment not to do business with racketeers, not to tolerate corrupt practices on their sites, and not to allow themselves to be the victims of fraud, waste and abuse. They must also share among themselves, and with law enforcement, information on corruption and racketeering. When these government agencies become part of the solution, rather than part of the problem, we will be far along the road to meaningful reform. Indeed, all government agencies which intersect with the construction industry have an important role to play.

Racketeering in the construction industry is also a civil liberties issue. The rights of construction workers have been trampled for generations. It is time that the highly active civil liberties groups based in New York City speak out for the correction of these systemic abuses.

The successful implementation of a comprehensive crime-control strategy requires the broadest possible support. This means looking beyond government for industry participants and groups to join a constituency for reform. The consumers of construction are obvious candidates for membership; the large corporations that own or rent buildings must scrutinize whom they are paying and for what. Likewise, the consumer protection groups must speak for the small consumers of real estate in demanding an end to scams, skims, ripoffs and frauds. But corruption and racketeering in the construction industry is more than a real estate issue; it is a civic issue and a quality of life issue. All New Yorkers should take notice of how their roads, bridges, hospitals, prisons, pollution plants, water tunnels and public buildings are being constructed. The next decade will determine whether New York City can rebuild its infrastructure and built-environment. If the challenge cannot be met, the quality of life in the nation's largest and greatest city will inevitably decline.

The project on which we are embarked—reforming business as usual in the New York City construction industry—will be made much easier if we have support from key groups within the construction industry. The largest private developers are often looked on as industry leaders. Fundamental change, at least in the private sector, will be hard to achieve if they are opposed, or even indifferent, to reform. Industry leaders must open their eyes to its crime problems; take responsibility for working with government to resolve the problems; bring their own ideas, energies, and resources to bear; and use their considerable influence to press for reform. Thus, as we conclude our *Final Report*, we renew our invitation to these leaders to work with us to create the kind of industry and the kind of business environment of which all New Yorkers can be proud.

We have emphasized the central role of labor racketeering in the industry's overall crime problems. It would be naive to expect incumbent labor racketeers to join a reform effort. Nevertheless, the great majority of New York City labor officials are honest men and women fighting to maintain and enrich the great traditions of the American labor movement. Their unwillingness to denounce and take action against racketeers, who undermine and tarnish the very movement honest workers are striving to nourish and embellish, is puzzling and frustrating. We emphatically reject the notion that being anti-labor racketeering is the equivalent of being anti-labor. Quite the reverse is true. It is anti-labor to embrace the regimes of racketeers who perpetuate their power through violence, intimidation, fraud and blacklisting, and who, in exchange for bribes, sell out their members' contractual rights.

Despite all of the power that is aligned against them, "dissident" workers in many construction unions are willing to raise their voices against incumbent racketeers. Many of these "dissidents" have suffered personally—both economically and physically—for their refusal to submit silently to union tyranny. We conclude by dedicating our *Final Report* to these courageous men and women whose faith in American values, institutions and laws has been an inspiration to us during our labors on this project.

Tables

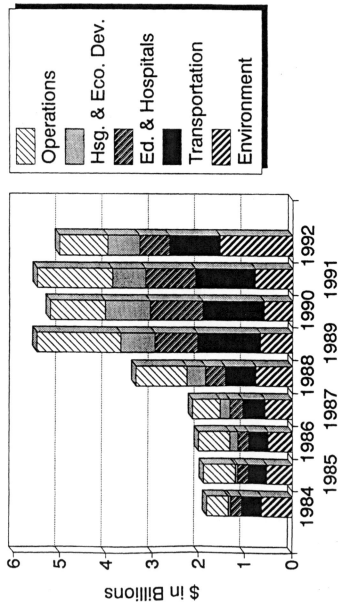

TABLE 1

Past and Projected Capital Commitments
FY 1984–1992 ($ in Billions)

TABLE 2

A Summary of the Process of Regulation of Private Construction in New York City

I. PRE-PLAN REVIEW	II. PLAN REVIEW	III. ON-SITE INSPECTION	IV. REVIEW / APPROVAL
CITY PLANNING COMMISSION Reviews project for compliance with zoning resolution.	**DEPARTMENT OF BUILDINGS** Reviews plans, issues building permits, considers provisions for egress, fire safety and compliance with zoning regulations.	**DEPARTMENT OF BUILDINGS** Inspects and approves excavation, concrete form and reinforcement, steel frame construction, interiors, elevator construction, electrical and boiler installation, hoisting, rigging, cranes and derricks.	**DEPARTMENT OF BUILDINGS** Reviews each stage of construction progress; grants temporary and then permanent certificate of occupancy.
BOARD OF STANDARDS AND APPEALS Hears appeals from rulings of Planning Commission and DOB.	**DEPARTMENT OF ENVIRONMENTAL PROTECTION** Issues water and sewer access permits and asbestos certification.	**DEPARTMENT OF ENVIRONMENTAL PROTECTION** Approves effluent facilities, asbestos removal, and sewer inspection and construction.	
LANDMARKS COMMISSION Designates and protects L/M structures; reviews applications for exceptions to Landmark status.	**DEPARTMENT OF TERMINALS AND INTERNATIONAL TRADE** Approves construction in waterfront areas.	**DEPARTMENT OF TRANSPORTATION** Grants permission for use and disruption of public streets and highways.	
		DEPARTMENT OF GENERAL SERVICES Construction and inspection of City owned buildings.	
		DEPARTMENT OF HOUSING PRESERVATION AND DEVELOPMENT Issues demolition permits, and approves changes during renovation.	
		FIRE DEPARTMENT Approves compliance with codes before occupancy.	

TABLE 3

Filings Required Prior to New Building Construction

Before construction of a new building begins, the following filings must
be examined and approved by a variety of different agencies:

1. House number certification.
2. Verification of metes and bounds.
3. Legal grade certification.
4. Plan (2 sets) showing architectural, structural, and mechanical
   parts of the building and zoning calculations prepared by a registered architect or licensed engineer.
5. Survey plan by a licensed surveyor.
6. Docket information sheet with a statement that a copy of this form
   has been sent to the appropriate community board.
7. Plumbing, mechanical equipment and tank installation application.
8. Single occupancy building form indicating whether the application
   is for new construction on a site which previously contained an
   SRO building.
9. Permanent inspection record card with block and lot number.
10. Fee calculation and payment.
11. Index form indicating status of the project in order to track viola-
    tions and progress toward certificate of occupancy.
12. Statement of responsibility by architect or engineer.
13. Statement of responsibility from other engineers involved.
14. Sewer information, sewer plan approval.
15. Miscellaneous sprinkler/standpipe application.
16. Letter from owner authorizing filing of plans for reconstruction of
    street/sidewalk at the Department of Transportation, Bureau of
    Highways.
17. Elevator construction application.
18. Place of assembly application.
19. Emergency generator application.
20. Fire alarm certification.
21. Borings or soil data.
22. Concrete design mix and certification of professional engineer or
    registered architect supervising concrete construction.
23. Fire protection plan.
24. Contractor's site safety statement for "major" buildings; 15 or more
    stories, or 220 feet in height, or with a lot coverage of 100,000 square
    feet or more regardless of height.

TABLE 4

Ten-Year Capital Plan, 1989–1998
($ in millions)

Environmental Protection
- Equipment $ 85
- Sewers   1,830
- Water Mains   2,759
- Water Pollution Control   2,588
- Water Supply   1,272

Subtotal Environmental Protection   8,535

Transportation
- Mass Transit   15,279
- Highways & Transit Operations   6,095
- Highway & Waterway Bridges   2,705

Subtotal Transportation   24,079

Education & Hospitals
- Education   5,189
- Higher Education   74
- Hospitals   2,582

Subtotal Education & Hospitals   7,845

Housing & Economic Development
- Housing   5,114
- Economic Development   562
- Port Development   189

Subtotal Housing & Economic Development   5,865

City Operations & Facilities
- Corrections   694
- Fire   309
- Police   360
- Public Buildings   722
- Sanitation   4,218
- Parks   1,837
- Other   2,842

Subtotal City Operations   10,982

TOTAL   **$57,306**

TABLE 5

Abbreviations

AFL-CIO	American Federation of Labor—Congress of Industrial Organizations
ALJ	Administrative Law Judge
AUD	Association for Union Democracy
BCA	Building Contractors Association
BOCA	Building Officials and Code Administrators International
BOE	Board of Estimate (New York City)
CAGNY	Contractors Association of Greater New York
CEQR	City Environmental Quality Review
CIAF	Certified Investigative Auditing Firm
CIP	Capital Improvement Program
CISF	Construction Industry Strike Force
CMR	Community Management Review
CPA	Certified Public Accountant
CPL	Criminal Procedure Law (New York State)
CPLR	Civil Practice Law and Rules (New York State)
CPMRB	Corruption Prevention and Management Review Bureau (New York City Department of Investigation)
DBE	Disadvantaged Business Enterprise
DEP	Department of Environmental Protection (New York City)
DOB	Department of Buildings (New York City)
DOI	Department of Investigation (New York City)
EAO	Engineering Audit Officer
ERISA	Employee Retirement Income Security Act
FCI	Federal Chandros Incorporated
GCA	General Contractors Association
GPO	Government Printing Office
HPD	Department of Housing and Preservation (New York City)
IBEW	International Brotherhood of Electrical Workers
LBE	Locally Based Enterprise
LILREX	Long Island Labor Racketeering and Extortion (FBI code name for undercover investigation)
LMRA	Labor-Management Relations Act (also known as the Taft-Hartley Act)
LMRDA	Labor-Management Reporting and Disclosure Act (also known as the Landrum-Griffin Act)
MBE	Minority Business Enterprise
NLRA	National Labor Relations Act (also known as the Wagner Act)
NLRB	National Labor Relations Board
OATH	Office of Administrative Trials and Hearings (New York City)

OCCA	Organized Crime Control Act (New York State)
OCCP	Office of Construction Corruption Prevention
OCTF	Organized Crime Task Force (New York State)
OLMS	Office of Labor Management Standards (U.S. Department of Labor)
OLR	Office of Labor Racketeering (U.S. Department of Labor)
OPWBA	Office of Pension and Welfare Benefits Administration (U.S. Department of Labor)
OUMA	Office of Union Members Advocacy
RICO	Racketeer Influenced and Corrupt Organizations Act
SEC	Securities and Exchange Commission (United States)
SIC	Commission of Investigation (New York State)
ULURP	Uniform Land Use Review Procedure
UTT	United Tremont Trades
WBE	Women's Business Enterprise
WTF	Working teamster foreman

Printed in the United States
60910LVS00002B/130-204